Pittsburgh Series in Composition, Literacy, and Culture

David Bartholomae and Jean Ferguson Carr, Editors

Literacy Online

The Promise (and Peril) of Reading and Writing with Computers

Myron C. Tuman, Editor

UNIVERSITY OF PITTSBURGH PRESS

Pittsburgh and London

Published by the University of Pittsburgh Press, Pittsburgh, Pa. 15260
Copyright © 1992, University of Pittsburgh Press
All rights reserved
Eurospan, London
Manufactured in the United States of America
Printed on acid-free paper

Literacy online : the promise (and peril) of reading and writing with computers/
Myron C. Tuman, editor.
    p.   cm. — (Pittsburgh series in composition, literacy, and culture)
Includes bibliographical references.
ISBN 0-8229-3701-8. — ISBN 0-8229-5465-6 (pbk.)
States — Computer-assisted instruction   3. Language arts — United States — Computer-as-
sisted instruction.   4. English language — Composition and exercises — Study and teach-
ing — United States — Computer-assisted instruction.   I. Tuman, Myron C., 1946–
II. Series.
LC149.5.L58   1992   91-50754
371.334 — dc20   CIP
A CIP catalogue record for this book is available from the British Library

"Hypertext, Metatext, and the Electronic Canon" is adapted from material appearing in
Hypertext: THE CONVERGENCE OF CONTEMPORARY CRITICAL THEORY AND TECHNOLOGY by
George Landow; reprinted by permission of the Johns Hopkins University Press.

"Opening Hypertext: A Memoir," copyright © 1990, Theodore Holm Nelson, is an excerpt from
his forthcoming book, World Enough.

Figures appearing in Helen J. Schwartz, "'Dominion Everywhere': Computers as Cultural
Artifacts," are from SEEN and provided by CONDUIT, 1-800-365-9774.

For Paula, Kathryn, and Dawn —
my mother and daughters

Contents

Acknowledgments

All these essays were first presented at Tuscaloosa, Alabama, in October 1989, as part of the Sixteenth Annual University of Alabama Symposium on English and American Literature. It was an exciting and memorable occasion for all the participants, three days and nights filled with that most heartening form of human communication, extended conversation. We all realized that here, outside the more narrowly focused interests of our departments and, in some cases, of our own professions, we were among kindred spirits. The discussions at the end of the five sections of this book represent an attempt to recapture the gist, if not the sponta- neity, of these official sessions. The issues raised in each of the questions came up in these conversations; the answers themselves were drafted and collected in the months following the symposium. Specifically, each participant was asked to respond to a specific question, and these initial responses were shared with the group, with a number of participants in turn providing additional responses.

I would like to thank all the participants for taking the time to organize their second thoughts in the Discussions, thus preserving a public record of the unofficial proceedings that are often the life of a conference. I am also grateful for the support the symposium itself has enjoyed from Claudia Johnson, department chair; James Yarbrough, dean of the college of Arts and Sciences; and James Taafe, academic vice-president. This particular symposium also benefitted from the stewardship of Doug Jones, acting academic vice-president, during crucial planning and funding stages. Finally, let me add a word of thanks to the many people who attended the symposium and who, ever since, have continued to inquire as to when these proceedings would appear. As much as anything, this sustained enthusiasm confirms the sense we all had at the time, that the issues raised here strike a resonant chord within contemporary educators.

LITERACY ONLINE

First Thoughts

Myron C. Tuman

One would think that by now it is a cliché to affirm that computer technology is likely to revolutionize both our practice and our understanding of literacy. We are living in an age that at times seems almost obsessed with the crisis (or crises) in literacy and with the power of computers. Does it not seem natural, therefore, that educational leaders should routinely see in computers an answer to many of the most pressing problems of contemporary reading and writing instruction?

Yet the literacy debates of the 1980s often either ignored computers or treated them as obstacles. We might expect E. D. Hirsch in *Cultural Literacy*, for example, to see in computer technology a possible way to provide all Americans with ready access to the knowledge base about culture that he feels is essential for full literacy (a suggestion Victor Raskin offers in this volume). Yet Hirsch has but a single reference to computers, and that not very positive: "The more computers we have, the more we need shared fairy tales, Greek myths, historical images, and so on" (Hirsch 31). Rather than representing a potential cure for our reading and writing ills, technology in the form of increased specialization is for Hirsch part of a disease, for which the "antidote . . . is to reinvigorate the unspecialized domain of literate discourse." Literacy and technological change are thus opposing cultural forces: "Advancing technology, with its constant need for fast and complex communications, has made literacy more essential to commerce and domestic life" (3).

It takes only a little manipulation, however, to postulate a different relationship between literacy and technology—as most of the authors in this volume do, seeing in the proliferation of computers, for example, the possibility for extending literacy by making more accessible all sorts of stored materials, pictures as well as texts. Such an approach would have us reword Hirsch's sentence (in effect reversing his assertion), thus: Advancing technology, with its increasing ability to provide fast and natural communications of text, voice, and graphics, has simplified the literacy skills essential for commerce and domestic life.

As Raskin explains in this volume, continuing progress in artificial intelligence is making our interacting with computers easier and more natural, creating the possibility that people with minimal reading and writing skills will someday be able to send and receive complex "written" communications via computers with only minimal input (perhaps through voice commands) on their part. Rather than heightening the demands of literacy, technology in this sense may well relieve us of many of the traditional burdens entailed in transcribing and decoding texts.

Admittedly, not everyone associated with literacy education can be expected to welcome such relief, to be enthralled by the thought that reading and writing may entail less, not more, work. For the iconoclastic Hirsch and, as we shall see, for many of his staunchest opponents, ease in manipulating text is hardly the issue. What is the issue—as articulated by a large group that has publicly identified itself as just such opponents (the sixty elementary, secondary, and college teachers of the English Coalition, who, representing eight professional organizations, met for three weeks during the summer of 1987 to chart the future of American language education)—is the fact that computer technology is making our ability to use critical (and largely traditional) reading and writing skills both more necessary and more difficult to attain: "The information explosion makes learning how to read and write absolutely vital for living, because without these abilities students will not be able to assimilate, evaluate, and control the immense amount of knowledge and the great number of messages which are produced every day. The development of new media similarly requires of citizens an enhanced ability to use different ways of reading and writing" (English Coalition 86).

In the work of Hirsch and of the drafters of the English Coalition, in opposition on so many points, we can see the limits of the literacy debates of the 1980s. Technology is one of the prime aspects of culture that literacy must overcome, not the source of a possible cultural reorientation as profound in its implications (for literacy education and practically everything else) as the industrial revolution of the last two centuries. In the literacy debates of the recent past, no one was inclined to see a word processor as a transitional step either to a radical new way of conceiving text (as Jay Bolter suggests in this volume) or, with the ready integration of graphics, to a radical new way of organizing knowledge itself (as Pamela McCorduck and Richard Lanham suggest). It was instead more likely portrayed as a turbo-charged typewriter, which enables individuals to write more (or at least faster) and perhaps to undertake more revisions. Similarly, a CD-ROM containing the text of the complete works of Shakespeare provides a more efficient vehicle for traditional literary scholarship; it is not a first step toward the creation of a vast hypertext that will subsume all English literature in a single database, dissolving, as it were, the traditional boundaries not just between individual works but between authors and ages as well and altering our existing notions of literature and the act of reading itself. In other words, what is lacking in recent attitudes to literacy is the recognition of how technology, in defining the medium of communication, creates the very atmosphere in which we function, creates what Greg Ulmer in *Teletheory* refers to as "the conditions of explanation itself" (xii) — and in so doing hides as background, as given, as universal truths, many of our most basic assumptions about the nature of literacy.

As Raymond Williams notes in *Keywords*, while the term *original* in preindustrial, craft-based culture referred to something's authenticity or its affinity with what had come first, with industrialism its meaning became essentially reversed, so in the nineteenth century it referrred to something's inventiveness or its lack of antecedent. This shift in semantics is mirrored in changes across industrial culture — including the emergence and widespread implementation, in the last decades of the nineteenth century and the first of the twentieth century, of a new, modern model of education designed to enhance both individual initiative and complex interdependent specialization — leading, among other things, to the dual (and to some seemingly contradictory) emphasis, in college composition courses, on both the personal essay and the research paper. The goal of this modern model of literacy was to produce not Hirsch's eighteenth-century autonomous producer and informed citizen but that personality designed for the new industrial age — self-motivated, self-governing workers and reflective, critical thinkers, people whose education makes them capable of thinking for themselves, which is a necessary condition for anyone to thrive in a world where the knowledge base is constantly expanding.

What can be readily overlooked in this educational reform is the promulgation of a new model of literacy, one that contained conceptions of both reading and writing that, while appearing commonsensical today, were truly revolutionary a hundred years ago. In preindustrial America (and in most of the preindustrial world even today), reading was defined largely in terms of the ability to recite socially important (often religious or nationalist) texts; and writing, when it was taught at all, was defined in terms of the ability to transcribe texts (hence the emphasis on penmanship and spelling). It is only with the great tide of industrialism that the now-pervasive definitions of reading and writing as the abilities to comprehend and to create new material were established. At the heart of this new model is the ability of readers to arrive at—and writers, in turn, to express—a new understanding based solely on the silent, solitary contemplation of written language. Is it any wonder that educators motivated by this new model of literacy have long placed such emphasis on process? It makes little sense to focus on a fixed product when what is valued most is the insight contained in the text that has yet to be read or yet to be written.

Even more important than process in the modern model of literacy is the crucial role afforded the notion of ever higher (or deeper) levels of understanding, an understanding most often defined by the adjective *critical*. The English Coalition, as a consensus report of current thinking in English studies, reveals the persistence of this attachment to the belief that the overriding goal of literacy is to afford students the power coming from (or at least expressed in) a *critical* understanding of our world. While there are, throughout the English Coalition's report, constant references to the need to recognize different ways and purposes for reading and writing (as with Hirsch), all are based on the notion of our exerting critical control over information. "In an information age, citizens need to make meaning—rather than merely consume information—in informal, formal, imaginative, and analytic ways and in many settings" (27). Making meaning with language thus becomes a crucial step for individuals exerting control over experience generally; or as Wayne Booth notes in his foreword to the report, there was wide agreement among the sixty participants in "'teaching

English' as the best way we know of 'enfranchising,' 'liberating,' 'enabling,' 'empowering,' those who will make the future" (x).

The English Coalition remains closely wedded to the demand that individuals reject what is given (usually described as trite, hackneyed) to search for new, more powerful explanations or expressions. The goal of literacy is not greater efficiency in manipulating text (hence the widespread disparagement, among leaders in composition, of the teaching of mechanics or the dependence on computers or on technology generally) but a heightened sensitivity to the new ideas of others and, just as importantly, new ideas we generate ourselves. Behind the cliché that writing is "a means of discovery — a way to experiment with the ideas of the course, to explore their implications, and to find out what [the students] themselves think" (English Coalition 30) — resides the historical imperative of industrial culture for greater understanding and control of the outer world and the inner self, an imperative that is expressed collectively as the technological control of nature and individually as the critical understanding of experience.

This ideal of critical discourse in the form of ever more powerful understanding of experience had its corollary, as Jay Bolter demonstrates in *Turing's Man,* in industrial culture's quest for ever more powerful forms of energy. Bolter notes that the spiritual quest for understanding so clearly manifested in Goethe's Faust parallels what he calls our pursuit of "the politics and economics of infinity": "If nature could never be completely dominated, completely transformed into capital, that too was the glory of the entrepreneur — his work was never done. Mechanisms must always be made more exact, metals converted into stronger alloys, new sources of power exploited on a grander scale" (227). Or, to paraphrase in the language of the modern model of literacy: If human experience could never be completely reconstructed, completely transformed into understanding, that too was the glory of the critic — his work was never done. Observations must always be made more exact, information connected to more powerful explanations, new techniques of criticism exploited on a grander scale.

At the very foundation of our modern notion of literacy, therefore, is a pervasive belief in the possibility of sustained material progress. That such a belief is admittedly harder to sustain, with the evidence of the environmental ravages of industrialism mounting daily, is likely to inspire increasing attacks on modern literacy practices and education, from the left as well as the right. Just how the new postindustrial technology (and computers in particular) will affect our practice and our understanding of literacy may be the single most pressing question in literacy education today, and, although the authors of the essays collected here do not represent a unified response to this question, they all differ from the disputants of the literacy debates of the 1980s in recognizing the extent to which computers will reshape not just how we read and write and, by extension, how we teach these skills but our very understanding of basic terms such as *reading, writing,* and *text.*

Computers and New Forms of Texts

Part 1 of this volume explores the scope of these reshapings, in particular how the immense retrieval powers of computers are subtly and irrevocably eroding the status of the independent, unified text—the basis of literary study and, by extension, reading instruction this century. As Jay Bolter argues, the full impact of this new technology on literacy will be felt only when we regularly use computers not for word processing, but for reading. (Hence the general lack of interest of the contributors in what has been the most pressing question of the first generation of writing teachers to use computers—the impact of word processing on the students' ability to write college essays and other traditional assignments.) Although we will be able to read traditional texts like Shakespeare's plays on computers, such traditional reading greatly limits the power of computers—it is as if our only use for the motion-picture camera was to film plays, or for television to view radio performances. We will be "reading" Shakespeare on computers (that is, using the full power of the new medium) only when we move freely through the full corpus of Shakespeare's work—and eventually all ancillary materials on Shakespeare, the Elizabethan age, and even all of literature—finding and bringing together in this limitless database (what Ted Nelson calls the *docuverse*) that precise material (pictures as well as text) that we want.

In "Literature in the Electronic Writing Space," Bolter emphasizes the continuity between hypertext—here in the form of the new literary genre of interactive fiction—and more traditional forms of writing. Bolter demonstrates how the interactive story "Afternoon" extends certain essential aspects of print literacy. What changes is the image of the deist author, a godlike figure who embodies meaning in texts that are then sent forth to be received by compliant readers. While postmodern literary criticism has argued forcefully against this model, it is the reader-driven basis of electronic reading that, Bolter contends, is changing directly and in practical ways the role of the author, and of literature itself. Certain emerging language practices, he contends, parallel those of preliterate Greece.

In "Opening Hypertext: A Memoir," Ted Nelson traces his lifelong involvement with hypertext, from his first experience of the concept and subsequent coining of the term to his current involvement with promoting a system for universal, open, hypertext publishing. Whereas Bolter focuses on a relatively small-scale collection of linked screens—systems that are often created and thus controlled by an individual, what Liora Alschuler calls "hand-crafted" hypertext (343-61), —Nelson is talking about an entirely new, interactive mechanism for publishing (and thus distributing) everything that is printed. Theoretically, Nelson argues, there is only one hypertext— the *docuverse*, or sum total of all that is represented in writing. But what are the technical and moral issues involved in designing an electronic publishing and storage system for such an all-encompassing hypertext—a system designed, at least in theory, to replace five centuries of traditional book publishing and distribution? Nelson's project Xanadu, some twenty-five years in the making and now in commercial development by the major software developer Autodesk, offers one solution to this challenge.

Computers and New Forms of Teaching English

How we organize language instruction in part reflects our understanding of literacy. Preindustrial cultures, for example, tend to emphasize the mimetic role of pedagogy, organizing the reading and writing curriculum around the notion of careful reproduction of existing texts and existing knowledge. Hence the typical emphasis, in nineteenth-century American language instruction, on neatness and mechanical correction as the keys to writing and on oral recitation as the key to reading. Twentieth- century English studies, however, have emphasized the expressive, not mimetic, component of language instruction. We have tended to define writing in terms of the ability to create a new text—one that says something new and interesting—and to define reading in terms of the ability to comprehend the new texts of others. The two essays in Part 2 consider the extent to which computers undermine, or in other ways affect, such long-standing conceptions.

In "Hypertext, Metatext, and the Electronic Canon," George Landow considers how relying upon hypertexts in a literature class can aid our close reading of individual texts by providing novice readers with the web of connections expert readers have always had. The computer-based, reader-driven reading of literature, Landow argues, threatens to transform the very nature of literary education. The fundamental nature of reader, author, and text all change, when all readers are given the technological power that was formerly reserved only for the most erudite—to make links quickly and effortlessly from one text and one citation to another.

In "'Dominion Everywhere': Computers as Cultural Artifacts," Helen Schwartz sees the dangers as well as the opportunities that confront us, as she reviews software that has been developed for teaching writing and literature (including her own award-winning program *SEEN*). Computer programs, she argues, which have until recently been designed to facilitate conventional writing tasks, have the power of reifying the traditional role of reader and author, and the traditional importance of the printed text. New instructional programs, however, have the power of embodying (what she calls *instantiating*) new, more cooperative relationships between readers and writers based largely upon the shared and malleable notion of electronic texts. Students in electronic writing classes, she concludes, for better or worse will soon be confronting a new model of literacy at the level of classroom practice.

Computers and New Forms of Critical Thought

In our culture we continue to place such high value on literacy in large part because of our belief in the pivotal role that reading and writing play in promoting critical thought. We believe that through intellectual analysis, especially that form involving reading and writing, individuals increase their power to control their own lives.

Implicit in our understanding of literacy, in other words, is a sense of the deep psychological connections between human reason and personal freedom: we are free to choose partly because our powers of analysis help us see the real choices before us. At first glance, computers appear only to enhance human freedom (as Nelson claims) by offering us so much more information and seemingly so many more choices.

Yet, as Schwartz notes, not all choices are equal. Indeed, some choices may be like selecting between fast-food restaurants at an interstate exit: for example, between McDonald's and Burger King, competitors driven to imitate each other by the same market-driven economic model, or between Taco Bell and Kentucky Fried Chicken, two outlets of the same corporation. At the heart of critical thought may reside, not the option to choose, but the ability to imagine an alternative to what is given. The two essays in Part 3 of this volume consider the extent to which computers impact our ability to think and act critically.

For Stanley Aronowitz, a professional is a member of that class of workers signaled out by society for the ability to exercise critical judgment within some well-defined domain. In "Looking Out: The Impact of Computers on the Lives of Professionals," he looks closely at the actual uses of computers in three work sites where large numbers of engineers are employed, to consider the impact of technological change on the ability—first of professionals and eventually of intellectuals in general—to maintain their autonomy. Just as computer-aided design offers engineers the possibility, not the guarantee, of an enhanced professional life, so society as a whole has no assurance that either the power or the playfulness of computers will necessarily increase our ability to exercise greater control over our collective existence.

In what sorts of new ways we will use computer-based reading and writing to understand that existence is the subject of Greg Ulmer's "Grammatology (in the Stacks) of Hypermedia, a Simulation." This piece is clearly of a different order from the others in this collection— while other authors speculate about the future, Ulmer attempts to enact it. At the center of Ulmer's piece is the insight that, as with film, the function of critical discourse within the apparatus of computers is likely to take on an entirely new form, possibly the playful, pastiche-like form he presents here. No other article makes as apparent the kinds of changes involved in computer-mediated discourse; in what sense such discourse represents a valid form of critical inquiry seems to be the precise question Ulmer's "simulation" raises.

Computers and New Forms of Administrative Control

The history of literacy is inevitably connected to the histories of institutions designed for the purpose of transmitting literacy skills—in our century most notably the school and indirectly the state. Educational sociologists have long pointed out the connection between the factory and traditional patterns of instruction, even in such small matters as the arrangement of seats and the use of fixed class periods regulated by clocks. Given such a past, it seems natural to expect that fundamental changes in society as a whole, brought about by the widespread introduction of computers, will also lead to changes in the organization of literacy education. The two essays in Part 4 of this volume consider the extent to which these changes will lead to greater, or at least more efficient, administrative control of students and citizens.

In "The Electronic Panopticon: Censorship, Control, and Indoctrination in a Post-Typographic Culture," Eugene Provenzo examines the power of the computer to reshape the very representation of our physical world. While computer-based literacy, with its reliance upon graphics as well as words, has the power of liberating us from the tyranny of the author and the text, it is, Provenzo argues, fraught with dangers. The photograph, which during the last 150 years has been taken as the model of truthful representation, can now be digitally manipulated. New computer-based imaging techniques threaten to blur the distinction between history and fiction, truth and ideology, in troubling ways presaged in George Orwell's 1984.

In "Naturalizing the Computer: English Online," Victor Raskin describes the interface between the computational power of computers and the needs of users. As computers become the dominant instrument of literacy, Raskin argues, the arena of our interaction (the interface) becomes an issue involving cultural values as well as formal design. His essay examines the possibilities and dangers in a world dominated by computers with a totally natural language interface, that is, a world of computers with which we can interact as if they were other people. His (reassuring?) conclusion is that computers are no more dangerous than the people who create them.

Computers and New Forms of Knowledge

Reading and writing have evolved over thousands of years, not just as means of communication, but as means of organizing and formulating knowledge. As theorists like Walter Ong and Eric Havelock have articulated, there is legend and myth without literacy, but no history; persuasive speech making, but no rhetoric; religious feeling, but no theology; folklore and commonplaces, but no philosophy. Largely through the introspection of writing and reading, we have gained both increasing control of the natural world and increasing insight into our own selves—it is probably not a coincidence that the most intricately woven, psychologically introspective novels of Henry James and Marcel Proust (much less the works of Freud himself) appeared during the time of unprecedented industrial expansion, the age Henry Adams saw represented in the all-powerful electric dynamo.

The knowledge of the world afforded by James and Proust, as well as Freud and Adams—all high priests of literacy—is, as if by definition, mediated through the abstraction of language. The sensual riches of the novel are products of pure imagination; the printed page itself is typically devoid of aesthetic interest. The two essays in Part 5 consider the ways in which computers reverse this dominant cultural tradition, in part by integrating text and graphics. Just what is to be gained (and what lost) by our coming to know the world through pictures as well as words?

In "Digital Rhetoric: Theory, Practice, and Property," Richard Lanham argues that the full promise of the new technology lies in the power of ordinary users to exercise direct control, often through computer manipulation, of our culture's dominant signs and symbols. Whereas book (or codex) culture was marked by a narrowing of the range of experience deemed appropriate for classroom study, computer-based rhetoric will compel students and teachers alike to become engaged in questions (both serious and playful) of more immediate interest. Our renewed interest in understanding all texts as events (and not just as artifacts), Lanham concludes, signals the rebirth of rhetoric.

The primary purpose for art in preliterate culture, Pamela McCorduck contends in "How We Knew, How We Know, How We Will Know," was epistemological, not aesthetic; the earliest cave paintings were a means of organizing and representing collective knowledge. While manuscript culture often relied heavily on pictures, writing, in the age of the book, increasingly relied on the unadorned word to carry greatest weight. Computer-based writing, McCorduck states, will inevitably involve the closer integration of word and picture. Being literate in the future will involve an expanded ability to create and interpret graphic images. The old saw, that you don't know something unless you can put it into writing, is not so much wrong as it is incomplete.

The issue raised by McCorduck and Lanham in this last section, like those raised in the preceding four sections, collectively begin to unravel the cloth of literacy that for most of this century has remained largely untouched by revisionist critiques from both the left and the right. Will our literate activities with computers (as George Landow and Ted Nelson suggest) represent merely an extension, however elaborate, of current critical activities, a more powerful means of helping more students attain deeper understanding? Or will these activities (as Bolter, Lanham, and McCorduck suggest) lead to different but in key ways better (more sensuous? more holistic?) forms of understanding? Or might these literate activities threaten the very notion of critical understanding, either as Stanley Aronowitz suggests by substituting manipulation for analysis or as Eugene Provenzo suggests by undermining the stability of reality and hence the very possibility of critique? How can we probe a world that seems to change, as if magically, before our eyes? Or (as Helen Schwartz suggests) does it all depend on choices we have yet to make? Of the thinkers represented here only Victor Raskin would have us relax, comforted with the thought that we are likely to use computers to do the same kinds of (nasty, mean-spirited) things to each other that we have always done.

What should soon be apparent in this volume is the extent to which these essays (and the responses they elicited) represent a serious effort to redefine the parameters of the literacy debates of the last decades. If nothing else, the materials collected here reveal something of the vast changes in our intellectual life that are likely to follow the rapid expansion in the power and availability of computers. For too long (to use McLuhan's metaphor) we have been driving into the future, looking through the rearview mirror. As we have focused on the challenge of Hirsch and the response of the English Coalition, we have as it were driven into a new country, where the terrain is largely shaped by electronic technology. It is as if the terrain we stand on has shifted—with many of us about to look up to discover the debates of the recent past rendered quaint, and the playful speculations of computer enthusiasts transformed into pressing questions of public policy. We are all soon likely, in other words, to be responding to the questions raised here about reading and writing with computers, not as futurists or theorists, but as teachers, parents, and citizens faced with immediate and difficult educational decisions. No one could claim that the contributors here have all the right answers—what hundred people, what thousand responses, would have such answers? And besides who could know? The writings collected here at least raise many of the right questions. This volume represents one of the first attempts to define the literacy debates of the 1990s, debates that may well continue into the twenty-first century.

> 1 <
COMPUTERS
and New Forms of Texts

Literature in the Electronic
Writing Space

Jay David Bolter

In the last decade the computer has proved itself an important writing tool. Programs for word processing have shown that the machine can be used by scholars and professional writers as well as scientists to handle text and graphics as well as numbers and mathematical structures. Now widely accepted as an aid for writing and revising, the computer has in many cases replaced the typewriter and the printing press. At the same time, it is becoming clear that word processing and desktop publishing do not exploit the full power of the computer as a technology for writing. The purpose of word processing is to generate perfect typed documents; the purpose of desktop publishing is to create camera-ready copy for publication in print. In other words, these programs use the computer to prepare texts that will eventually be translated back into the older medium of ink on paper.

The word processor is still a transitional tool; it marks the transition between conventional writing for print and fully electronic writing. Even this transitional tool has had an impact on literacy. Everyone who uses a word processor notices that revision becomes easier: heavily revised and often longer texts are the result. Together word processors and laser printers make it possible for small organizations and individuals to publish their own newsletters, pamphlets, and even books. Indeed, the word processor is turning us all into typographers: we are more conscious than ever of the type styles, fonts, and page layout that constitute the printed page. But for that reason word processing is not a revolution in the way we conceive of text. The computer as word processor does not provide us with a new space for writing and reading; instead, it gives us a space that is an electronic image of the familiar typed or printed page.

Fully electronic writing uses the computer as a medium in its own right—both for the creation and for the reading of texts. It is only when both reading and writing are done on the computer screen that the computer can display in full measure its unique qualities as a writing space.[1] As soon as we stop thinking about the text as a printed page, we are freed of the primary constraint of the page. In a printed book or typed document, the text is presented in one fixed order. Printed texts are normally meant to be read in linear order, paragraph by paragraph, from first page to last. The computer allows us to define units of text of any size and to present those units in a variety of orders, depending upon the needs and wishes of the reader. An electronic text is fluid, adjustable right up to the moment of reading. Indeed an electronic text only exists in the act of reading—in the interaction between the reader and the textual structure.

The computer's capacity to create such fluid textual structures and present them interactively to the reader has been named hypertext. (Hypertext was pioneered and named by Ted Nelson, the author of the following essay.) Consider the simple example in Figure 1. A paragraph of prose is presented on the computer screen and can be read in the conventional manner. But each of the boldfaced words is also linked to another paragraph of explanatory prose. The reader can select any such word and open it to reveal the second paragraph. This might seem to be nothing more than an automated version of the footnote that has been used in printed books for centuries. But there is an important distinction. The second paragraph also contains bold-faced words that open onto other paragraphs. The process of reference can continue indefinitely in the computer, as it cannot do with footnotes in a printed book. A hypertext is organized as a web of related textual elements: the author creates the elements and defines their relations and then hands the structure to the reader. Effective reading can only be done on the computer screen, because only the computer can handle the links between elements and take the reader effortlessly to the next text.

The computer as hypertext constitutes a new writing space with qualities unlike those of the previous spaces of handwriting and printing. No longer ancillary to printing, the computer as hypertext earns a distinct place in the history of writing. The shift from printed book to electronic hypertext becomes a watershed as important as the shift from manuscript to print in the fifteenth century. As Elizabeth

The view of originality was far different in the Middle Ages prior to printing, as Elizabeth **Eisenstein** has shown. She cites a passage from the thirteenth-century Saint `Bonaventura` explaining the four ways of making a book: one can be a scribe, a compiler, a commentator, or an author. Bonaventura conceives of writing as a craft: copying and composing are simply two ways of producing books. He does not even mention the possibility that a writer could work without reference to written authority. It is a commonplace but nonetheless true to say that Western medieval authors relied heavily upon written authorities (the Church fathers, ancient and early medieval encyclopedias, Aristotle, and so on). In the East, too, **Byzantine writers** very often spent their time compiling and commenting upon ancient Greek poems and histories: they seemed to have believed that their own best contribution would be in abridging, arranging and making available the works of the past.

In this hypertext each boldfaced word or phrase is linked to another paragraph.

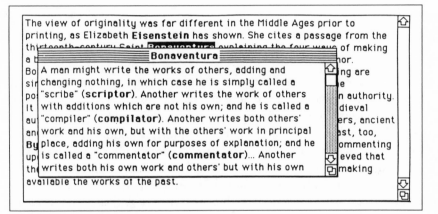

Bonaventura

A man might write the works of others, adding and changing nothing, in which case he is simply called a "scribe" (**scriptor**). Another writes the work of others with additions which are not his own; and he is called a "compiler" (**compilator**). Another writes both others' work and his own, but with the others' work in principal place, adding his own for purposes of explanation; and he is called a "commentator" (**commentator**)... Another writes both his own work and others' but with his own

When a link is activated, the appropriate paragraph appears in a new window on the screen.

Fig. 1.

Eisenstein explains in *The Printing Press as an Agent of Change,* the introduction of printing was a technical change that transformed the way science was practiced and the attitude of humanists toward the ancient and modern texts they studied. The printing press affected styles of writing and genres of literature. In fact, each technology of writing has had this effect. Since the invention of the Greek alphabet, there have been three principal media—the papyrus roll, the hand-written codex, and the printed book—and each has fostered certain attitudes toward the act of writing and the nature of written text. The electronic medium will do the same.

In describing the changes brought about by printing, Eisenstein stresses the ability of the press to preserve and stabilize both words and images with a greater degree of accuracy than handwriting could provide. It was the fixity of the printed text that encouraged exacting textual criticism in humanistic scholarship and the drive for greater mathematical precision and descriptive accuracy in the sciences. Now, however, the computer is calling into question the idea of fixity: in place of the stable printed text, the computer offers us a fluid and in-teractive text. The computer promises, therefore, to reverse the quali-ties that Eisenstein identified in the printing revolution, and this reversal may have important consequences for the humanities and the sciences.

The Electronic Book

The immediate consequences of hypertextual writing will be in pedagogy and scholarship, where electronic texts are already coming into use. George Landow is exploring the pedagogy of hypertext: as he describes in his essay later in this volume, Landow has used the Intermedia system at Brown University to create electronic materials for a course in Victorian literature.[2] The resulting hypertext, called Context32, shows how the computer can assist the student in a new and more active engagement with both primary and secondary mate-rials. It is not only students who need to be active readers. Scholars too practice the kind of active and interactive reading for which hypertext is ideal. Everything from student essays to scholarly commentaries can and no doubt will be recast in this new electronic form. It will soon become clear that hypertext can serve for all kinds of books and printed materials.

Hypertext calls for a redefinition of the book, for our current definition depends heavily upon our long experience with print. Above all, hypertext challenges our sense that each book is a com-plete, separate, and unique expression of its author. A printed book is an artifact that you can hold in your hand; it is a sequence of pages bound between two covers. Physically and metaphorically, a printed book claims to cover a subject. But in fact no book is complete in itself. Any book contains echoes, references, and often direct quotations, from other books. All the books on a given subject form a network of facts, insights, arguments. In the computer, this network can be expressed as a series of hypertextual links. The reader can be reading one text, branch quickly to another, then go back to the first text or on to a third. Dozens or hundreds of texts by different authors can be stored on the same disk (and thousands on a CD-ROM), so that the separateness or individual identity of texts tends to break down. Hypertext encourages us to think of all texts as occupying the same writing space, and to regard any one author as simply adding new elements and links to that space. In a sense, all an author adds is new links among previous elements. In the world of hypertext, to write is to make connections.

Once we begin to see writing as connecting, we are carried easily from the individual text to great collective texts, from the individual book to the encyclopedia and library as a collection of texts. Such collections already exist in machine-readable form: not only medical and scientific bibliographies and Supreme Court decisions, but traditional literary texts as well. Most of ancient Greek literature from Homer to the Empire period is now available on a CD-ROM. [3] We can look forward to the day when whole libraries of modern works will also be available in this format. But the real revolution will come as we find sophisticated ways of organizing these electronic databases. The computer permits multiple organizations—so that texts in the database can be arranged alphabetically, and by topic, and ultimately also by association. In other words, these databases will be filled with hypertextual links describing interesting paths through the material. (The pathways can function like the footnotes we saw in our simple example.) In a fully hypertextual library, readers will be able to choose any of the existing paths, or define a new path, through the materials they are reading and perhaps leave that path for other readers to follow if they choose. What we get from this speculation is a vision of the library as an encompassing hypertextual book in which everyone can read and everyone can add his or her own writing. This is surely a utopian vision (and like all utopias it could be a nightmare as well as a paradise), but it is certainly the direction in which hypertextual writing will take us. Hypertext will give us new interactive encyclopedias and libraries as well as new individual books.

How to write these new individual and collective books and how to exploit the new writing space will be, I think, central tasks for our literate culture in the coming decades. We shall have to reconsider the relationships between author, text, and reader. In the technology of print, an author creates a text, which is reproduced in thousands of identical copies and sent out to an audience of passive readers. But the computer, as it works against the fixity of the text, calls into question the authority of the author. So the computer as hypertext raises fundamental questions of literary theory. And, in a curious way, hypertext is a vindication of postmodern literary theory. For the past two decades, postmodern theorists from reader-response critics to deconstructionists have been talking about text in terms that are strikingly appropriate to hypertext in the computer. When Wolfgang Iser and Stanley Fish argue that the reader constitutes the text in the act of reading, they are describing hypertext. When the deconstructionists emphasize that a text is unlimited, that it expands to include its own interpretations—they are describing a hypertext, which grows with the addition of new links and elements. When Roland Barthes draws his famous distinction between the work and the text, he is giving a perfect characterization of the difference between writing in a printed book and writing by computer.

It is uncanny how well postmodern pronouncements seem to fit the computer. The irony is that postmodern theorists have been doing this without knowing it. Their methods have always been directed in the first instance to printed or written texts, not to electronic writing; their aim has been to upset our complacent notions of conventional printed literature. And their work has been controversial, to many shocking, when applied to literature in print. But when we read the same work with the computer in mind, it becomes indisputable, obvious, indeed (as mathematicians like to say) almost trivially true. Perhaps the best way to understand postmodern theory is to see it as a final product of the late age of printing. Its function is to clear the field of the metaphysical wreckage of the age of printing so that the computer as hypertext can take its place.

"Afternoon"

Let us look more closely at an example of hypertext: a short story called "Afternoon," written by the novelist and educator Michael Joyce. Designed to be read on the Macintosh computer, "Afternoon" functions much like the example shown above in Figure 1. The story is divided into short episodes: each episode is a word, sentence, or paragraph. You, as reader, control the movement between episodes by typing a response or by clicking with the mouse on the screen. Nothing happens until you make a response. As soon as you do type or click, the program compares your response to a list of anticipated responses and branches to an appropriate new episode. "Afternoon" is a hypertextual network of connections between these episodes. The reader cannot change the prose of the story: all the prose, as well as the structure of interrelations, was created by Michael Joyce.

The story itself begins:

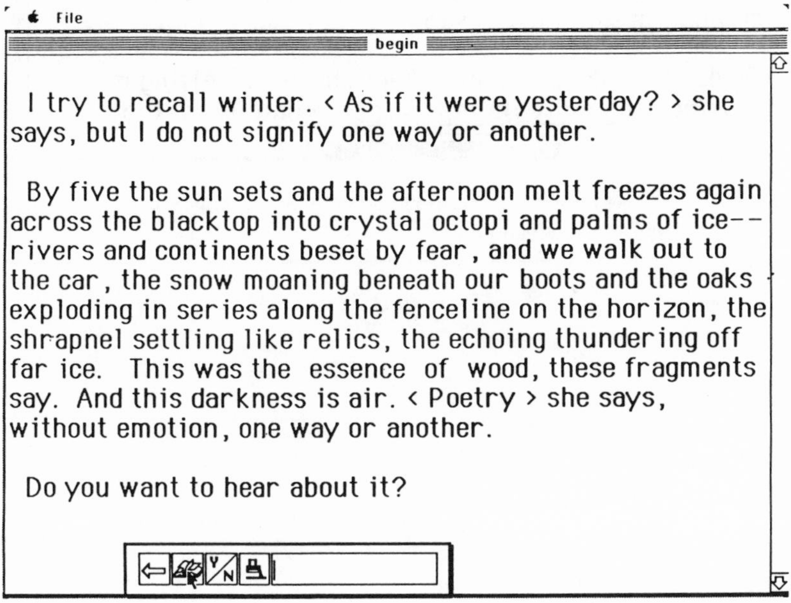

** File**

begin

I try to recall winter. < As if it were yesterday? > she says, but I do not signify one way or another.

By five the sun sets and the afternoon melt freezes again across the blacktop into crystal octopi and palms of ice-- rivers and continents beset by fear, and we walk out to the car, the snow moaning beneath our boots and the oaks exploding in series along the fenceline on the horizon, the shrapnel settling like relics, the echoing thundering off far ice. This was the essence of wood, these fragments say. And this darkness is air. < Poetry > she says, without emotion, one way or another.

Do you want to hear about it?

"Afternoon, a Story," copyright © 1987, Michael Joyce, published by Eastgate Systems of Cambridge, Mass. Reprinted with permission of the author.

Fig. 2.

As the reader, you may respond by typing *yes* or *no*. If you type *yes*, you see this new screen:

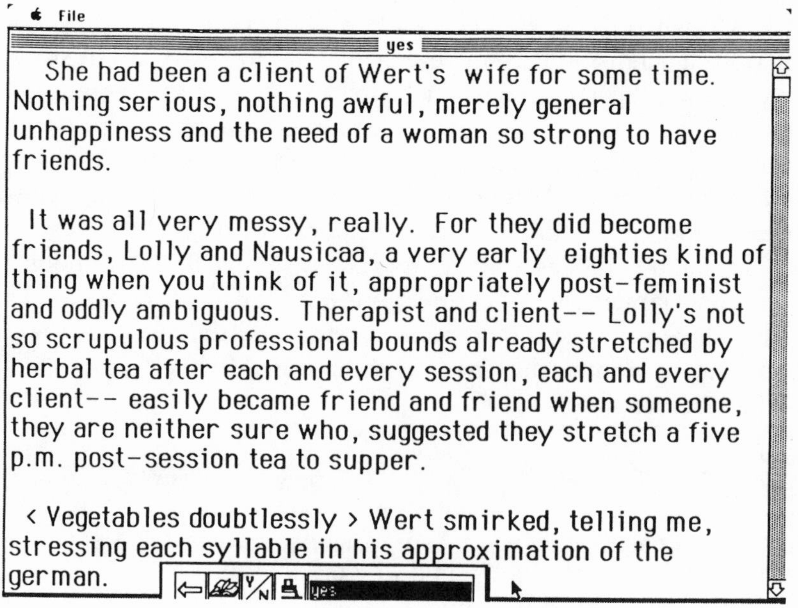

"Afternoon, a Story," copyright © 1987, Michael Joyce, published by Eastgate Systems of Cambridge, Mass. Reprinted with permission of the author.

Fig. 3.

If you type *no*, another episode appears:

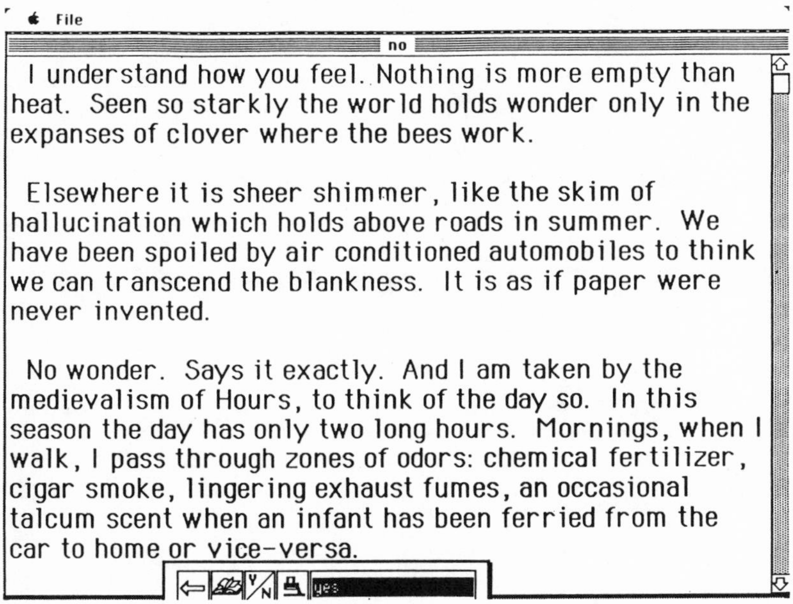

```
 ┌────────────────────────────────────────────────────────┐
 │  🍎  File                                              │
 │══════════════════════ no ═════════════════════════════ │
 │   I understand how you feel. Nothing is more empty than │▲
 │  heat.  Seen so starkly the world holds wonder only in │
 │  the expanses of clover where the bees work.           │
 │                                                        │
 │   Elsewhere it is sheer shimmer, like the skim of      │
 │  hallucination which holds above roads in summer.  We  │
 │  have been spoiled by air conditioned automobiles to   │
 │  think we can transcend the blankness.  It is as if    │
 │  paper were never invented.                            │
 │                                                        │
 │   No wonder.  Says it exactly.  And I am taken by the  │
 │  medievalism of Hours, to think of the day so.  In this│
 │  season the day has only two long hours.  Mornings,    │
 │  when I walk, I pass through zones of odors: chemical   │
 │  fertilizer, cigar smoke, lingering exhaust fumes, an  │
 │  occasional talcum scent when an infant has been       │
 │  ferried from the car to home or vice-versa.           │
 │       ⇐ 📝 Y/N 🖨 yes                                  │▼
 └────────────────────────────────────────────────────────┘
```

"Afternoon, a Story," copyright © 1987, Michael Joyce, published by Eastgate Systems of Cambridge, Mass. Reprinted with permission of the author.

Fig. 4.

The story does not let you go quite that easily: you are directed back into the structure by other routes. You may also respond by selecting any word on the screen and highlighting it with the mouse. The computer takes this word as your response. The word "yields" and opens onto a new episode. There are more than 500 different episodes and more than 900 branches in the story's network. There may be half a dozen or more different branches for any episode, half a dozen different directions that your reading can take.

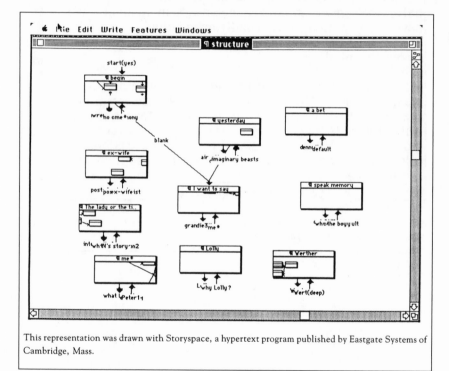

This representation was drawn with Storyspace, a hypertext program published by Eastgate Systems of Cambridge, Mass.

Fig. 5. A fragment of the network of "Afternoon." Boxes represent episodes; arrows represent links between episodes.

I will not try to summarize the story. Such a summary of any fiction is misleading. It is particularly misleading in the case of interactive fiction, because the experience of reading the story *is* the story and that experience changes with each reading. But I will note that "Afternoon" is not a soap opera with multiple plots. Indeed, there is not much plot in any of the possible readings of "Afternoon." The events are ambiguous, and the story focuses on the characters' reactions to those ambiguities. At the heart of "Afternoon" there is mystery: the narrator's son may or may not have been in an automobile accident. I think there is no unequivocal solution to this mystery in any reading of the story. But in almost all readings, the reader is compelled to follow the father as he tries to establish the fate of his son. The father's quest also becomes the reader's—to establish what really happened to the son. The episodes the reader visits will determine the answer he or she receives. In that sense, "Afternoon" becomes an allegory of the act of reading. The reader's own participation in the story becomes the story.

"Afternoon" is text as pure texture. It is the sum of all possible readings, the sum of all the paths the reader can take in exploring the space of the text. The branching itself is part of the text. The branches are the points at which you, as reader, assert your presence in the story. Within each episode, "Afternoon" is a conventional story: that is, it is conventionally ordered prose (occasionally poetry). But at each branch the reader has the opportunity to determine the text, in collaboration with the author who arranged the branches.

In the early 1960s, there was an experimental printed fiction called *Composition #1*, which consisted of about 150 loose and unnumbered pages of prose (Spencer 209-12). The reader was instructed to shuffle the pages and read the result. This experiment could be called the end of the printed novel, an experiment in which the author tore up the book in order to break free of the constraint of linearity. "Afternoon" and hypertexts in general are quite different from that kind of (admittedly decadent) experiment in print. "Afternoon" is not aleatory fiction, because the author can exercise any degree of control over the choices the reader makes. "Afternoon" can be and sometimes is a linear story, because occasionally there is only one path leading from a given episode. At other times "Afternoon" expands to give the reader dozens of choices, but even then the choices are far from random, and they do not impress the reader as haphazard.

Reading and Rereading

A few minutes spent at the computer with "Afternoon" make it clear that electronic hypertext is a new kind of writing. A text that changes before our eyes challenges our assumptions about the nature of literature. On the other hand, "Afternoon" is in a literary tradition: we have no difficulty recognizing it as a coherent act of imagination, as a story, with characters who interact and conflict. Both the novelty and the familiarity of a hypertext like "Afternoon" deserve our attention.

As a reader of "Afternoon," I am struck by the importance of repetition in the story. I often returned to the same episode—sometimes intentionally, sometimes in spite of my best efforts—and yet at each return the episode was different because it was approached along a different path. Repetition has been a quality of literature since the invention of writing. Writing allows an author to repeat his or her own words and to allude to the words of others. And repetition or exact reproduction is the essence of writing and certainly of the technology of printing. Printing makes us confident that every reader of a novel does in fact read the same words. When we take a book from the shelf, we can assume that it holds the same text it held a week or a year before. If we say that a book is different when we reread it, we mean that we as readers have changed, not the text. At the very least we have changed in that we have read the text before and therefore possess it as a structure of episodes, images, or words in our memory. In the case of an electronic text, however, both we and the text change with each reading because the number and order of the episodes change. What does repetition mean in these new circumstances? After several rereadings, "Afternoon" becomes a network of narrative elements that is taken over into the reader's mind. In this sense, an electronic text like "Afternoon" is not meant to be read, but always reread.

Now this was the comment that the literary critic Joseph Frank made about *Ulysses*: he said that James Joyce's *Ulysses* could not be read, but only reread (Frank 19). And in a sense this is true of all consciously traditional or allusive literature. It is true of the *Aeneid* and it is true in another sense of the *Iliad*. Literature rooted in an established tradition, either written or oral, invites the reader to be rereading even on a first reading. Of course, if we are not familiar with the tradition, then our first reading really is a first reading, for we must build the context of the work as we proceed. Many readers today are first readers of the *Iliad* or the *Aeneid*, for whom the experience of reading ancient epic is like the experience of reading a modern novel.

In any case, such traditional literature is judged by the success of the rereading—by its capacity to manifest or elaborate the tradition to which it belongs. In periods when invention and apparent freedom from tradition are valued, the first reading will be regarded as something special. Since the romantics, we have assumed that the first reading is privileged because as first readers we are fresh to experience the author's invention. Our own literature today is characterized by extreme diversity in its relation to tradition. Authors are free to borrow from any tradition they happen to know: Greek mythology, African poetry, Native American ritual, the Bible, Indonesian shadow theater, or the I Ching. The task of contemporary literature is to build its own tradition "on the run"—to create in the reader's mind its own network of associated narrative elements. This the electronic medium can do far more assuredly than print, for the electronic text itself is the network and therefore is the tradition. Reading an electronic text can be both a rereading and a first reading at the same time. We, as readers, are always rereading, in the sense that we can manipulate the text as if it were already part of our tradition. We never break free of the linear experience of reading, but links among elements in the network do free us from that single reading order that is required of a first reading in print. As a network, the text provides its own context. An electronic text may never repeat itself in the conventional sense, but we may always read the text as if it were a repetition.

Making the Text

If electronic text is always a repetition, then what becomes of the notion of originality in writing? Who is the author? In electronic writing, reader and author share in the act of making the text and therefore in the responsibility for the result. The shared responsibility is apparent in "Afternoon," where the reader is drawn into the search for information about the narrator's son, until the reader becomes almost an accomplice in the son's death. In any hypertext, the text originates in an interaction that neither author nor reader can completely predict or control. The problem of the origin of a text and of originality in the text is therefore redefined by the electronic writing space.

The definition of literary creativity, of what it means to make a text, has always depended in part upon the contemporary technology of writing. Our own standards of originality have developed only in the last few hundred years and again under the influence of the printing press. The legal concept of copyright, which protects the originality of our texts, could arise only after the printing press made it both possible and financially worthwhile to produce identical copies. In this late age of print, our culture still believes firmly in the originality of all good writing and still establishes a hierarchy of texts on the basis of originality. Every poem or play must be highly original. In nonfiction, writing an original essay is more valued than editing a volume of essays or producing a translation, for we presume that it requires more creativity and therefore makes a greater contribution to produce an essay than to arrange and present the ideas of others.

The view of originality was far different in the Middle Ages prior to printing, as Elizabeth Eisenstein has shown in *The Printing Revolution in Early Europe*. She cites a passage from the thirteenth-century Saint Bonaventura explaining the four ways of making a book: one can be a scribe, a compiler, a commentator, or an author. Bonaventura conceives of writing as a craft: copying and composing are simply two ways of producing books. He does not even mention the possibility that a writer could produce a wholly original work, without reference to previous written authority (84-85). It is a commonplace (but nonetheless true) to say that Western medieval authors relied heavily upon written authorities (the Church fathers, ancient and early medieval encyclopedias, Aristotle, and so on). In the East, too, Byzantine writers often spent their time compiling and commenting upon ancient Greek poems and histories: they seem to have believed that their own best contribution could be in abridging, arranging, and making available the works of the past.

In the ancient world itself, artistic ability was often measured by standards other than original invention. Greek tragedies took for their plots stories that were hundreds of years old: originality consisted in the fresh use of traditional materials. In Homeric epic too, making the text meant telling a traditional story in a particularly effective fashion. The stories of the Greeks at Troy and indeed all Greek mythology existed as a shared network of elements in the minds of Homeric bards and their audiences. A good performance was one that used familiar elements well, which the audience could judge because they were always "rereading" the poet's performance. Homer's poems were the first in this tradition to be written down, and they are the only ones to survive whole, so that the *Iliad* and *Odyssey* now constitute their own genre.

All writing is genre-writing in a loose sense, but strict genres (from Greek New Comedy and Roman pastoral to the Gothic novel) are also examples of formulaic, or what we might call Homeric, writing. Today, the strict genre is enormously popular—including pulp romances, detective stories, spy novels, and science fiction (which is probably several genres). The irony is that today's serious literature is eclectic, since authors are free to pick elements from any genres of the past and to put them together in any collation. Yet the reading public for this eclectic serious fiction is tiny compared with the reading public for strict genre fiction: pulp romances outsell all other kinds of fiction in the United States (Radway 19-45). Each genre defines a mythic structure, and, when the genre is rigid as in Greek New Comedy or modern harlequins, we have the impression that the author is dropping elements into predetermined slots. Fans of the genre expect a fixed structure. Like the audience for Homeric poetry, they do not want their authors to stray beyond the perceived limits of the genre. They want each instance of the genre to be new in detail yet familiar in essence.

Genre-writing brings us back to electronic fiction, for any single electronic fiction is a genre in itself. The reader of an electronic text functions like the writer of a genre text, or like a poet in the Greek oral tradition. At the very least, the electronic reader is dropping into slots episodes that he or she selects from the preconceived materials of the author. The reader becomes a writer because the reader too is putting together symbols to form a text. Instead of letters or words, the unit symbols may be sentences, paragraphs, or sections, but they are symbols nonetheless, capable of defining different texts by rearrangement.

If in the electronic medium the reader takes on the role of a traditional author, the author too has a new relation to the tradition, since he or she is creating not one text, but a whole family. "Afternoon" is not one story, but a series of stories that share characters, conflicts, and the same generic structure. Some of these stories contradict others or play satirically upon the "genre," but all the stories that can possibly be generated from the web of "Afternoon" belong to the same family. An electronic fiction is not only a fictional universe, but a universe of possible fictions. Fictional universes are common in the history of literature: they may be collective creations, such as Homeric mythology or Authurian legend, or individual (such as Balzac's Paris or Faulkner's Yoknapatawpha County). However, a single author has never been able to control the fictions that derive from that universe. In the electronic writing space the author becomes an author at one remove; guarding the text with less zeal than in printed or written fiction, the author is more tolerant of change in his or her fictional world. The author sets up the outlines, defines the limits of possible thought and action in the fiction, but the author leaves to the reader the responsibility of exploring the space within those limits. The electronic medium makes for a religion of art that is more like enlightened deism than like the stern Calvinism espoused by the literary world in the nineteenth century. Traditionalists will perhaps claim that, as with deism, such a religion is no religion at all.

The deist author of the electronic writing space complicates the role of the reader by expanding it in both directions. By participating in the creation of the textual structure, the reader becomes at the same time both author and audience. In previous technologies, authors were always their own first readers. Now readers too can become their own readers, aware that their choices are affecting the text as they read. This awareness must lead to a greater self-consciousness, to the realization that readers can no longer judge the text without judging their own contributions. If the result is not successful, the fault may lie with the original author who created a poor structure or with the reader who has made poor choices in exploring that structure. Moreover, if we arrange the writing space so that the reader's choices can be saved, then the reader may give the newly constituted text to others to read. The first reader becomes an author for a second reader, and the chain of authors and readers may then continue indefinitely.

We have a long tradition of readers who become authors for other readers; we now call such readers literary critics. Their job is to write texts about texts—to explain and transmit literature to their audience. Many critics in the twentieth century have asserted that such critical interpretation is essential to the act of reading. Furthermore, we are all critics when we read, given that we cannot avoid interpretation. That fact becomes obvious in the reading of electronic texts, where, like observers in quantum physics, we cannot read without affecting the text. Even when we read in print, we fashion or elaborate a conceptual text from the text upon the page. Literary critics are readers whose fashioned or elaborated texts are deemed worthy to be published and given to other readers. Critical interpretation as an endless play of text upon text fits perfectly into the electronic writing space.

Loss and Gain

These are some of the ways in which electronic fiction helps us rethink the nature of fiction, and indeed the nature of writing. My example of hypertext has been an interactive fiction; the same qualities of impermanence and interactivity belong to all uses of electronic text. Certainly these qualities contradict established criteria of good writing in the medium of print. The shift from print to computer will close off familiar avenues at the same time as it opens new possibilities. Perhaps every important change in the technology of writing entails loss (by the criteria of the old technology) as well as gain. The introduction of alphabetic writing in Greece, for example, doomed the art of Homeric oral poetry; it replaced the technique of spontaneous composition before an audience with the more labored technique of writing and revising alone. The vivid narrative of Homeric poetry was lost, but it was replaced by a more introspective and metrically sophisticated lyric poetry.

We can already begin to identify those aspects of literacy that will be lost in the shift from print to computer. We will lose a sense of the sanctity of the text: the assurance that Shakespeare's plays have always been and will always remain the same, an immutable resource available to all readers. Of course, it is possible to copy and preserve texts of Shakespeare's plays in the electronic medium. In fact, electronic technology can produce copies with greater ease and accuracy than print technology can. But in a world of hypertext the reader's attitude toward the text changes. The original text no longer seems inviolate; the reader is invited to move in and through the text adding his or her own notes. Any text becomes a temporary structure in a changing web of relations with other, past and future, textual structures. In the culture that reads and writes electronically, the original text loses its privileged status.

It becomes hard to say what constitutes the original text. If an author is writing in and for the electronic medium, the text is constantly changing even before it reaches the reader. Almost any electronic text will exist in multiple versions: which version, then, is the Urtext? The author may still try to manage those versions and release only one, but the author may not succeed. In fact, there are already several versions of "Afternoon," and at least one in Europe, although Michael Joyce does not know how it got there. Electronic texts mutate and migrate like computer viruses, often against the will of their creators. Once a text is sent out into the world, it will continue to grow and change as long as it continues to attract readers. The technology of printing gave rise to, or at least greatly fostered, the scholarly desire to establish and maintain the original text. This drive for scholarly accuracy became the definition of classical scholarship in the nineteenth and twentieth centuries, when classicists collated medieval manuscripts letter by letter in an effort to establish the original texts of Greek and Roman authors. And classical scholarship became the model for the source study of modern texts. Ironically, in the case of ancient texts, scholars were trying to restore what probably never existed. What was the definitive original text for an ancient playwright like Euripides: his own copy, the actors' parts (if they existed), or the official Athenian state copy that was made decades after Euripides' death? Even scholars of modern printed texts know how difficult it is to establish the original text. There are usually several typed or written drafts, and there is always the impossible question of what the author intended to add or revise. The recent controversy over the new edition of *Ulysses* should remind us (if we need reminding) that the original text may itself be an incoherent notion. Those who pursue the original text are pursuing an ideal appropriate to the age of print. It is doubly ironic that scholars should be so concerned to establish an Urtext for *Ulysses*, because *Ulysses* is a text that looks forward to the associative quality of electronic writing.

Along with the sanctity of the original text, electronic technology also threatens the idea of the literary canon. Electronic texts are by definition all interrelated. No electronic text has well-defined borders; instead, each text reaches out to join with other (prior and future) texts. It therefore becomes impossible to isolate and canonize a few great texts and authors. Electronic technology leads us to question whether it was ever appropriate to define such an exclusive canon. We cannot say where Euripides ends and the actors' interpolations or the critics' interpretations begin: all form a textual web. It is not simply that we do not have the knowledge of the original text in Euripides' case. The same is true of Shakespeare and of James Joyce. Indeed, it would seem obvious in the case of Joyce that *Finnegans Wake* or even *Ulysses* cannot be isolated and read apart from the texts from which they borrow and the interpretive texts they have generated. Thus, the current debate between those who support a traditional canon and those who reject it is really a debate over the nature of reading and writing.[4] Those who uphold the canon opt for a kind of authoritative writing and respectful reading that is appropriate to the technology of print. They draw a necessary and firm distinction between the author and the reader. At least some of those who reject the canon envision a more fluid relationship between author and reader—the relationship posited in a hypertext in the electronic medium. Here again recent critical theory, which speaks of empowering the reader and breaking down the hierarchies of the traditional canon, is anticipating electronic text.

The sense of anticipation for the possibilities of electronic text will not diminish the feeling of loss. The loss of the great text as a touchstone and of the great author as authority is real and unavoidable. All that can be said by way of consolation is that we must not identify the qualities of literature in print as necessary qualities of all literature. Literature will continue in the electronic medium, although the relationship between author, reader, and text must change. In particular, although the authority of the author diminishes in this new medium, the author does not disappear from the equation. There is no longer one author, but two, as reader joins author in the making of the text. The ideal of print was that the author embodied an experience in words, and the reader revived or relived that experience in reading. In the electronic medium the reader recapitulates the experience of the author, not passively, but rather as new author. What the reader recapitulates is the experience of writing itself. The first author (there is no good term, since the author is always also a reader) sets up a textual structure by working with and against the limitations of language and the various cultural codes available. In exploring the text, the reader-as-author must work with and against the structural limitations set by the first author. To make this exploration possible for the reader, the first author has relinquished some degree of control. The reader cannot read just anything but must still move within a structure set up by the first author. All readings will run along paths suggested or made possible by the first author—unless readers can make their own paths, which requires that the first author relinquish more control. For example, all readings of "Afternoon" will involve the narrator, Peter, and his odd collection of friends and lovers. No amount of work on the part of the reader could produce a convincing reading of "Afternoon" as a medieval mystery play or a Homeric epic. In electronic texts, at least the first generation of such text that I am envisioning, there is always a structure for the reader to explore, although the structure may change in response to that exploration.

Myron Tuman has drawn the distinction between reading-as-assimilation and reading-as-accommodation. Readers assimilate when they enter into a playful relation with the text and so alter the textual world to fit their preconceptions. Readers accommodate when they change themselves to fit the world. A sophisticated reader is one who combines "constructive assimilation" with "deliberative accommodation." Assimilation is constructive when it exhibits a "structural complexity that reflects real rather than fanciful transformative powers." And accommodation is deliberative when it is "freely chosen by us and not controlled by whatever happens to be before us at the moment" (Tuman 80).[5] I see no reason why this characterization cannot apply to electronic reading and writing as well as to earlier technologies. With electronic text, it seems clear that reading is always both assimilation and accommodation: both the reader and the text change with each reading. But reading in any medium is always, at least figuratively, both assimilation and accommodation. Readers always appropriate the text to fit their preconceptions. If they did not do so to some degree, the text would be incomprehensible. In the world of print, most texts and indeed the most popular texts are ones that encourage assimilation. They encourage readers to get lost in a textual world that in fact challenges none of their assumptions. (I am thinking here of most of the books that really top the best-seller lists: from harlequin romances, to celebrity biographies, to volumes of religious and secular advice.) The question for any particular text and for each technology of writing is one of ratios: of passive to active reading, of assimilation to accommodation. Notice that these categories are defined in such a way that they approach one another: they oscillate between opposition and mediation. Constructive play passes over into freely chosen accommodation. Is this not exactly what a good reader of hypertextual fiction does? When we choose to follow a certain path in "Afternoon," we are submitting to the structure Michael Joyce has laid down, but we are at the same time aware that our playful choices make a difference.

If the question is whether electronic writing fosters passive or active reading, then the answer is that it fosters both. Hypertext can be extended to video as well as verbal text, and it seems likely that passive readers will prefer watching images to reading words. Video hypertext will therefore be far more popular than verbal hypertexts—just as television is today vastly more popular than printed books. No doubt we will have the electronic equivalent of harlequin romances, probably in the form of electronic soap operas, in which the viewer gets to choose who is killed off and who sleeps with whom. But hypertext also permits a new kind of "serious" (the word better suits the technology of print) fiction in which the reader actively engages the textual structure. These engaging hypertexts may also include video images as well as or in place of verbal text. The difference is that the images will be used semiotically—as elements in the textual structure that the reader must confront. When the computer is used to record and present a structure of verbal, visual, or aural elements, the result has as much right to be called text as do the products of print technology or handwriting.

Landow's Context32 shows how images can be used textually. In this system an image may be displayed on the screen—say a map of London. Sections of the image are actively linked to other texts. If the student selects, say, Fleet Street, he or she may be taken to one text, discussing the press in Victorian England; other locations on the map will take the student elsewhere. So the elements of the graphic have become textual elements, signs that refer to other signs. This same technique can also be used with video. In fact, hypertext can integrate image into text more completely than print can—for in print, graphs and diagrams usually occupy a space that is different from and subordinate to the verbal text. As Richard Lanham puts it in his penetrating contribution to this volume, the electronic text can "renegotiate" the ratio between alphabetic and iconic elements in writing. It becomes possible in the computer's writing space to write with graphs, images, and icons as well as with words. This graphic writing constitutes the new *ecphrasis* that Lanham foresees for electronic writing. It permits the reader/viewer to oscillate between looking *through* the images to the text "below" and looking *at* the images as pictorial elements.[6]

Looking At and Looking Through

Hypertext makes its formal structure visible and operative: the structure is embodied in the links between episodes. When we are reading an episode, we may succeed in looking through the text to the imagined world. But whenever we come to a link, we must look at the text, as a series of possibilities that we as readers can activate. We move back and forth between reading the verbal text and reading the structure. In "Afternoon" we may get lost in Peter's compelling narrative of his search for his son, but the need to make choices keeps pulling us back to the fact that we are participating in the making of a fiction. And we are constantly reviewing the nature of these choices as we read. In "Afternoon," as in all hypertexts, the links have the same status as the verbal episodes. We are made aware of the oscillations as never before: they become the explicit measure of our encounter with the text.

These oscillations constitute the rhythm of the hypertext, and they can be rapid or slow. A hypertext can have short episodes with many links, or it can have longer episodes where the reader remains a conventional reader and can therefore get lost in the text for relatively long periods of time. The mechanism for branching can also require more or less effort on the part of the reader. If there is little effort, then the reader may not be interrupted as forcefully. For example, in "Afternoon" the reader can just hit the return key and move effortlessly from episode to episode. This activity is hardly more self-conscious than turning the page of a printed book. At other times, the reader may intervene more actively in the text by typing a word or choosing one from the text. Whenever the reader does intervene, he or she is brought up short and is made to look at the structure of the hypertext.

The reader's control of a hypertext can be expressed as the ratio between looking at and looking through the text, between the experience of reading the words and the new experience of choosing the path. What, then, is the ideal ratio between the two? If the ideal of the printed book is the unselfconsciously transparent text, then what is the ideal of the electronic book? It is a text that is hypertextual at all levels, down to the finest granularity of words or even letters or graphic elements. "Afternoon," like all the current hypertexts I know of, consists mainly of relatively large units of texts joined by links. Only the order of these episodes can be recombined. But the ideal hypertext would be one in which all elements are subject to recombination. A hypertext wants in fact to be nothing but a network of links. Proposals like Ted Nelson's Xanadu, presented in the following paper, reflect just this ideal. The conceptual structure of Xanadu is such that (in theory though not in practice) all the verbal texts in the world could be reduced to pointers to a single set of alphabetic characters. Such a conceptual reduction lies behind all proposals for universal hypertexts. Certainly this ideal could be only approximately realized by any working hypertext, just as the ideal of print (the fixed, unchanging, monumental volume) could be only approximately attained by any real printed book.

How would such a hypertext be read? If every textual element is also a link to something else, then the reader is constantly being called on to participate in the making of the text. The oscillation between looking through and looking at becomes so rapid that the two experiences merge. The formal structure of the hypertext is then always present to the reader as he or she reads. This would be the antithesis of escapist literature: there would be no escaping the text as a structure of elements. In this ideal hypertext, looking at is simply looking through to another level. Every textual element is a sign pointing to some other element. The hypertext is a network of signs, and there is no way out of the network. Reading such a hypertext would be hard work. It would require the constant engagement of the reader with the text as texture and would therefore be in the tradition of good critical reading in all of the previous technologies of writing.

Computing as Writing

We have seen how the computer as hypertext can broaden our understanding of text as a fluid structure of verbal and visual elements. As we learn to read interactive fiction, we gain a new insight into the more pragmatic forms of electronic writing, such as textual databases and electronic messaging. Finally, we see that the computer itself can be best understood as a new technology for reading and writing. In all its various uses, including scientific and industrial ones, the computer reads and writes symbolic information in its new and peculiar writing space. For the scientist, the machine reads and writes the language of mathematics. For industrial processing, the computer sends symbolic commands to electro-mechanical devices that control machinery. Computer programming too is a kind of writing: it is the art of writing texts that in turn write other texts. Even artificial intelligence, which is the quintessence of computer programming, is a special kind of computer writing, literally a genre of (science) fiction. Wherever and however we use computers, we are turning the world into a digital text; we are textualizing the world. All the computer can ever do is to read and write text, if we take the word *text* to mean in the largest sense all systems of discrete symbols. I find this an exciting prospect because it places our work with computers and writing at the center of the computer revolution. We as humanists know and care about reading and writing, and it is therefore our responsibility to help make sense and to make good use of this new technology of literacy.

Notes

1. There is a fuller discussion of the electronic writing space (with the example "Afternoon") and its impact upon critical theory in my book *Writing Space;* see also my article "Beyond Word Processing."

2. See also his "Hypertext in Literary Education, Criticism, and Scholarship."

3. These texts have been transferred by the Thesaurus Linguae Graecae under the direction of Theodor Brunner, University of California at Irvine.

4. See, for example, the September 1983 issue of *Critical Inquiry* devoted to the canon. See also Robert Scholes, "Aiming a Canon at the Curriculum," and William Bennett, *To Reclaim a Legacy.*

5. See also the final chapter of the same work (169-84).

6. See also Lanham's comprehensive article "The Electronic Word."

Opening Hypertext: A Memoir

Theodor Holm Nelson

I think a lot about paradigms. The term in its present sense was popularized by Thomas Kuhn in his book *The Structure of Scientific Revolutions*. Let me just define *paradigm* as an idea too big to get through the door. A paradigm is so much a part of the way you think that you are not even aware of it. When I started thinking about this, I realized that the most important arguments, the most difficult arguments, are those you could call paradigm arguments, arguments where two different people are speaking inside two different paradigms, and they cannot understand what the other person is saying, or how that person could possibly believe it. Religious arguments are paradigm arguments, political arguments tend to be paradigm arguments, arguments with your parents, arguments with your children—in all these there is just no comprehending how the other people could possibly say that, or what they could mean, or what they could be thinking. Paradigm arguments are like two people wearing divers' helmets decorated with colored glass trying to see in—as if trying to see the face of the other person through prisms—even so close, the optical refractions in all directions confuse the image.

I have tried for many years to convert people to a new paradigm, not just to the idea of hypertext, but to the idea of a new literature. And it has taken me thirty years to see how difficult it is for many people even to imagine an idea of this size, let alone accept it.

We are entering a new era. Not merely where computers are ubiquitous, but where they are, like cassette players, everywhere cheap, fast, exciting, powerful, and vivid. Even the equivalent of a hot workstation of today should cost only a few hundred dollars (except for the screen). So, thinking about computers the way they are now, expensively filling desktops, is pointless. We must consider how life and the world will be when computers become articles as casual as fashion watches. So we must plan now for when every kid has the equivalent of a Sun workstation. Sure, the school systems won't be able to afford them; but the kids will have them, possibly on their lunch boxes.

However, separate "computers," with nothing to show on their wonderful screens, are no more useful than record players with no record industry. I am concerned about what that supply of information is going to be, and how it will be a part of, and support, our freedoms.

One thing I have to mention is freedom. It is my job always to mention freedom because I do not hear most speakers at computer conferences mention freedom. THE PURPOSE OF COMPUTERS IS HU- MAN FREEDOM. And anybody who thinks it is the other way around— that computers are tools of oppression—is stewing in very old cliches and has not been paying attention.

I have a vision for the year 2020; I like to call it the 20/20 vision. Think of everyone at screens: a billion screens around the planet. And each person at a screen will be able to extract from a great common pool any fragment of whatever is published, with automatic royalty and no red tape.

Why automatic royalty? Why shouldn't it be free? Because design- ing such a system doesn't stop with the computer software. The design has to include a viable economic basis.

A greater issue is the conceptual framework, the system of order, which will provide a viable structure for people's minds and people's lives. (Ideally this system of order has to be in some way based on what we know works, especially paper publishing.)

Some kind of unified documentary universe of hypertext is histori- cally inevitable; designers around the world are pushing toward this in software, communications, and everything else. Everywhere you hear, "Yes we are going to have shared documents in this great system." But we don't hear more about this conceptual structure of unification.

It cannot be like databases, tables of alleged facts. Today's massive and contradictory information, and people's complication overload, have brought us to the end of the usefulness of the database model. The question is what lies ahead. I think we know that it will be some form of hypertext. But what?

Getting the Idea

To reminisce in this personal fashion at a learned conference may in some ways be inappropriate, but I thought you might like to hear some of the odder connections in my work, and I thought you might like to share and enjoy them.

From boyhood I was a fierce intellectual, absorbed in the interconnection of all ideas. When I saw that typewriters and file cards could not possibly handle these interconnections, and that computers might, I did the only possible thing. First came my private dream of a writer's console — but because this was lonely and pointless it led to the dream of an open hypertext publishing system based on new forms of interconnection.

While my involvement with hypertext in certain ways dates from my earliest years as a schoolboy in Greenwich Village, and indirectly from college extracurriculars in theater, film, and publishing, it was as a graduate student in the fall of 1960 that I would say my actual enlightenment took place. My efforts to finish writing a book of philosophy, then called *Truth, Man, and Choice,* had fallen through, in part (I realized) because of the extreme difficulty I had organizing the ideas.

When you want to express a complex of ideas, there are many threads that you can take as governing organizational structures. So many different expository lines are possible — then the more you want to say, the more ideas you have, and the more potential expository threads need liberating. It is the choice among them — the truncation of some of these thoughts, and their continuation and forward referencing and backward referencing — that is the process of writing: picking things up and putting them down, trying to remind the reader of things you said before. In other words, you take a structured complex of thought (I like to call it a *structangle*) that you are trying to communicate, and you break it into individual sequential parts that can be put end to end, and this is a wholly artificial process, a breakdown not intrinsic to the structure of thought you are trying to convey, but based upon the fact that it has to be published eventually in a sequence.

So I was fresh from my failure to complete *Truth, Man, and Choice* when I took my first computer course. And suddenly everything I had done fell into place. In my manual for the IBM 7090 was a picture of a CRT — a cathode ray tube — hooked up to the machine for display; and in a copy of *Datamation* I saw a computer screen with a map on it; and it was perfectly clear from reading the manual (even though they were giving all these numerical examples) that the computer could handle text; and it was perfectly clear that price was going to come down as integrated circuits became available.

Wait a minute, I thought: screen with graphics, storage of texts, cheap machines—these meant that writing no longer had to be sequential. The preposterous extrinsic activity of taking the struc-tangle of thought and breaking it into pieces could be dismissed. It was no longer a problem.

Not only the writer's lot, but the reader's, could be uplifted. All readers could take a more sophisticated approach. The sophisticated reader picks up a book, looks perhaps at the first page, the last page, the middle, hefts the book, flips it, holds it upside down, and then begins reading the parts of interest. Yet the writer, and editor, and publisher have until now been united in a conspiracy to pretend you are going to read this book from beginning to end, to behoove would-be authors to sequence their words under this fictitious rubric. Whereas when we can produce writings for the sophisticated reader, we can throw away the sequential presentation stuff and just say, "Here's this, this, and this—go for it!" and thus create a structure best designed for that engaged reader to explore.

So in this epiphany and its aftershocks, in October or November 1960, I went very quickly through a lot of possibilities.

1. *Branching literature.* I looked at branching text and graphics as they were in 1960—then called "computer-assisted instruction"—and found nothing of interest for a general literature. People were doing good things for teaching skills, for teaching arithmetic, but what good did these do for education: education as the presentation of concepts, education as the intercomparing of alternative points of view? Noth-ing. In education we want to understand opposite and conflicting points of view, in depth, as expounded by those who believe them. The problem with a survey course, even today, is the approach "Well, Jung said this, and Freud said that, and Adler said that," presented evenhandedly, in boring fashion, without the passion and conviction with which an advocate would present it. So in my mind I propounded my first computer project, "The Thousand Theories Program." It would present a thousand different viewpoints about the whole realm of human knowledge. That project became hypertext.

As I thought of branching documents in the fall of 1960, over the course of several weeks I had a fourfold vision. First, there would be new documents, a new literary genre, of branching, nonsequential writings on the computer screen. Second, these branching documents would constitute a great new literature, but they would subsume the old, since all existing books of paper would be transferred to the new computer medium as well. In other words, all literature would go online and extend to a new branching generality. Third, there would be a new delivery system, a distributed network of relatively small computers that concentrated on acquiring, storing, and feeding these materials from and to users. Fourth, this would be a franchised delivery system, licensing its specialized storage and delivery software to vendors throughout the world, with copyright supported by an automatic royalty system.

I am surprised to say it still looks to me as if this is what will happen.[1]

2. *Organizing, visualizing, and intercomparing ideas.* As I said earlier, the process of writing—a primary example of organizing thought—is complex. We need screen tools not just for seeing bare outlines, as today's software allows, but for intercomparing alternative structures. And here we have scarcely begun in 1990, let alone in 1960.

It was obvious that word processing and outline processing (which I started imagining immediately) were helpful but inadequate. What relevance does writing a sequential document have? We want deep understanding. We want version control. We want to be able to write one version, then bring out of that a transmogrification, a new unfolding, another structure. Then we want to see how this deep structure in the second draft relates to the structure in the first draft. This problem of intercomparing alternative structures goes beyond mere sequence; it seemed to me fundamental. We must be able to intercompare things in depth, whether or not they are sequential. This is the problem—deep intercomparison among complex structures.

So my first design, which became by stages the Xanadu project, was a system for presenting deep alternatives in the organization of the same material.[2] That was to be my term project thirty years ago, actually only being finished now.[3]

3. *Constructs.* I began to ask, What overall structures might be useful as ways to organize things? For instance, outlines as we know them are a construct. We need constructs for intercomparison and

outlining, and for the parallel visualization of alternatives and comparisons of all kinds.

The Handle in the Rock

I had crossed enough fields, and looked at the lives of enough innovators, to know that I was onto something. I knew I was the first in the world to be onto this. I had enough vision to recognize a handle when I saw it sticking out of a rock. This was like Arthur's sword in the stone; but it was not the handle of a weapon, it was the handle of some other great tool, one I would need in all my academic and creative work.

The wild surmise on a peak in Darien, Balboa looking at the Pacific: "Holy smoke!" I saw this as the vehicle that would allow me to do more work faster, and thus satisfy all my ambitions.

So I decided I would not try to finish another book until I had the tools—proper, decent tools to allow the deep comparison of complex structures on the computer screen. I thought it would take from three to six months. And these same deep intercomparison tools (I call them *thinkertoys*) would be necessary for holding hypertext. I thought that hypertext would replace the printed word by 1962. As I said in *Literary Machines,* I mistook a clear view for a short distance.

There were no decent tools by 1962, or by 1982, and indeed they do not yet exist on earth—good strong writing systems with deep intercomparison of versions. Instead we have trivial word processing, outline processing, desktop publishing; and the important stuff—intercomparison tools and structures like those I have called *zippered lists*—is ignored, not comprehended, and not yet built.

Selecting the Word

I kept on designing, in my various garrets. By 1964 I realized the historical importance of choosing the right word for this new kind of text that would reshape the world.

Now, I hold with Mark Twain that the difference between the right word and the almost-right word is the difference between the lightning and the lightning bug. There are so many ways the choice of a phrase can slant people's thinking, and I wanted to help them think right. Suppose we made up some stupid word like *teachotechnics* or *showmanshipnogogy*? It would seem to be a branch of something else, not the new field of its own that seemed so clear to me.

Then I thought of the right word. *Hypertext* was an audacious choice: *hyper-* has a bad odor in some fields and can suggest agitation and pathology, as it does in medicine and psychology. But in other sciences *hyper-* connotes extension and generality, as in the mathematical *hyperspace,* and this was the connotation I wanted to give the idea.

In the fall of 1965 I published the first papers with the word *hypertext* and gave my first paper. It was before the Association for Computing Machinery in Cleveland. This was starting at the top, and it got a great reception. Briefly.

From there it was downhill, downhill for years, and then decades; perhaps largely, I now realize, because no one understood the idea. I now see this deep misunderstanding as a paradigm problem, and confusion as predestined; but in those days I could not understand why others did not understand.

Occasionally, in the present day, people come up to me and say they were inspired by that first talk in Cleveland. But at the time, I didn't hear about it.

Indeed, I didn't realize during those early years that people may have thought I was clinically insane. And, if paranoia is to believe what others do not believe, then clearly I was paranoid. That definition leaves us two cures: on the one hand, the paranoid can be persuaded to accept the views of everyone else. That is the low road. Or, on the other hand, by the paranoid's effort and persistence he can persuade others to adopt the same view, thus freeing himself of the malady. This was my therapy of choice.

The Problems in the 1960s and 1970s

I put aside the overall vision of the future hypertext literature, and the problems it might create, although they frequently came into my thoughts. In the 1960s I concentrated on two issues: what separate hypertexts would be like, and the kinds of organizing constructs that might create some manner of orderliness.

In my first paper, in 1965, I concentrated on the organizing constructs. (I also hoped these might improve the prospect for a unifying literature.) In particular, I came up with structures I called *zippered lists,* which I described in my first paper (but never implemented as such). Zippered lists have been with me since, as an idea both for organizing and for visualizing.

After that, in the late sixties, I concentrated on hypertexts that individuals could produce—that is, individual works or chunks with jumps between them on the screen. This is roughly where most of the field is now—facilitating individual hypertexts that take over the whole system (such as Hypercard).

Around 1967 I began to see that the real problem was different. The real problem is not merely the creation of organizing constructs, or the individual hypertext unit, but how to merge into a coherent and unified literature the many different hypertextual and hypermedia objects being created, and to comprise these many contributions—created under different rules, with different graphics, with different styles of interaction—into a unified literature, a unifying system that we may all access through whatever machine we use.

Throughout the seventies, the issue that crowded my mind was how to design this overall structured literature in which many hypertexts, documents, and authors could participate—how to devise some system of order that put every contribution on an equitable basis with every other—unlike most of the other computer-based text and media of that time, and now. In the paper world we have this equitable basis: because books are compatible, they can be read with the same equipment, and they meld into a common literature.

This too redounds to the issue of freedom. Look at the petty tyrants on the networks of today—the sysops on the computer bulletin boards, the leaders of electronic conferences who delete whatever they don't like. Who chose them? Who baptized these particular guys as the arbiters of taste and propriety? At least in the magazine world, editors tend to have some principled basis for operation that others know of in advance. In tomorrow's electronic literature, we must have a system to which all participants are welcome whether or not anyone likes their contributions.

And so it is with paper: you can publish books and send them where you will. Paper literature at large is open, though some of its byways are not. What is to be the electronic equivalent?

Personal Computers

In the late seventies came personal computers. (I needn't regale you with the so-called personal computer revolution.) As luck would have it, I had just published a book, called *Computer Lib*, that predicted personal computing and the explosion of computer graphics, and the accuracy of my predictions surprised many people. Many of them are still coming true.

My involvement with the so-called personal computer revolution remains a bittersweet experience for me, because only part of the dream came through, even with the great interest in hypertext today. I've been compared by Stuart Brand to Thomas Paine; I've also been compared to Leon Trotsky. In every revolution, you see, there is someone who says, "Wait a minute! We haven't gone far enough! Don't stop now, or we betray our principles!"

And I say that the purpose of computers is human freedom. But who has yet been made free by computers?

The revolution most important to me will be the revolution in access to ideas: a grand open hypertext system that will let anyone explore all the ideas there are in the world, as expounded by those who believe in them and with all the color and vitality that belong to that exposition.

I suppose I am an elitist, because I think highly intellectual controversies are important. I'm also a populist, because I think everyone has the right to take the elitist approach to ideas: start where you want to start and do your own thing. I want to give, to every kid, the same privileges, the same freedom of ideas, that Bertrand Russell had as a kid, and Bucky Fuller had, and I had—to every kid, everywhere. I want to make the world safe for smart children, so that all children are safe to be smart.

The Xanagroup

Computer Lib, and the notoriety it brought, brought also coworkers. In 1979 an unusual group came together to build the world repository I've been talking about.

The group included some remarkable people: especially Roger Gregory, a former mathematics graduate student from the University of Michigan, irascible technocritic and generalist. Mark Miller, one of the more remarkable minds of our time, as a Yale student read every word of *Computer Lib,* and he lectured a seminar at Swarthmore on historical version intercomparison, from a page in my book I thought no one had ever read. He is now the key designer of tomorrow's Xanadu system. Another who worked with the team for a time was K. Eric Drexler, the physicist who predicts nanotechnology in his book *Engines of Creation.*

I had done the best I could with the design of the Xanadu system to that point. What I really did, it turned out, was find the people who could come in and take it over.

For the first part of the summer of 1979, we sat on a porch in Swarthmore, Pennsylvania, considering the question Is it mathematically possible to supply billions of readers at screens with the exact paragraph, sentence, fragment, illustration, or footnote, photograph, or piece of movie that each requires, immediately? Even if the number of the stored documents and the number of the links between them grow into trillions? And this was a fundamental question.

I am not a mathematician; those guys were. And after two months spent looking at every possible method we could propose, we came to the conclusion Yes, it could be done. This was a heavy responsibility.

Had that not been the case, we would have disbanded, shaken hands, and said "Well, that great hope is out of the question; let's look for something smaller to do with our lives."

But no. It was determined that this was feasible, and then we argued about the structure of such a system, and we agreed on how it should work and the meaning of freedom in such a system. We agreed specifically on the rights of the user—for example, that no one can see or keep a record of your reading and that you may publish freely. Fundamentals. We arrived at complete agreement—astonishing for the most captious group of people I ever met, unable to agree on what to have for dinner. Yet we agreed on all of this. Then they said something that shook me to my core: they said, "OK, Ted—we understand what has to be done; go away."

Years ensued. We worked hard and survived. And in 1988, half of the Xanadu project—Xanadu Operating Company (XOC), the branch of the project concerned with developing the software—was bought by mighty Autodesk, Inc., for an undisclosed sum. And since then the group—substantially the same group, a decade later—has been working on a product to embody these principles.

A Generalized Structure for Electronic Literature

The conceptual structure of an information system is perhaps its most vital aspect. This is more true for a system that must hold and supply millions of documents and their interconnections. Now I want to redefine the terms *document* and *literature*. As a moralist of words, I want the redefinitions to be faithful to the old meanings and yet open the door to the future. So let me define a *document* as an information package created by someone at a given time. This is subtly erosive of the computer notion of databases. A database is a collection of information that's allegedly true, and people talk about "all knowledge in a database." I leave the representation of knowledge to the artificial intelligencers; let them try. Meanwhile I know what a document is, and storing these documents and giving people rapid access to them— this is our focus, and it is an immediate and powerful goal for us all.

A document is a package of information; it has a creator, a date of creation, and presumably a point of view.

So now let's take the word *literature* and see again if we can re-understand it, in a way that does justice to its old meaning and opens the door to tomorrow. I say that literature is a connected system of documents. So the literature in biomechanical engineering, the literature in literary criticism, the literature in sociology—each of these is a literature because the connections within it are dense. And all writing taken together is a literature, too, albeit with less dense connections. So we can think of individual literatures as galaxies and of all literature as the universe or, as I prefer to say, the *docuverse*.

Very well. How can we expand literature to the world of tomorrow? Literature (I have noticed—and this seems to be a new insight for people) is a debugged system. Literature has been working well for thousands of years. By this I mean the system of studying and storing individual documents and following their interconnections. This person quotes that person; each point of view is perfectly expressed in principle by its owner because that person gets to express it any way they want.

Even so we must have a way of unifying under a common accessibility the so-called information explosion. Sure, there are all these books and all these magazines—but are you reading more this year than last year? Probably not, because you have an absolute number of hours. And how long can you spend in the stacks?

The real issue is literature—all literature. The problem is to create a unifying and principled basis for the interconnection of everything that everyone says, to maintain the integrity of each document, and yet to allow everything to be deeply interconnected. So the issue is one of *grand hypertext,* as I call it, and of the literature of tomorrow, and of how to create a conceptual framework satisfactory for indefinite growth.

I would like to propose a sort of Gaia hypothesis of literature: that a literature, or all literature, is a living system that maintains stability and brings needed things to the surface, just as (according to Lovelock's thesis) Gaia brings to the surface of the water those calciferous blooms that are required to adjust the temperature of the planet. These blooms, although never before suspected, now appear as white splotches in the Atlantic Ocean when viewed from space. So too may the literary system bring to the surface those issues that the time is right to concentrate on. But these are speculations.

In this grand vision the document is the central concept. The integrity of that original document is vital, but people everywhere have to be able in their turn to use it any way they wish, to quote from it and arrange it for their use—just as when you buy a book you can cut it up and rearrange the pieces. You must be able to do that electronically.

How do we reconcile this cutting up with the integrity of the original? That is, I think, the fundamental idea of the Xanadu project.

Transclusion

Our unifying structure in the Xanadu project maintains the integrity of all original materials and yet allows individuals to quote and anthologize in any way they wish. How can we do it? The answer we call *transclusion,* a simple idea, like *quotation* but not quite.

When you cite something, you ordinarily insert a copy of the quoted material from the original, or quoted, document into the new, or quoting, document. In the Xanadu model we use transclusion instead:

now you have a hidden pointer in the data structure of the second document, which points to the original and tells the computer-based reading machine where to get it. So the material is not copied from the original; it remains in the documentary space of the original and is brought anew from the original to each reader.

Let us see what this does in various contexts.

1. *Copyright.* This system allows all the appropriate desiderata of copyright to be achieved: one, payment for the originator; two, credit for the originator; three, nothing is misquoted; four, nothing is out of context. How could I mean nothing is out of context? Well, the inquiring user may immediately ask for the context of the original and see it. (This has to be interactive — you can't have the context of every quotation hovering in the background of your own document, but if the material is taken as needed from the original, then the context is as easily obtained as the quotation.)

So that's what transclusion does for copyright. It makes the copyright system work without complication, and with the freest arbitrary usage. Now you may create, through transclusion, any anthology you wish, using any sort of quotation, rearranged any way in your own document. Thus anyone is free to revise anything without affecting the integrity of the original and without permission, since no copy is made until the reader buys the copies through the automatic reading machine.

2. *Versioning by the owner.* If you are the originator of a document and create a second version, that second version is a transclusion of all the original parts you wish to retain, put into that new order, plus any new material. So readers of the new version can compare it side by side with their notes on the old version, seeing all the differences. The old remains accessible, and the integrity and intercorrespondence of both is maintained.

3. *Versioning by anyone else* (celluloid overlays). Anyone, even a stranger, may also revise this document. The revised version, also consisting of transclusions and new material, becomes then that stranger's version of the document.

Thus each new version is like a celluloid overlay, varying the document's contents without modifying its original storage. This is how we maintain, with utter clarity of origin and convenience, the sources of every fragment: transcluding all the portions that are still there and making whatever changes the new context requires. (Note that the principal difference between changes by the document's owner and changes by the stranger concern ownership of the account: the original owner has a right to the original name and author-name unmodified, the stranger must find another designation.)

Open Hypertext Publishing

Hope for the future lies in the accessibility of open hypermedia publishing. Not only may anyone publish a document and any reader draw out any part, as mentioned in our 20/20 vision, but anyone may publish connections to any part, visible wherever they are attached. Some authors may find this disconcerting. But it is fair. If I can put footnotes on other people's documents, then they can put them on mine (though I may not always look forward to such exchanges).

It is entirely possible that without open hypermedia publishing we are dead, for, as Eric Drexler argues in *Engines of Creation,* so many technological dangers in the future will mean there is only a narrow keyhole of survival for the human race and for the planet. In this struggle to save the planet, I believe nations and corporations must confront each other and work out serious negotiations, especially those concerning toxic waste, rain forests, and endangered species. Small-scale examples of tough negotiations may be seen in arms control, international whaling, and union-management relations. In each of these, we see natural interests balanced by complex schedules; good faith negotiations, such as union negotiations, require a complex understanding with many comparisons in great detail of lists of wants and proposed concessions. In such a world, the ability to intercompare these matters is a fundamental issue. I believe this today as much as I did when I began my first hypertext design some thirty years ago.

The purpose of computers is human freedom, and so the purpose of hypertext is overview and understanding; and this, by the way, is why I disapprove of any hypertext (like Michael Joyce's "Afternoon" discussed by Jay Bolter) that does not show you the interconnective structure.

Our objective at the Xanadu project has been not to fulfill the needs of industry, or to make things happen a little faster or more efficiently. Ours has been the only proper objective: to make a new world. Don't think of the universal electronic docuverse, of open hypertext publishing with transclusion, as my dream; it's your dream too, if you will only feel it. I want you to see, to feel in your gut, what open hypertext publishing can do for the life of the mind, and perhaps for the life of the planet. Open hypertext publishing is the manifest destiny of free society. It is fair, it is powerful, and it is coming.

Notes

1. For further information see my book *Literary Machines* from Mindful Press, 3020 Bridgeway #295, Sausalito CA 94965.

2. "Xanadu" is a trademark of the author for computer software and services, licensed to Autodesk, Inc.

3. For information on the current status of Xanadu software, contact XOC, Inc., 550 California Ave., Palo Alto, CA 94306.

Discussion

TUMAN. While hypertext undermines the boundaries that have traditionally separated author, reader, and text, a hand-crafted hypertext like Joyce's "Afternoon" seems only to explore a small and relatively safe part of this new territory. What happens when such an author-controlled work gets placed within a larger hypertext publishing system like Xanadu, where it becomes as easy to make links outside as inside the original story, when Joyce's paths become only one possible set of options available to the reader? Doesn't such a possibility or eventuality lead to a more radical rethinking of literacy than you have indicated?

BOLTER. The territory explored by "Afternoon" is neither small nor particularly safe. It is true that episodes in this hypertext are fixed by the author, but there is still enormous room for the reader to wander, to reread, and to misread creatively. "Afternoon" already illustrates the principle lesson of hypertext: to write is to reorder the elements of a writing system. "Afternoon" is a writing system whose elements are verbal episodes ranging in length from a single word to several sentences. The reader of a hypertext becomes a writer because he or she can construct the text within constraints imposed by the system. We could allow the reader to construct the text at a different grain—to add new links or to modify the verbal texts. Interesting hypertexts would result, but they would be no more or less valid as literary texts.

We can think of a spectrum that runs from conventional printed texts (which are purely linear and allow the reader to interact only figuratively, not operatively) through texts like "Afternoon" to texts that allow the reader to intervene and rewrite at any level of structure. None of these is better than the other—any more than we could say that loosely structured Homeric poetry (the product of an oral tradition that was flexible and to some degree interactive) is better than the highly linear narrative structures of Virgil's or Milton's epics. Any point along the spectrum can produce compelling results. Electronic technology permits the author to vary the level of reader interaction, allowing the reader various degrees of freedom.

But the reader's freedom can never be absolute. The rhetoric of hypertext (and all of us who work in hypertext are guilty of this exaggeration) tends to be a rhetoric of liberation. We sometimes talk as if the goal of electronic writing is to set the reader free from all arbitrary fixity and stability of the print culture. In fact, hypertext simply entangles the reader in nets (or networks) of a different order. Readers are tempted to believe themselves free of all control, only to be caught by two kinds of constraints—the constraints of the computer system and the constraints of the writing system the computer embodies. The computer system aims to be transparent, but it can never achieve that goal. The reader must interact with the computer in some way (typing, moving the mouse, or speaking into a microphone) and therefore must know and obey the rules of interaction. The writing system may be any combination of words, graphics, and video. But, as semiotics and postmodern theory in general have shown us, all such verbal and graphic writing must function in terms of codes and conventions. The reader can neither ignore nor circumvent these codes and conventions.

Like all previous forms of writing, hypertext depends upon the interaction of many such codes. A system like Xanadu would put many millions of verbal and visual texts at the reader's disposal. The reader turns into a writer by using links to connect fragments of these texts into new patterns. The hypertextual reading is both operationally and figuratively dependent upon the written tradition; it is simply that the written tradition is much larger in Xanadu than it ever was in a printed library. The whole point of Xanadu (and hypertext in general) is to tie each reader/writer more firmly into the textual tradition.

McCorduck.   Having now read "Afternoon" a few times, and in a few different ways, I agree completely with Jay that the territory explored by the story is neither small nor safe. The same is true for the disk version of Jay's own *Writing Space*. I am also learning to write with the hypertext tool *Storyspace*, which certainly turns your head around!

Tuman.   We are used to talking about reading largely in vertical terms of higher or deeper levels of understanding—contrasting, for example, a shallow, superficial reading with one that is probing, profound. Does the advent of hypertext, and its largely horizontal language of links, paths, and webs suggested by both Bolter and Nelson, signal the advent of a new geography of understanding?

PROVENZO.   The advent of hypertext, not only hierarchically but also symbolically, signals the advent of a new geography of understanding. Landow and others can address the hierarchical issues most effectively—let me explore the symbolic side.

It should be noted that with the Gutenberg revolution, the technology of the book made it possible to create and disseminate new ideas. Architecture was transformed, for example, by the creation of pattern books that could be cheaply reproduced and widely circulated. Symbolic representations, while certainly not new in their association with written language, became redefined and transformed. Changes in typography and the symbolic function and presentation of text date back to the earliest years of printing. Italic printing, for example, has its origins during this period. According to legend, the great Venetian humanist and printer Aldus Mantius developed italic type so he could compress more text onto a single page. The design for italic was based on models of cursive handwriting then in use in the papal chancery.

Italic typefaces are significant because they provide a standard typeface with a second dimension. Thus an italic type accompanying a standard, more linear, roman face has imbedded in it a secondary message. The introduction and use of italics may seem a trivial issue. In fact it represents a small but important example of how the new technology of print transformed the process of writing. While, technically, italic handwriting was possible before the invention of print, it was not developed. Even if it had been, it would not have been practical. When italic is written by calligraphers today, it represents merely a particular style of writing. *It is not typically used to offset or emphasize a specific point or concept in a text, as is the case in this sentence.*

The introduction of new graphic means of presentation—ones made possible by the print and typographic revolution of the fifteenth and sixteenth centuries—reflects a radical reconceptualization of the meaning of text. The implication of these changes across different fields was profound.

Examples of new iconic forms emerging as part of contemporary computer culture include forms as diverse as the Space Invader

Warriors from the arcade game, Mario from the Nintendo game system, and the various icons and symbols included as part of the Macintosh system (the "trash can" and so on). I am convinced that iconic and symbolic forms as exciting as those that emerged from the Renaissance will come into being through the use of hypertext and hypermedia.

A simple example demonstrating this point could, for example, take place through the creation of electronic rebuses. A rebus is a representation of a word or phrase by pictures and/or symbols. The popular television game *Concentration* uses rebuses as the basis for its puzzles. Rebuses were widely included in children's game and activity books during the nineteenth century. Hypertext has the potential to reinvent the rebus as a form. Imagine, for example, a word processor that creates a rebus every time you write something. It might have a screen with a small narrow window at the base showing the word or sentence being written and its symbolic representation immediately above it. Animation and color could be added. Using a hypertext-based rebus writer one could write "I saw the brown dog jump, and then jump even higher." The symbolic representation of the construction could include words, rebus constructions, symbols, and animations. Imagine such a system being given to a grade-schooler: as a classroom word processor, one that might include a system for putting anything written into the computer into a synthesized speech package that could be played back, or as yet another window that presents the sentence in a phonetic form such as the Initial Teaching Alphabet. Using hypertext techniques, a system such as this is not only a possibility but would be relatively easy to execute.

Systems such as a computerized rebus writer are relatively primitive compared to what will probably emerge for use as part of hypertext systems during the next ten or fifteen years. It is perfectly plausible to imagine symbolic/iconic writing systems being developed for the composition of poetry. The sort of elaborate word and special textual presentations that are found in the work of poets such as e. e. cummings will probably go through a further process of evolution and development. Verbs will literally become active—where appropriate, migrating across the computer. Exclamation points will explode as they emphasize their point. A word like *unfold* may literally do what it says. Or one like *disappear* may literally disappear. Sound will be incorporated into textual and visual materials. Thus, the reader will not only see the "brown dog" jump higher and higher, he will hear him bark at the moon as well. Text, visual representations, and sound will combine to give new meaning to the phrase *to be literate*.

> 2 <
COMPUTERS
and New Forms of Teaching English

Hypertext, Metatext, and the Electronic Canon

George P. Landow

Many of our assumptions about education and its institutions derive from the printed book. We assume, for example, that education, particularly in the humanities or social sciences, requires books or simulacra of them produced by xerography. We also assume that the texts we read belong in some way to the authors who created them, despite ample evidence that few books have much in them that is properly considered novel or original. We make many assumptions about the role and strategies of education—assumptions that we take to be natural, inevitable, and hardly worth questioning—that derive largely from the information medium which originally generated them and with which they have so long been associated. We assume for example that when we teach a novel, say, *Great Expectations*, our students will read it, study it in essential isolation from any biographical, political, religious, or other contexts, and, if particularly sophisticated, consider it from the vantage points of one or more critical approaches. Unless pressed to do so, our students, we assume, will not compare it to other works they have read, even in the same course, and they will assume, in turn, that they are not supposed to introduce materials from other courses too frequently or at all into their readings of *Great Expectations*.

Education was not always thus, and hypertext, a new electronic information medium, promises to make changes as radical as those made five centuries ago by Gutenberg. Because hypertext changes our basic experience of the texts we read, we can expect that it will also change our corollary assumptions about literary education, the curriculum, and the canon that shapes it and is in turn shaped by it.

Suppose that instead of reading a printed book, our student—let's call her Jane Lee—sat down to read *Great Expectations* for her introductory survey course in a different information medium, one that placed greatest emphasis upon making and following connections, one that, moreover, made little distinction between reader and writer. Jane sits down at a computer console with a large screen on which she encounters three-dimensional images of folders lying on a desk top.[1] Touching the folder labeled "Literature" with her fingertip, she opens it, finds another series of folders bearing names of various languages and nations and chooses "English." Upon opening the English folder, she encounters others inside bearing names of authors (Dickens, Lessing), movements or periods (aestheticism, Victorian), and concepts or approaches (literary techniques, feminism). Touching the folder for Charles Dickens, she opens it and finds a series of documents and additional folders that include several graphics documents some of whose titles include the word *overview*. Choosing "Dickens overview," she finds a familiar graphic directory in which the name of the novelist appears together with his portrait and dates within a rectangle at the center. Surrounding this rectangle are a number of other rectangles bearing various texts, including "Biography," "Literary Relations," "Cultural Context: Victorianism," "Literary Techniques: Imagery," "Political and Economic Context," "Religion," and "Works." Choosing "Works," she opens a complete list of the novelist's works, which appears on the lower left of her computer screen; then she opens *Great Expectations*, which appears in the center of her screen, to the page at which she had last been reading the paperback copy she left in her room. (Approximately thirty seconds have elapsed since Jane first sat down to work.)

Reaching her hand to the top of the screen, Jane opens a menu marked "Preferences," which allows her to configure her electronic copy of *Great Expectations* as she wishes. At her last session she had chosen to view the text as it appeared when first published serially, but now she changes to the kind and size of font she has found in the past to be the most comfortable for reading. After completing the last pages of the final chapter, Jane returns to "Preferences" and requests to see the text as fully linked as possible. To the right of the text immediately appears a dynamic concept map showing connections to that part of the text on screen. Choosing among variant readings, comments by various critics, Dickens's original notes, and earlier and later novels by Dickens and other authors that might have relevance, she first looks at essays comparing Jane Austen's *Pride and Prejudice* to *Great Expectations*, after which she opens her electronic notepad and adds a few remarks to those from earlier sessions.

Returning to the overview with which she began, Jane now looks through materials on the novelist's life, choosing to examine first a brief biographical essay and next more detailed studies of his childhood and of the years during which he wrote *Great Expectations*. These materials in turn lead to others on contemporary social and political conditions. Returning again to the overview, she examines the range of documents linked to the section on conditions of life. As someone who has considered a career in medicine, she picks the public health overview, which leads to materials on sanitary conditions, nutrition, and diseases—materials that have been created by a faculty member in another department at another university for his course in Victorian social history. Some of these images, statistics, and essays link to questions about the degree to which Dickens wrote as a realist and what the term *realist* might mean in the nineteenth-century context. These materials, like those on urban history, were written not by her instructor but by a member of the Department of Comparative Literature. Thinking that some of these materials might help with her forthcoming term paper, Jane places private links, which no one else can see, from them to her notepad.

Returning yet again to the overview, she opens another one for the literary relations of *Great Expectations* and examines the range of works read in the survey and other courses she has taken. Coming upon Graham Swift's *Waterland* (1983), which she read in a course on contemporary British literature, she touches the icon representing it and learns that one can obtain Barry Fishman's honors thesis on Swift, all the reviews the novel received on its initial publication, forty-five brief essays by students at her university, as well as the text of the novel. Using the keyboard of her computer, she types in "*Great Expectations, Waterland*" and instantly receives a menu listing six essays comparing the two novels in terms of theme and individual techniques. One of the essays appears to be way off the mark, and she adds a response to it, which automatically links to this other essay.

Her interest piqued, she now looks further at Swift's novel, encountering, among other materials, a graphic presentation of novels in English published in chronological proximity to it. Finding materials on works by Penelope Lively, Jan Morris, Jane Gardam, T. Coraghessan Boyle, Robert Coover, Timothy Mo, Salman Rushdie, Chinua Achebe, and Wole Soyinka, she decides to make a note inquiring if they, too, have obvious connections to *Great Expectations*. Leaving this note for other members of her discussion section to find when they use this hypermedia system, she decides to freeze her session and go to dinner.

Jane has been reading hypertext; and systems with most of the capacities described already exist and have been employed to support the kind of reading Jane has been doing.

Ted Nelson has defined hypertext as *"non-sequential writing*—text that branches and allows choices to the reader, best read at an interactive screen. As popularly conceived, this is a series of text chunks connected by links which offer the reader different pathways" (2).[2] Hypertext is probably best described, however, as multisequential, rather than nonsequential, since it is characterized by the fact that readers can take various paths through a set of documents—what Nelson calls the *docuverse*— rather than by the fact that they cannot take any path.

By allowing readers to choose their own reading paths, hypertext cedes to the reader some of the authority that both manuscript and print grant to the author and thereby fulfills Roland Barthes's call in *S/Z* for a text in which the reader takes a more active, determining role 4). As the authors of "Reading and Writing the Electronic Book" point out, hypertext blurs the boundary between author and reader in two ways.[3] First, by permitting various paths through a group of documents (one can no longer write "one document or text"), it makes readers, rather than writers, control the materials they read and the order in which they read them. Second, true hypertext, such as the Intermedia system developed at Brown University, permits readers to become authors by adding electronic links between materials created by others and also by creating materials themselves.[4]

This new information medium has broad implications for literature and literary education. Experienced as a writing medium (that is, conceived from the vantage point of the author), electronically linked text demands a new rhetoric and a new stylistics. It raises fundamental questions about plot, characterization, narrative line, and other aspects of fiction.[5] Looking at electronically linked text from the author's position reveals that it radically changes notions of authorial property and collaborative work.

Seen from the literature teacher's point of view, hypertext offers many new possibilities. I have elsewhere discussed using hypertext to stimulate critical thinking and to provide information difficult to introduce into lecture or discussion.[6] In the following pages I would like to discuss the educational implications of hypertext that derive from one of its fundamental qualities—its existence in the form of a collection of electronically linked materials. I shall examine, in other words, the educational implications of hypertext as the inevitable creator of a *metatext*.

In contrast to print technology, which foregrounds the physical separateness of each text, hypertext reifies the connections between works and thus presents each work as fundamentally connected to others. Hypertext, in other words, embodies or instantiates Roland Barthes's notions of the individual text as the center of a network. As he explains in S/Z,

> literature itself is never anything but a single text: the one text is
> not an (inductive) access to a Model, but entrance into a
> network with a thousand entrances; to take this entrance is to
> aim, ultimately, not at a legal structure of norms and departures,
> a narrative or poetic Law, but at a perspective (of fragments, of
> voices from other texts, other codes), whose vanishing point is
> nonetheless ceaselessly pushed back, mysteriously opened. (12)

Electronic linking, which generates the fundamental characteristics of hypertext, changes many of the characteristics of text that derive from print, particularly from the physical isolation of the printed work. By inserting the individual text into a network of other texts, this information medium creates a new kind of textual entity—a metatext or hypermedia corpus.

Such bodies of electronically linked documents have an essential openness and, unlike a printed document, never reach completion. In this way hypertext fulfills Barthes's description in S/Z of the "ideal text" whose

> networks are many and interact, without any one of them being
> able to surpass the rest; this text is a galaxy of signifiers, not a
> structure of signified; it has no beginning; it is reversible; we gain

access to it by several entrances, none of which can be authoritatively declared to be the main one; the codes it mobilizes extend as far as the eye can reach, they are indeterminable . . . the systems of meaning can take over this absolutely plural text, but their number is never closed, based as it is on the infinity of language. (6)

Conventional notions of completeness and boundary do not apply to hypertext. Its essential novelty makes it difficult to define and describe in older terms, since these terms (which derive from another educational and information technology) have hidden assumptions inappropriate to hypertext. Hypertext materials—by definition open-ended, expandable, and incomplete—call into question conventional notions of the fixed, bounded text. If one put a work conventionally considered complete, such as the *Encylopaedia Britannica,* into a hypertext format, it would immediately become "incomplete." Electronic linking opens up a text by providing large numbers of points to which other texts can attach themselves. Barthes explains that "as nothing exists outside the text, there is never a whole of the text" (6). The fixity and physical isolation of book technology, which permits standardization and relatively easy reproduction, necessarily closes off such possibilities. Hypertext opens them up, and this opening up has important potential for culture and education.

Reconfiguring Instructors

For teachers a hypermedia corpus or metatext offers a far more efficient means of developing, preserving, and obtaining access to course materials than has existed before. One of the greatest problems in course development is that it takes such a long time and that the materials developed, however pioneering or brilliant, rarely transfer to another teacher's course because they rarely match exactly another's needs. The same difficulties apply to one's own work in different courses: many times teachers expend time and energy developing materials that have potential use in other courses they teach, but they do not make use of them because of the time necessary for adaptation.

A hypertext corpus allows a more efficient means of preserving the products of past endeavors because it requires so much less effort to select and reorganize them. A body of hypertext materials functions, in other words, as an easily accessible electronic institutional memory. It records and retains materials, and, although preserving the individual work, it has a flexibility impossible with print. Therefore, because the individual block of text or text unit can be electronically linked in different ways, teachers and students can arrive at it from different directions. Having created a set of materials on, say, the realistic novel, for an introductory course that reads works by Charles Dickens, one can easily link them to materials for another course that reads either other works by Dickens or works by Elizabeth Gaskell or Anthony Trollope. Furthermore, once one has created materials, questioning, qualifying, or adding to them becomes very easy.

Hypertext also provides a wonderfully efficient means of teaching courses in one discipline that need the support of another because it permits us to teach in the *virtual presence* of other teachers from other disciplines. Using an analogy with optics, computer scientists speak of "virtual machines," created by an operating system that provides individual users with the experience of working on their own individual machines when they in fact share a system with as many as several hundred others.

Computing makes great use of this kind of "virtual" existence: since text processing is a matter of manipulating computer-manipulated codes, all texts that the writer encounters on the screen are virtual, rather than real, texts in two senses: first, according to conventional usage, they only become texts when printed on paper in so-called hard copy. Second, once a writer places some portion of that text in the computer's memory, any work upon that text encounters a virtual text in another sense—the original resides in memory and the reader works on an electronic copy until such time as the two converge when the text is "saved" by placing the changes in memory. At this point texts in the reader's memory and in the computer's memory coincide.

Virtual presence characterizes all technology of cultural memory based on writing and symbol systems: since we all manipulate cultural codes (particularly language, but also mathematics and other symbols) in slightly different ways, each record of an utterance conveys a sense of the one who makes that utterance. Hypermedia differs from print technology, however, in several crucial ways that amplify this notion of virtual presence. Because the essential connectivity of hypermedia removes the isolation of individual texts, the author of that text receives a greater presence. The characteristic flexibility of this reader-centered information technology means that anyone who has contributed material to the entire corpus or metatext is potentially always present to any reader.

Since any one institution, no matter how small, includes specialists from different disciplines, the hypertext materials contributed by its faculty and students will inevitably be interdisciplinary. For example, someone teaching a plant cell biology course can draw upon the materials created by courses in closely related fields, such as animal cell biology, as well as courses in more distant fields, such as chemistry and biochemistry or the history and philosophy of science. Similarly, the instructor of an English course that concentrates on literary technique of the nineteenth-century novel can nonetheless draw upon relevant materials in political, social, urban, technological, and religious history. Teachers frequently allude in passing to aspects of the larger context, but the limitations of time and the need to cover the central concerns of the course often present students with a decontextualized, distorted view of individual texts. By having related materials always accessible, teachers who have hypertext systems available can teach collaboratively with them in several ways: They can simply permit students to encounter related materials during browsing, or they may suggest relevant areas students can investigate. Taking a more active approach, they can create assignments that model the way a professional draws upon several approaches, disciplines, or bodies of material.

Hypertext furnishes an especially efficient, convenient means of teaching interdisciplinary courses, and it thereby solves some of the main problems of such approaches to teaching. At the same time one suspects that work across disciplines, no matter how difficult, provides valuable perspectives for student and teacher, one realizes that the term itself now often bears a kind of stigma. Indeed, interdisciplinary teaching no longer has the glamor it once did, and there are several obvious reasons for this lack of interest. First, the need to deal with several disciplines has meant that some or all end up being treated superficially or only from the point of view of a single discipline. A more important reason for university administrators to look askance at interdisciplinary teaching, however, is that it often requires faculty and administration to make extraordinarily heavy commitments, particularly when such courses involve teams of two or more instructors. University administrators, faced with dispensing always scarce resources, understandably often have little enthusiasm for interdisciplinary teaching, so much so that from their point of view the term *interdisciplinary* might be taken to mean "that which should not be done."

When work across disciplinary lines becomes productive enough to become common, it also changes status and is no longer considered interdisciplinary. Few, for instance, consider biochemistry an interdisciplinary field. It has become a field, a discipline, unto itself. On the other hand, a course covering Victorian biology, geology, and literature would still be considered interdisciplinary, because one does not expect to encounter these fields studied together. Assuming that one wishes to teach such a course—I for one, would find it quite interesting—how would one go about teaching it today? A member of an English department might wait until his or her sabbatical, assuming there is one coming, and then spend that time working up the necessary materials in the associated sciences. Conversely, he or she might find biology and geology faculty members and convince them to teach a course as a team; then together they might seek to gain course credit, released time from their departments, or the administrative mechanism that would enable them to carry out this plan.

In contrast to previous educational technology, hypertext offers the possibility of each instructor's easily gaining access to materials created by content experts in different disciplines and to the virtual presence of teachers from these disciplines. Teaching at an institution where educational hypertext systems are available and in wide use, one has a much greater chance of successfully carrying out interdisciplinary projects. Thus, if one works, as I do, with an educational metatext to which geologists and biologists have contributed, then one discovers that all of one's teaching becomes potentially—indeed, inevitably—interdisciplinary. Simply by linking one's materials on literature or history to those created by workers in another discipline (say, biology), one automatically transforms one's materials into interdisciplinary ones. At Brown such use of an interdisciplinary educational metatext, which has clearly only reached its first stages, occurs readily. Materials on Tennyson, Dickens, and Victorian science developed for my English courses link to timelines and essays that Peter Heywood, professor of biology, has created for his course in cellular biology, and essays on the technological and political context of Graham Swift's *Waterland* similarly link to the hypermedia corpus Professor Richard Smoke created for an upperclass course on nuclear arms and arms control.

Since much of my own work with hypertext involves teaching literary survey courses, the question has arisen whether Intermedia and other such systems might have a natural bias toward historical approaches. Are we not in danger, a sceptic might query, of reducing the imaginative text to a historical artifact, creating a situation where all reading becomes a variation of John Livingstone Lowes's reading of "Kubla Khan"? Four years' experience of teaching with the support of a hypertext system convinces me of the opposite—namely, that this medium, which can indeed present historical connections, most easily encourages text-centered approaches. Linking across document boundaries permits linking across disciplines and theoretical approaches as well as chronological periods. The connectivity of hypertext supports either synchronic or diachronic approaches, though if the medium has an inherent bias, it would be toward the ahistorical. Subsequent uses of Intermedia, such as the *In Memoriam* project, demonstrate its value in recording and presenting intratextual and intertextual relations.[7]

The connectivity that encourages integrating one discipline with another also encourages integrating all of one's teaching, so that one's efforts function synergistically. A hypermedia corpus preserves and makes easily available one's past efforts as well as those of others. Its emphasis upon connectivity also encourages one to relate all of one's interests at those points that touch upon one another. This integrative quality of hypertext, when combined with its ease of use, also offers a means of efficiently integrating one's scholarly work and work-in-progress with one's teaching. All the qualities of connectivity, preservation, and accessibility that make hypertext an enormously valuable teaching resource make it equally valuable as a scholarly tool. In particular, one can link portions of text or data upon which one is working (whether they take the form of primary texts, statistics, chemical analyses, or visual materials) and integrate these into courses. Such methods, which we have already tested in undergraduate and graduate courses at Brown, allow faculty to explore their own primary interests while simultaneously showing students how a particular discipline arrives at the materials, the "truths of the discipline," it presents to students as worthy of their knowledge. Such an approach, which can be used to emphasize the more problematic aspects of a discipline, accustoms students to the notion that for the researcher and theorist many key problems and ideas remain in flux. This approach has a further effect, for it is a particularly efficient means to introduce students to the culture of a discipline, which is one of the most important aspects of teaching.

Hypermedia linking permits teachers to introduce beginners in a field to the way advanced students think and work, also giving beginners access to materials at a variety of levels of difficulty. These materials (which the instructor can make easily available to all, or only to advanced students) permit the teacher to introduce students more efficiently to the actual work of a discipline, which is often characterized by competing schools of thought as opposed to textbook presentations.

Reconfiguring the Student

Because hypertext interlinks and interweaves a variety of materials at differing levels of difficulty and expertise, it encourages both exploration and self-paced instruction. For students, hypertext promises increasingly reader-centered encounters with text. In the first place, experiencing a text as part of a network of navigable relations provides a means of gaining quick access to a far wider range of background and contextual materials than has ever been possible before. Students in schools with adequate libraries have always had the materials available, but availability and accessibility are not the same. Until students know how to formulate questions, particularly about the relation of primary materials to others, they are unlikely to perceive a need to investigate context, much less know how to use the library resources to do so.

Even more important than having a means to acquire factual material is having a means to learn what can be done with such material when one has it in hand. Critical thinking involves interrelating many things. Since the essence of hypertext lies in its making connections, it accustoms students to make connections among materials they encounter. A major component of critical thinking is the habit of seeking the way various causes impinge upon a single phenomenon and then evaluating their relative importance, and hypertext encourages these habits.

Hypertext can also teach a novice reader the habit of nonsequential reading—which is characteristic of more advanced study—and hence becomes an efficient means of learning to read student anthologies as well as scholarly apparatus, prefaces, and the like. Hypertext, with its nonsequential format, efficiently models the kind of text characteristic of scholarly and scientific writing. These forms of writing require readers to leave the main text and venture out to consider footnotes, evidence of statistics and other authorities, and the like. The Brown experience suggests that using hypertext teaches students to read in this advanced manner. This effect upon reading, which first appears in students' better use of anthologies and standard textbooks, exemplifies the way Intermedia and appropriate materials quickly get students up to speed.

Another important effect of educational hypertext appears in the fact that it connects materials to other materials that students encounter in separate parts of a single course and in other courses in the same and other disciplines. This first effect, which results from the benign asynchronicity of hypertext, permits students to perceive connections among subjects and materials encountered at different times in a single course, and it is not adequately described as "integration" or "unification." Despite attempts to encourage students to relate materials read in a course to one another, experience shows they tend to concentrate on each week's work and then go on to the next. When they finish *Pride and Prejudice* and begin reading another work, say, *Great Expectation,* they tend not to think about any diachronic or synchronic relations between the two novels, unless specifically directed to do so by an assignment. Evidence gathered by the assessment team that evaluated the effects of Intermedia strongly suggests that hypertext changes these habits (Beeman et al. 107-8, 150-51). The team reports that students in the section using hypertext had become so accustomed to ranging throughout the course they found it odd that students in other sections did not do so. This result is particularly interesting, since the students still read all the primary works in print;

they worked with hypertext only to obtain reading questions, background materials, and models for integration. A student in another course that had a hypertext component pointed out that he experienced using this body of electronically linked documents as similar to taking the final exam every week—not that it produced high levels of stress but it inevitably led him to create a synthesis of the materials each time he encountered new ones.[8]

In similar fashion hypertext provides a means of integrating subject materials of a single course with other courses. Students, particularly novice students, continually encounter problems created by necessary academic specialization and separation of single disciplines into individual courses. Hypertext's intrinsic capacity to join varying materials creates a learning environment in which materials supporting separate courses exist in closer interrelationships than is possible with conventional educational technology. As students read through materials for a biology or a philosophy course, they will encounter materials supporting other courses and thereby perceive relationships between courses and disciplines.

Hypertext also offers a means of experiencing the way a subject expert makes connections and formulates inquiries. One strength of hypertext lies in its use of linking to model the kinds of connections that experts in a particular field make. By exploring such links, students benefit from the experience of experts in a field, without being confined by that as students would be in a workbook or book approach. In Figure 1, for example, we can see how electronic linking recontextualizes individual works and thereby almost inevitably reconfigures the literary canon and curriculum. At the left of the screen appears the text of Wole Soyinka's poem "Ulysses," which contains a note informing readers that by touching a linker marker (the Intermedia equivalent of a footnote number or symbol) they can encounter "modern and earlier works about Ulysses and discussion." To the right of Soyinka's poem appears the text of the Nausicaa section of Joyce's *Ulysses* and, to the right of that, material on Tennyson's "Ulysses." At the lower right appears a graphic concept map that organizes materials on the literary canon controversy into documents grouped according to definitions, advocates, feminist views, race and ethnicity, individual authors, and the canon. Exploring Intermedia materials with the aide of this overview leads to many articles, including those by

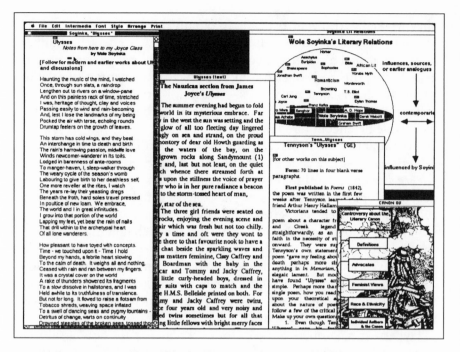

Fig. 1. Three versions of *Ulysses:* Electronic intertextuality.

students on Soyinka's role in the canon and the controversy about it. "Wole Soyinka's Literary Relations," which appears at the upper right, permits readers to organize their search in terms of questions involving intertextuality.[9]

Hypertext thus provides novices with the means to learn, quickly and easily, the culture of a discipline. The reader in Figure 2 has activated the marker above the phrase "Literature" in the "Indian Subcontinent Overview" and thereby darkened icons representing overview or directory documents for three texts—Anita Desai's *In Custody,* Sara Suleri's *Meatless Days,* and Salman Rushdie's *Shame.* Clicking upon a link marker (once, if the marker is already activated, or twice if not) produces the Link Menu, a system feature that, unlike Web View, provides not only the title of the linked documents but also the names the author assigned to the linked blocks or sections within that document. In contrast to the hierarchically organized overviews created by the author, the Web View created by the system automat-

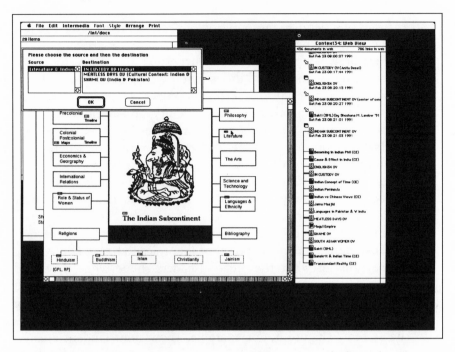

Fig. 2. Making one's way through the metatext by using either the Link Menu or the Web View.

ically shows titled icons representing all documents connected to the active document. Hypertext materials allow students to experience the way an expert works in an individual discipline, and it follows that they also provide students with an efficient means to learn the vocabulary, strategies, and other aspects of a discipline that constitute its particular culture. As in so many other areas of learning, hypertext empowers students by allowing them to master materials quickly.

The capacity of hypertext to inculcate the novice with the culture of a specific discipline and subject might suggest that this new information medium had an almost totalitarian capacity to model encounters with texts. The intrinsically antihierarchical nature of hypertext, however, undercuts such possibilities and makes it a means of efficiently adapting the materials to individual needs. A body of hypertext materials functions as a customized electronic library that makes available materials as they are needed—and not, as lectures and other forms of scheduled presentation of necessity must often do, just when the schedule permits.

The infinitely adaptable nature of hypertext also gives students a way of working up to their abilities by providing access to sophisticated, advanced materials. Hypertext permits the student to encounter a range of materials that vary in difficulty, and authors no longer have to pitch their materials to different levels of expertise and difficulty. Students, even novice students, who wish to explore individual topics in more depth have the opportunity to follow their curiosity and inclination as far as they wish. At the same time, more advanced students always have available more basic materials for easy review when necessary.

The reader-centered, reader-controlled characteristics of hypertext also offer student-readers the power of shaping and hence controlling major portions of what they read. Readers shape what they read according to their own needs; they explore at their own rate and according to their own interests. In practical terms the ease of using hypertext means that any student can contribute documents and links to the system. (Figure 3, for example, shows four student-created documents linked to the "South Asian Women Overview.") Students can thus experience the way contributions in various fields are made.

Nontraditional Students: The Distant Learner

For those interested in the efficient and just distribution of costly educational resources, hypertext offers students at one institution a way to share resources found at another. By permitting one to move from relatively familiar areas to less familiar ones, a hypertext corpus similarly encourages the autodidact, the resumed education student, and the student with little access to instructors to acquire the habit of making those connections which constitute the liberally educated mind. By placing the distant learner in the virtual presence of many instructors, hypertext effectively disperses the resources the instructors have created and allows the individual access to some of the major benefits of an institutional affiliation without costing either party time and money.

The combination of the reader's control and the virtual presence of a large number of authors makes hypermedia metatext well suited for

Fig. 3. Student-created documents linked to the "South Asian Women Overview."

use by distant learners—for those nonconventional students pursuing their learning outside the usual institutional setting. The strengths that make hypertext a powerful means of enhancing education in conventional institutions also make it the perfect means of informing, assisting, and inspiring the unconventional student.

Reconfiguring the Canon and Curriculum

The same factors—connectivity, virtual presence, and shifting of the balance between writer and reader—that prompt major, perhaps radical, shifts in teaching, learning, and the organization of both activities inevitably have the potential to affect the related notions of canon and curriculum. The literary canon as we know it is largely a product of book technology and the economic forces that play upon it.[10]

For a work to enter the literary canon—or, more properly, to be entered into the canon—is to gain certain obvious privileges. This passive grammatical construction, which accurately describes the manner in which a book or painting receives the stamp of cultural approval, reminds us that those in positions of power decide what enters this select inner circle. The gatekeepers of the fortress of high culture include influential critics, museum directors and their boards of trustees, and more lowly scholars and teachers. One of the chief signs of the canon appears in those middlebrow anthologies, those hangers on of high culture that, in the Victorian period, took the form of pop anthologies like F. T. Palgrave's *Golden Treasury* and, today, take that of major college anthologies. In America, to have gained entrance to the Norton or Oxford anthology is to have achieved not necessarily greatness but what is more important, certainly, the possibility of being read. (That is why it matters that so few women writers have managed to gain entrance to such anthologies.)

One sees the privileges of canonization in the notion that something is a work of art or literature, for the classification of some object or event as a work of art enters it into a form of the canon. Such an act of categorization endows a work with certain values, meanings, and modes of being perceived. A work of art, as some modern aestheticians have pointed out, is functionally what someone somewhere takes to be a work of art. Saying it's so makes it so. If one says the found object is a work of art, then it is; and having become one (however temporarily) it gains a certain status, the most important factor of which is simply that it is looked at in a certain way. Taken as a work of art, the object is contemplated aesthetically, regarded as the occasion for aesthetic pleasure, or possibly for aesthetic outrage. It enters, one might say, the canon of art, and the Western world of galleries permits it to inhabit, for a time, a physical space that is taken by the acculturated to signify, "Hey, there. This is a work of art. I'm not (simply) an object for holding open a door. Look at me carefully." If that object is sold, bartered, or given *as a work of art* to one who recognizes the game or accedes in the demand to play one's role in it, then the work of art gains a capacity to generate a special space around it that signals it to be an object of special notice and of a special way of noticing.

Similarly, belonging to the canon confers status—social, political, economic, aesthetic, none of which can easily be extricated from the others. Belonging to the canon is a guarantee of quality, and that guarantee of high aesthetic quality serves as a promise, a contract, that announces to the viewer, "Here is something to be enjoyed as an aesthetic object. Complex, difficult, privileged, the object before you has been winnowed by the sensitive few and the not-so-sensitive many, and it will re*pay* your attention. You will receive a frisson; at least you're supposed to, and if you don't, well, perhaps there's something wrong with your apparatus." Such an announcement of status by the poem, painting, building, sonata, or dance that has appeared ensconced within a canon serves, as I have indicated, a powerful separating purpose: it immediately stands forth, different, better, to be valued, loved, enjoyed. It is the wheat winnowed from the chaff, the rare survivor, and has all the privileges of that survival.

Anyone who has studied literature in a secondary school or university in the Western world knows what that means. It means that the works in the canon get read, read by neophyte students and supposedly expert teachers. It also means that to read these privileged works is itself a privilege and a sign of privilege. It is also a sign that one has been canonized oneself—beautified by the experience of being introduced to beauty, admitted to the ranks of those in the inner circle who are acquainted with the canon and can judge what belongs and what does not.

This canon, it turns out, appears far more limited to the neophyte reader than it does to the instructor, for few read what lies beyond the reading list; few know that one can read beyond since what lies beyond is by definition dull, darkened, dreary. One can look at this power, this territoriality of the canonized work in two ways. Gaining entrance clearly allows a work to be enjoyed; failing to do so thrusts it into the limbo of the unnoticed, unread, unenjoyed, unexisting. Canonization permits members of the canon to enter the gaze and to exist. Like the painting accepted as a painting (and not, say, a mere decorative object or even paint spill), it receives a conceptual frame. Although one can remark upon the obvious facts that frames confine and separate, precisely such appearance within the frame guarantees its aesthetic contemplation—its capacity to make a viewer respect it, take it with respect.

The narrowness of the frame and the confinement within such a small gallery of framed objects produce yet another effect. The framed object, the member of the canon, gains intensification, not only from its segregation but also from the fact that, residing in comparative isolation, it gains splendor: on the one hand canonization permits the canonized work to be seen, and on the other, since there are relatively few objects thus privileged, canonization intensifies the gaze. Not only are potentially distracting objects removed from the spectator's purview, but those that are left benefit from their isolation, as they, and they alone, receive attention (or bear the burden of it).

Not belonging to the canon has obvious ill effects. If belonging thrusts one into view, falling out of it or being absent or exiled from it keeps one out of view. One is in effect excommunicated. One is not permitted to partake of the divine refreshing acts of communion with the divinity, one is divorced from sacramental life and from participation in the eternal. One is also kept from communicating with others; one is exiled from community. Thus, among the harshest results of not belonging to the canon is that noncanonical works do not communicate with one another. A work outside the canon is forgotten, unnoticed; and if a canonical author is under discussion, any links between the uncanonical work and the canonical tend not to be noticed.

I write *tend* because under certain conditions, and with certain gazes, noncanonical works can turn up at the end of connections. But within the currently dominant information technology (that of print), such connections and such linkages to the canonical require almost heroic and certainly specialized efforts. The average, intelligent, educated reader, in other words, is not expected to be able to make such connections with the noncanonical work. For this reader connections do not exist. The connections are made among specialized works and by those readers (professionalized by scholarship) whose job involves exploring the reader's equivalent of darkest Africa of the nineteenth- and early twentieth-century imagination: the darkest stacks of the library where reside the unimportant, unnoticed books, those one is supposed not to know, not even to have seen. The situation not so strangely resembles that of the unknown dark continent that hardly was dark or unknown to itself or to its inhabitants but only to Europeans who labeled it so because to them, from their vantage point, it was out of view and perception. They did so for obviously political—indeed, obviously colonialist—reasons, and indeed one may inquire if this segregated, separated placement at a distance accurately figures the political economy of works canonized and uncanonized.

Like the colonial power—like, say, France, Germany, or England—the canonical work acts as a center—the center of the perceptual field, the center of values, the center of interest, the center, in short, of a web of meaningful interrelations. The noncanonical works act as colonies or as countries that are unknown and out of sight and mind. That is why feminists object to the omission or excision of female works from the canon for, by not appearing within the canon, works by women do not . . . appear. One solution to this more or less systematic dis-appearance of women's works is to expand the canon to include more great women's works recently discovered or else to change standards or definitions of the canon, as some feminist critics have done by arguing for the inclusion of diaries, letters, and other forms of nonfiction by women.

A second approach to solving problems created by the canon lies in creating an alternate tradition, an alternate canon. Toril Moi points to the major problems implicit in the idea of a feminist canon of great works (though she does not point to the possibility of reading without a canon) when she argues that all ideas of a canon derive from the humanist belief that "literature is an excellent instrument of education" and that the student becomes a better person by reading great works. The great author is great because he (occasionally even she) has managed to convey an "authentic vision of life." Furthermore, argues Moi,

> The literary canon of "great literature" ensures that it is this
> "representative experience" (one selected by male bourgeois
> critics) that is transmitted to future generations, rather than
> those deviant, unrepresentative experiences discoverable in much
> female, ethnic, and working-class writing. Anglo-American
> feminist criticism has waged war on this self-sufficient
> canonization of middle-class values. But they have rarely
> challenged the very notion of such a canon. (78)

Arguing that Elaine Showalter aims to create a "separate canon of women's writing, not to abolish all canons," Moi points out that "a new canon would not be intrinsically less oppressive than the old" (78).

Grandiose announcements that one is doing away with The Canon fall into two categories, resembling either the announcements, doomed to failure, that one is no longer going to speak in prose or those of the censor that in totalitarian fashion tell others what they cannot read. Doing away with the canon leaves one not with freedom but with hundreds of thousands of undiscriminated and hence unnoticeable works, with works we cannot see or notice or read. Better to recognize a canon, or numerous versions of one, and argue against it, revise it, add to it.

Having set forth some now-common notions of the positive and negative effects of a literary canon, I would like to express some reservations about the idea that it is particularly rigid. I have little doubt that a canon focuses attention, provides status, and screens noncanonical works from the attention of most people. That seems obvious. I do not believe the one canon about which I know very much, that for English and American literature, has ever been terribly rigid. The entire notion of world literature, great touchstones, and studying English academically has a comparatively brief history, and that history has seen almost continuous change and flux.

The history of Victorian literature, that area of literature to which I devote most of my attention, certainly shows over time astonishing changes of reputation. When I first encountered the Victorians (in undergraduate courses in college some thirty years ago), Tennyson, Browning, and Arnold claimed positions as the only major poets of the age, and Hopkins, when he was considered at all, appeared as a protomodernist in twentieth-century literature courses. In the following decades, Swinburne and the Pre-Raphaelites (first Dante Gabriel Rossetti and then his sister Christina) have appeared increasingly important, as has Elizabeth Barrett Browning, who had a major reputation during her own lifetime. Arnold, meanwhile, has faded badly. Such change in reputations is not new. Looking at older anthologies, one realizes that some of the poets whose reputations have of late taken a turn for the better had fairly strong ones in the 1930s and 1940s but then disappeared into a shade cast by modernism and the New Criticism.

Such evidence—which reminds us how ideological and critical fashions influence what we read as students and what we have our students read now—suggests, perhaps surprisingly, that the literary canon changes with astonishing speed. Only historical myopia could claim that the academic canon long resists the pressures of contemporary interests. In other words, no matter how rigid and restrictive it may be at any one moment, the canon has shown itself characterized by impermanence, even transience, and by openness to current academic fashion.

Nonetheless, the canon — particularly that most important part of it represented by what educational institutions offer students in secondary school and college courses — takes a certain amount of time to respond to present needs. One factor in such resistance to change derives from sincere interest and conviction — though, as we have seen, such conviction can change surprisingly quickly in the right circumstances (right for change, not necessarily right according to any other standard). Another factor, which every teacher encounters, derives from book technology, in particular from the need to capitalize a fixed number of copies of a particular work. Revising, making additions, taking into account new works, all require substantial expenditure of time and money; and the need to sell as many copies as possible to cover the costs of this expensive information technology means that one must pitch any particular textbook, anthology, or edition toward the largest possible number of potential purchasers.

As historians of print technology such as Marshall McLuhan and Elizabeth Eisenstein have long pointed out, the cost of book technology necessitates standardization. Although education inevitably benefits in many ways from such standardization, it is also inevitably harmed by it as well. Most of the great-books courses, which had so much to offer within all their limitations, require some fixed text or set of texts.

Although hypertext hardly provides a universal panacea for all the ills of American education, it does allow one to individualize any corpus of materials by allowing reader and writer to connect them to other contexts. In fact, the connectivity, virtual presence, and shifting of the balance between writer and reader that permit interdisciplinary team teaching do away with this kind of time lag, at the same time that they permit one to preserve the best parts of book technology and its associated culture. Let me give examples of what I mean. Suppose (as is the case) I teach a survey course in English literature, and I wish to include women writers. A few years ago, if one turned to the Oxford or Norton anthologies, one received the impression that a censor had gone through these books consciously eradicating the presence of women—from them and therefore from most beginning undergraduates' sense of literature. One could of course complain, and many did complain. After a number of years (say, seven or eight), a few suitable texts began to appear in these anthologies, though Norton also published an anthology of women's literature in English. All this new presence of women is certainly better than the former nonpresence of women, but entering them into the canon and curriculum takes and is taking a long time. What is worse, many of the texts that appear, at least in these anthologies, may well not be those one would have chosen.

Let us consider a second problem I have encountered introducing new materials into my teaching, one less likely to find redress anywhere as quickly as has the first. I refer to the difficulty of introducing into English literature courses works by authors of non-English ethnic backgrounds who write in English. This problem, which precisely typifies the difficulties of redefining the canon and the curriculum alike, arises because a good many of Britain's major authors during the past century have not been English. In England (whose citizens distinguish quite carefully among English, Welsh, Scots, and Irish) many major figures have not been English since the rise of modernism: Conrad was Polish, James American, Thomas Welsh, and Joyce and Yeats Irish. Generally, anthologies include these figures without placing too much emphasis on their non-Englishness, which shows a nice capacity to accommodate oneself to the realities of literary production.

Today the situation has become far more complex. In Great Britain's postcolonial era, if one wishes to suggest the nature of writing in English (which is how I define English literature), then one must include both writers of Commonwealth and ex-Commonwealth countries and also those with a wide range of ethnic origins who live and write in English in the United Kingdom. Surveying leading novelists writing in English in Britain, one comes upon important English men and women like Graham Swift, Jane Gardam, and Penelope Lively. Such a survey almost immediately brings up the matter of national origins. After all, among the novelists who have won prestigious prizes, of late, one must include Salman Rushdie (Pakistan), Kazuo Ishiguro (Japan), and Timothy Mo (Hong Kong), and, if one includes novels in English written by authors occasionally resident in Britain, one must include the works of the Nigerian Nobel Prize winner Wole

Soyinka, Chinua Achebe (Nigeria), and Anita Desai (India). And then there are all the Canadian, Australian, not to mention American, novelists who play important roles on the contemporary scene. The contemporary English novel, in other words, is and is not particularly English. The contemporary novel is English in that it is written in English, published in England, and widely read in England and the rest of Britain; it is not English in so far as its authors no longer necessarily have English ethnic origins or even live in England.

The canon, such as it is, has accommodated itself to such facts, and, while the academic world churns away attacking or defending the supposedly fearsome restrictions of the canon and the virtual impossibility of changing it, contemporary writers, their publishers, and readers make much of the discussion moot if not downright comical. The problem faced by the teacher of literature, then, is how in the case of contemporary English literature to accommodate the curriculum to a changing canon. One can include entire novels in a course on fiction, but that means that the new does not enter the curriculum very far. In fact, relying on print technology, the academic version of the expanded canon of contemporary literature will almost certainly take the same form as have inclusions of Afro-American literature: it will appear in separate courses and be experienced as essentially unconnected to the central, main, defining works.

Hypertext offers one solution to this problem. In my version of the standard survey course, which is a prerequisite for Brown English majors, I include works by Derek Walcott (Jamaica) and Wole Soyinka (Nigeria) and plan in future years to add fiction by Mo or Achebe. How can hypertext aid in conveying to students the ongoing redefinition, or rather self-redefinition, of English literature? First of all, since Soyinka writes poems alluding to *Ulysses* and *Gulliver's Travels,* one can easily create electronic links from materials on Joyce and Swift to Soyinka, thus effortlessly integrating the poems of this Nigerian author into the literary world of these Anglo-Irish writers.

Since hypertext linking also encourages students to violate the rigid structure of the standard week-by-week curriculum, it allows them to encounter examples of Soyinka's work or questions about its relation to earlier writers when reading Soyinka's works. By allowing students to range throughout the semester, hypertext permits them to see various kinds of connections—not only historical ones of influence or of reactions against a precursor text but equally interesting ones involving analogy. In so doing, this kind of educational technology effortlessly inserts new work within the total context.

Such contextualization, which is a major strength of hypermedia, has an additional advantage for the educator. One of the great difficulties of introducing someone like Soyinka into an English literature course, particularly one that emphasizes contextualization, involves the time and energy—not to mention additional training required— to add the necessary contextual information. In Context32, for example, one already has materials on British and continental history, religion, politics, technology, philosophy, and the like. Although Soyinka writes in English, received his undergraduate degree from Leeds, and wrote some of his work in England, he combines English and African contexts; therefore to create the context for him analogous to those created for Jonathan Swift and Robert Browning, one has to provide materials on colonial and postcolonial African history, politics, economics, geography, and religion. Since Soyinka combines English literary forms with Yoruba myth, one must provide information about that body of thought and encourage students to link it to Western and non-Western religions.

Such an enterprise, which encourages student participation, draws upon all the capacities of hypertext for team teaching, interdisciplinary approaches, and collaborative work, and also inevitably redefines the educational process, particularly the process by which so-called teaching materials develop. In particular, because hypertext corpora are inevitably open-ended, they are inevitably incomplete. They resist closure (which is one way of stating they never die), and they also resist appearing authoritative: they can provide information beyond a student's or a teacher's wildest expectations, yes, but they can never make that body of information appear to be the last and final word. Like literature itself, hypertext remains an open, changing, expanding system of relationships, one that allows one to read Soyinka without abandoning Homer.

Notes

1. Jane, it turns out, prefers to use her reading system in this way, just as she prefers to touch the screen rather than use a computer mouse or her keyboard. Others in her

class use a mouse or wear a circlet that translates head movements into directions to the computer, and they also prefer other visual metaphors, or (in the case of one or two students) none at all.

2. As Nelson further explains, "Hypertext can include sequential text, and is thus the most general form of writing" (3).

3. Nicole Yankelovich, Norman K. Meyrowitz, and Andries van Dam, in "Reading and Writing the Electronic Book," trace the concept of hypertext back to an article by Vannevar Bush, President Roosevelt's science advisor, in the 1945 *Atlantic Monthly* and provide both a history of the concept and the best introduction to its implications; see also James M. Nyce and Paul Kahn, "Innovation, Pragmatism, and Technological Continuity."

4. For a description of Intermedia, which was developed at the Institute for Research in Information and Scholarship (IRIS), Brown University, see Nicole Yankelovich, Bernard Haan, Norman K. Meyrowitz, and Stephen Drucker, "Intermedia: The Concept and Construction of a Seamless Information Environment." Jeffrey Conklin, "Hypertext: An Introduction and a Survey," provides a useful survey of systems at the time of its publication.

5. For more on the problem of the author, see my "Rhetoric of Hypermedia"; and for more on problems of fiction, see Carl Zimmer's "Floppy Fiction." Zimmer discusses the work of Stuart Moulthrop and Michael Joyce in creating hypermedia fictions.

6. For more on authorial property and collaboration, see my "Hypertext and Collaborative Work"; for more on problems of teaching, see my "Hypertext in Literary Education, Criticism, and Scholarship" and "Course Assignments Using Hypertext." "Hypertext in Literature" explains how the hypertext system developed at Brown relates to the other parts of the English courses it supports. Using illustrations, this article also recounts and explains a typical session of a student user.

7. Alan Howard, in "Hypermedia and the Future of Ethnography," exemplifies those who find hypertext's primary value in its application to nonhistorical fields. An early stage of the *In Memoriam* project—in which faculty, undergraduates, and graduate students linked variant readings, critical commentary, and three dozen clusters of images that run throughout the poem—is described in my "Hypertext in Literature" (192-93).

8. Professor Peter Heywood, who used Intermedia to support the teaching of an upper-level course in plant cell biology, reported another way hypertext materials free students from constraints. His students have to produce a term paper that takes into account all research published up to two weeks before they submit their papers. During more than fifteen years' experience with this exercise before using Intermedia, Professor Heywood said, a large number of papers came in late and almost all papers covered the first three weeks of the course; other subjects, no matter how much interest they held for students, came too late in the course for students to include them in such a complex exercise. After using Intermedia, however, all thirty-four students turned in their papers on time, and their topics ranged evenly throughout the semester's reading. He explains this enormous improvement by the fact that students working with materials on the cell membrane (a topic covered in the early weeks of

the course) readily observed connections with other topics (such as genetics or biotechnology) encountered later in the course. Students do not find themselves constrained by the necessary sequence of assignments and therefore efficiently move back and forth throughout the course.

9. The represented screen in this snapshot of an Intermedia session measures approximately 11 x 15 inches, and in order to make the text legible twelve-point type has been enlarged to eighteen. The smaller type in the original documents permits narrower documents, and this different document-width in turn makes the screen less crowded and easier to use than might appear from the snapshot.

10. Howard observes how these factors also shape—and constrain—the nature of research in a nonliterary field.

"Dominion Everywhere":
Computers as Cultural Artifacts

Helen J. Schwartz

In "Anecdote of the Jar," Wallace Stevens tells how a cultural product of humankind affects the surrounding landscape: "It took dominion everywhere." Stevens's jar teaches us that cultural notions are not only performed in ritual, in legal, and in religious functions, but are also made visible or "instantiated" in products which then help organize the surrounding field. We are free, Paolo Freire shows us, only when we realize that culture is human-made and therefore susceptible to change. But often it is hard for those within a culture to gain the critical distance to see culture as human-made.

Standing back and seeing an event as possibly problematic is a mode of critical thinking that takes some practice. At times, for example, science fiction can help us gain cultural distance by resituating a cultural norm; at other times, sci-fi merely extrapolates from the current situation and its values. For example, Richard Fleischer's film *Soylent Green* (based on Harry Harrison's *Make Room! Make Room!*) assumes that traditional food supplies will become inadequate for human needs, but it maintains a cultural taboo against cannibalism, the "solution" to world hunger that is the terrible conspiracy uncovered in the film. However, in the water-scarce ecology of Herbert's *Dune*, the notion of cannibalism (that one's bodily fluids belong to the clan and are due back to it upon the individual's death) is shown as a highly civilized, socially and morally responsible act.

Without a "problematizing" point of view, we are objects of culture. That is, culture (like Stevens's jar) generally organizes the field of experience and gains dominion to such an extent that certain notions become *reifications*—abstractions that become real forces, protected from scrutiny by taboos and enforced through social pressure. We can look at these favored notions critically only when we see them as *instantiations*—that is, when we problematize them as embodiments of ideas that can take that form *or* another form. The poet helps us see this option by writing "Anecdote of the Jar." The science-fiction writer may make this distancing available in popular culture. Without a problematizing point of view, however, people are generally only able to see culture as a human choice and as an instantiation of a worldview at times of drastic change (for example, after losing a war or during widespread social upheaval). The essays in this volume are attempts to combine the practice of analysis with a historically important transition—the integration of computers into meaning making throughout our culture—at a time when we are still aware enough of this transition to see it critically.

Computers can be seen as cultural artifacts of an especially interesting sort. Because they can be programmed to carry out a wide and growing array of tasks, their programs model cultural assumptions. They are useful—and potentially harmful—because they instantiate models of operation. For example, the productivity measures of word processing (tracking keystrokes produced versus the final number of characters in a document) reflect a time-in-motion assessment of work that has been superceded by a more holistic concept of motivation, rejecting the mechanistic view satirized by Chaplin in *Modern Times*. When unions fight to have such tracking disabled, they are fighting a theory of work effectiveness that is enforced in the computer programming, but whose reification they oppose.

Cultural mores provide stability within a culture, but they may become counterproductive in a changing environment. When cultural mores change, the process is usually very slow because those mores have been protected by taboo and buttressed by institutionalization. Kafka's "Penal Colony" shows the power of the Old Commandant living on in law and in enforcement beyond the creator's death and beyond the ability of the people to understand or encorporate that law meaningfully in their lives. The old ways still have power to hurt, to execute, but not to bring life or joy. Culture resists change to the extent that its tenets are reified; it is susceptible to change to the extent that its adherents see its tenets as merely a manifestation of human thought, emotion, and will.

It is important to see computers as cultural artifacts because they are so powerful as enforcers. The controversy about artificial intelligence gains heat, I believe, because people feel safe with computers as long as they are not intelligent and, by definition, cannot become intelligent. However, I would argue, the point is moot since, intelligent or not, computers are agents of human culture. They have no ambition, yet they implement the goals of those who design them to achieve their human ambitions. Computers are without compassion, but their inflexibility reflects either the lack of skill or the rigid rules of the people who invoke computer power. Expert systems may be smart, but they are never wise. They are unambiguous and leakproof. In 1984, Orwell feared the power of leaders to control the populace if interactive devices of surveillance and broadcast could be created; we see today that computers can provide such power. With the advent of personal computers and increasing miniaturization (with expanded capacity), such central control seems unlikely. Nevertheless, we need to be aware of computers as cultural artifacts not only in the ways we employ them, but also in the ways we program them.

The peril of computer power is that we can spawn theories that modify reality through their enforceability, just as Hitler's notions of racial purity significantly changed the demography of Europe. Another peril may seem to be more cognitive than cultural: inadequate realization of a theory in computer programming. Cognitively, the design of computer programs carries out theoretical assumptions, yet theories themselves are attempts to understand reality. When theories take on a power of their own through inexorable, leakproof, computer applications, the theory in the software becomes culturally powerful to change reality. Computer literacy courses usually have a component to explain that the automatic operation of the computer is not infallible but is only as good as the human-made assumptions on which it is based: "Garbage in, garbage out" is part of the folk wisdom of programmers. For example, although computer trading has made many people and organizations lots of money, when it contributes to the Black Monday stock market meltdown of 1987, its limits are painfully visible.

The advantage of computer power is that, if we are aware of computer programming and use as only one model of a solution, we have a powerful tool with which to test theories. In fact, in educational use, one provocative hypothesis (Collis) suggests that perhaps the most useful educational use of computers derives from the opportunity given to teachers to reexamine their assumptions about teaching.

Let me illustrate the perils and possibilities I've discovered in programming computers and implementing their use in education. I argue from the data I know best—my own odyssey as classroom teacher, programmer, and critic. The first software I used was a readability formula to give feedback about style to students in a business-writing class. Readability formulas, such as the Flesch Index, are based on the high correlation between reading difficulty and sentence length and word length in a text. That is, long sentences with big words are likely to be difficult to read. Now, although sentence length and word length are good indicators of reading difficulty (index variables), they do not cause it. To illustrate the difference between index variables and causal variables, consider the high correlation between water temperature and incidents of drowning: lots of drownings when water temperature is high; almost none when it is low. But if someone is drowning, you do not cool the water to save the victim. Although even early studies warned against using readability formulas to gauge difficulty (Charrow, Seltzer), those interested in enforcing plain English have often used readability formulas such as Flesch's to implement legal mandates (Pressman, Redish). It is easy enough to get a document to pass a readability test when one knows the formula is based on word length. And sentence length too. See?

But consider the possible uses of a readability formula in a classroom. At first, in a business-writing course, I required all my students to run the readability formula on their writing. However, my students rarely suffered from the gobbledegook syndrome so prevalent among bureaucrats and academics. The more common problem was overly simple sentence structure, or incomplete control of sentence boundaries, resulting in sentence fragments, run-on sentences, or sentences spliced together with only a comma. Even the ballpark index of complexity shown by readability formulas are confounded when they are run on these errors in students' writing. Sentence fragments produce an artificially low score (Schwartz, "Teaching"). Run-on sentences and comma splices produce artificially high scores. And a formula known to be based on word length and sentence length leads to a mechanistic sense of writing. The formula was helpful to only one of my students: the nurse with good writing skills who prepared a pamphlet on sickle cell anemia for an audience with as low as eighth-grade reading ability. Readability formulas are tempting to reify as standards (as though they were measuring causal variables instead of index variables), because they are so easy to implement as a test, either in a classroom or in plain-English law enforcement, but when we test the theory against reality, we find them inadequate and inaccurate in many cases.

Computer programs have been created not only to gauge writing texts but to help teach the process of writing. Here too I've discovered the dangers of reifying theory in the computer as enforcer as well as the power of computers to instantiate and test theory. Reification is not limited to computer use, however. Sherry Turkle, author of *The Second Self,* tells of her education in a French school where an outline was due the week before any paper was due. Turkle reports that she was never able to write this way; so she would draft the paper and then the outline, turn in the outline but reserve the paper for the next week. Turkle's teacher reified a procedure, but she could not enforce it. Similarly, software such as *Writing Is Thinking (WIT)* programs the standard procedure for essay writing—brainstorming, outlining, then drafting—but the software enforces this procedure. Many writing texts have held up this model as the recommended way to write, and, for many people on many occasions, such a writing process is indeed an efficient and useful one. But studies show there is a wide variation in actual writing processes—from person to person and from one occasion to the next (Bridwell et al.; Bridwell-Bowles et al.). Writing software that provides access to outlines before, during, and after drafting allows teachers to support a theory of writing as broad and as flexible as research shows in the practice of good writers.

Clearly there's a tradeoff in educational use of software for processes as complex as reading and writing. The greater the structure, the greater the teaching effect, but the inflexibility or reification of theory is also greater. In the development of my own software program *SEEN,* even though it won a national award for humanities software, I found myself needing to steer between theory as realized in the software and the questions raised by classroom observation and research. In the several reprogrammings the software has undergone, all changes have moved toward greater flexibility for the teacher or the student.

I started designing *SEEN* in 1980 and have been using it, research-ing its impact, and modifying it since then. The program includes idea-generating tutorials and idea-sharing bulletin boards. The program grew from my desire to encourage students to develop their ideas through writing, while also providing a safe social context in which to compare work with that of other students. I wanted to help students learn the approaches and epistemology of literary analysis. When students in my introductory literature classes asked me what I wanted in their papers, I realized they were trying to learn what my discipline considered to be evidence and how to argue it. In lectures and discussion I could model both the process and the product of literary analysis, but some students could not bridge the gap between my model and their paper. I wanted them to come up with their own ideas and to support those ideas by marshaling evidence. This was hard to do, whether in a small class or in a large introductory lecture. *SEEN* was an attempt to help students internalize disciplinary approaches to their reading and meaning making.

The program's first tutorial was on character analysis, asking the student to provide the name of a character, a literary work in which that character appeared, and a noun or adjective phrase that conveyed an opinion about that character. The choices of the student (for example, "Willy Loman" in "Death of a Salesman" is "a man betrayed by false values") are inserted in generic questions that then ask the student to consider various kinds of evidence in support of the thesis: for example, "what does Willy Loman *do* that shows Willy Loman is a man betrayed by false values?," "how do others react to Willy Loman in a way that shows Willy Loman is a man betrayed by false values?" and so on. Some of the questions are preceded by a yes/no question ("Does Willy Loman change?") so that a nonapplicable question can be skipped. Some involve a two-step process that can be iterated: for example, if the student can think of evidence against his or her thesis (that "Willy Loman is a man betrayed by false values"), that evidence is typed into the tutorial. A follow-up question asks if the student can explain the apparent justification. If so, the word *but* appears on the screen after the contrary evidence, and the student is directed to type an explanation (see Figure 1). The question can be answered as many times as the student can think of contrary evidence. The student's ideas can be printed out, stored on the student's disk, or posted on the built-in bulletin board that allows others to see the work of their peers, compare it to their own, and comment (as shown in Figure 2).

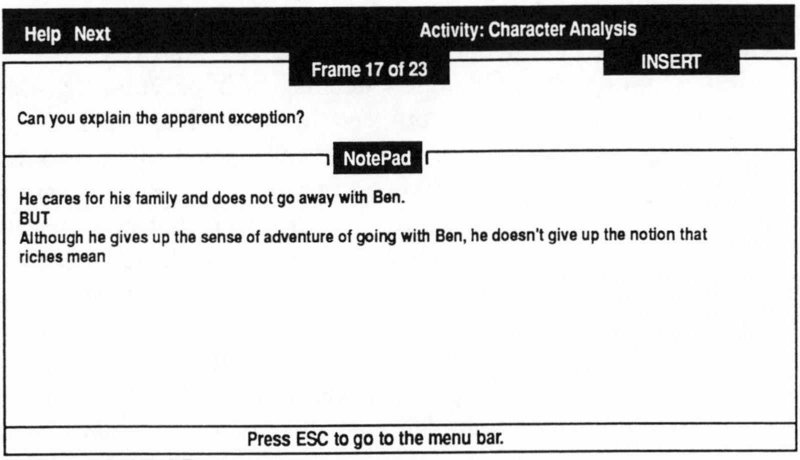

Courtesy of CONDUIT

Fig. 1. Example of a follow-up question in *SEEN*.

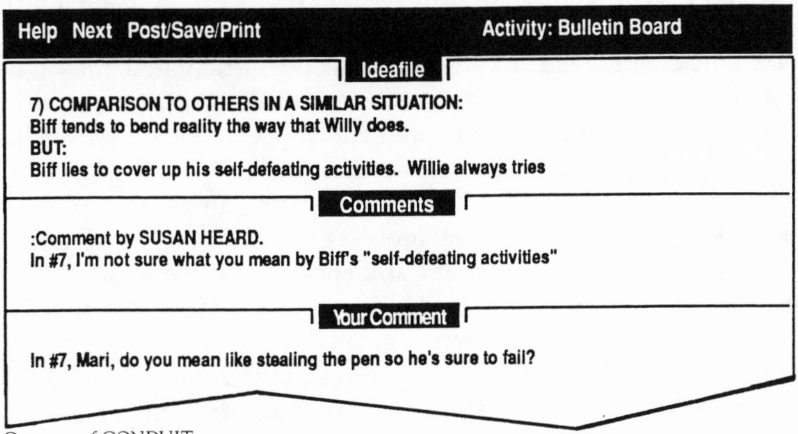

Courtesy of CONDUIT

Fig. 2. Scrolling ideafile and responses on Bulletin Board in *SEEN*.

Studies have suggested that repeated use of the program does lead students to internalize the questions, and this is shown by their marking their books in anticipation of using the computer (Schwartz, "Hypothesis"). A study at the University of Wisconsin has indicated that, although *SEEN*'s bulletin board does not guarantee students will provide perceptive comments or that writers will improve their ideas by building on criticism, for some students *SEEN* provides logistical support for peer- and teacher-sponsored direction (Hastings).

Even though the dynamic of the program seemed to be working, response by teachers and research on program use raised questions about the theoretical model of the New Criticism that underlay the tutorial on character analysis. Would the tutorial really help a student who had not yet established an opinion about a character? Poststructuralist theory emphasizes the constructive power of the reader in interpretation. And critics such as Louise Rosenblatt call for starting with the student's affective response. Frank Madden in a description of his software program *Literature Journal* called for a choice of tutorials so that students could start with an affective approach and then explore other theoretical approaches.

These criticisms and theories led me to conduct basic research on the process of reading and writing about literature. A pilot test at Carnegie Mellon employed "think-aloud protocols" to compare the reading/writing processes of college freshman to those of experts. Each participant read a short story aloud, articulated his or her responses to it, and then wrote an essay (while continuing to think aloud). Each participant completed this process twice, first reading and then immediately writing, and then with a second short story, reading it, using *SEEN*, and afterward writing an essay. This study (using *SEEN* as part of an actual process of writing) suggested the usefulness of the software in helping students develop ideas for an essay, but it also showed they needed help translating ideas into standard essay form. In contrast, expert readers did not need the software. Several developed ideas they incorporated in their essays, but they all, as poststructuralists, found the questions beside the point or counterproductive for their process of meaning making (Schwartz, "Reading").

A subsequent study aimed at ascertaining how critical approaches (or lack thereof) affected readers' ability to construct meaning from literature and convey it in an essay. Without using computers, I studied think-aloud protocols of three kinds of interpreters: college students, New Critics, and feminist critics. (Students ranged from eighteen- to forty-seven-year-olds and had never taken a college-level literature class. The expert readers, aged from twenty-five to fifty-five, were all teachers and had PhDs or post-baccalaureate study.) Again, each participant was asked to think aloud while reading and writing about one of the short stories used in the previous protocol study. SEEN was not used. Initial analysis suggests that students lack the approach to meaning making that critics have internalized, no matter what their theoretical approach, and this suggests the importance of providing tutorials to help students internalize approaches. Although a hypertext copy of the text might enrich interpretation of the text, the students' responses were often already rich and perceptive. What they lacked was the overarching questions that SEEN appears to inculcate with repeated use. For the expert critics, critical theory affected what they chose to write rather than what they saw in their reading. That is, theory guided the critics in choosing among their perceptions to shape an argument, but students usually lacked both a literary theory for selecting data as well as a schema about what was appropriate as topic in a literary essay. Probably the most interesting finding supports Madden's call for teaching a variety of approaches. People vary considerably in their reading process, just as research has shown that people vary widely in their writing processes. For example, some readers are very analytical, working primarily with the text and with literary concepts such as symbolism and linguistic register. Other readers favor an empathic process in which they evaluate episodes with reference to their own experience or "try on" a literary experience to gauge how they would react. These differences in style occur across categories and are not peculiar to either students, New Critics, or feminist critics.

What are the implications for teaching the higher literacy skills of interpretation? The need for different tutorials is clear, as instantiated in Madden's Literature Journal and now in the multiple tutorials in SEEN. In addition, the early version of SEEN was reprogrammed to include utilities for modifying a tutorial or creating a new one. Although this design decision meets objections about theoretical narrowness and provides a variety of approaches, it does not fully address the differences in reading styles suggested by the most recent think-aloud protocols. These concerns must be met, I believe, by the teacher's art of implementation and by creating additional software environments. For example, readers who like to "try on" an interpretation may be interested in the responses of other readers as they read a text, an approach that could be supported in a hypertext reading environment. Or, as a questionnaire answered by my students suggested, some students may prefer to word process an open response without tutorial questions (as is allowed in *SEEN*), or vary their choice of writing format (tutorial or journal response) from time to time. Or students may be asked to modify tutorials or write their own based on a study of their own reading style.

Artificial intelligence (AI) plays no part in the programming of *SEEN*, but the protocol research raises the question whether a more sophisticated heuristic would be useful or possible. In his discussion of a Natural Language Interface (NLI), Victor Raskin suggests that artificial intelligence may aim to do more than encode speech or text into machine-understandable commands, moving in addition into a higher cognitive level that would understand the *intent* of the user. This vision of a mental valet seems incredible, but barely conceivable, in the limited domain of goal-oriented action: saving textfiles, deciding whether to order more blood tests. *SEEN*, however, attempts to help the user *make* meaning, to raise questions and doubts. *SEEN* provides structured "trainer wheels," but as the protocols with experts using *SEEN* suggest, such a program becomes intrusive once the critic understands the process of literary interpretation.

The computer programs that teach or support literacy clearly incorporate theoretical assumptions about literacy, most clearly in structured teaching environments. Less structured, tool-like programs such as word processing and hypertext, however, also act as cultural artifacts. Word processing often wins the loyalty of writers, even when they recognize disadvantages to its use (Case). It makes the revision of text easier, but that capacity will not make writing better unless the writer is able to identify problems, diagnose them, and provide a remedy (Flower et al.). Therefore, simply providing a tool with features that help accomplished writers will not be sufficient for *instructional use*. Teachers must provide the context that shows writers how to revisualize a text before the computer can help with revision. Most teachers, however, need help recognizing what Selfe calls the "grammar" of the new technology—the uses that structure insights and writing unavailable with paper and pencil. Examples of this grammar include calling for three different orderings of a short text (cut and paste), searching for and highlighting key words by replacement (Balestri), and simple insertion of alternate views to force decisions about versions before deleting occurs (Sudol).

Despite the inherent benefits of certain word-processing features, the current design of most word processors also causes problems for writers in nonacademic (and academic) settings. Except with high resolution screens (as on the Macintosh), users have more difficulty reading from a screen than from hard copy (Haas and Hayes). And planning seems to suffer (Case, Grow, Haas), as writing grows looser and writers lose a sense of the whole text (Hansen and Haas).

Amelioration may be possible with high resolution screens and bigger screens that will show different views of a text, including built-in heuristics or templates, outliners, and graphic brainstorming. Several hypertextual programs provide views of the writing process that make structure not only graphic (as with doodled outlines) but dynamic as well. *Learning Tool* and *Storyspace* are constructive hypertexts with this feature. That is, in contrast to an exploratory hypertext in which the reader can only browse, constructive hypertexts allow the user to add to the hypertext as well as navigate existing material. (See Joyce on the terms *constructive* and *exploratory* hypertexts.) Constructive hypertexts allow writers to create objects that can be arranged to show graphically the relation of the parts. The most fascinating feature of *Storyspace*, in my view, is the ability to have text and a representation of the whole essay on screen at the same time, thus overcoming the writer's loss of a sense of the whole. Although I've not had a chance to use the program extensively myself and have some doubts about the modularization of writing, this program seems not only a solution to a problem, but (as with all hypertexts) a possible "prosthesis," as Ulmer uses the metaphor in *Teletheory*. Here we mean an ability to extend human powers in new and unpredictable ways, as Ong has argued that literacy changed human culture from the holistic vision of an oral culture to the analytic capacity of a literate culture.

Let's be clear what we mean by *prosthesis*. I mean not a replacement (a la Captain Hook) but an extension as with contact lenses or a megaphone. Think for a minute what music Mozart might have written if he'd had the finger length of Meadowlark Lemon, the Harlem Globetrotter who could hold a basketball with one hand. The music of a bionic Mozart might have been better, or maybe worse, but certainly different. This example forces us to consider that a technological extension or prosthesis may not necessarily be a benefit. Although Ma Bell intimates that the telephone is a technological prosthesis that improves the emotional quality of life, there is no guarantee that the caller reaching out and touching someone will not make an obscene phone call or an automated sales pitch with random dialing of phone numbers.

In computer technology, hypertext may qualify as a prosthesis because it can integrate the right-brained experience of graphics and the left-brained analysis of language. Reading hypertext can be nonlinear, and we can get different "views" of the same territory.

However, hypertext raises theoretical questions as well. Rhetoric has traditionally been defined as the art by which an author creates and conveys meaning to an audience in order to accomplish a purpose. Are the author's traditional rhetorical goals (informing, persuading, moving) achievable with the nondeterminacy of order in hypertext and the loss of coherence when pearls of text can be strung in a variety of ways? Or is hypertext useful only for making data accessible to the meaning-making activity of the reader? If so, then we should stop using the notion of *rhetoric* and refer only to *information processing,* a term that emphasizes the structuring of data and leaves open whether rhetorical meaning (an argument or thesis) is intended by the author or created by the reader. Does hypertext's openness necessarily involve the "death" of the author and the end of traditional notions of rhetoric—or is it simply a medium that instantiates that argument in deconstructive literary theory? Is the author "dead" in hypertext because he or she cannot constrain the response of the reader through normal plotting devices? Or is hypertext the medium that some authors' texts seem to have been longing for, such as Fowles's *The French Lieutenant's Woman,* Calvino's *If on a winter's night a traveler,* and Borges's "The Garden of Forking Paths" (now adapted to hypertext by Stuart Moulthrop in *Storyspace*). In these works, the authors seem to long for a more active participation by a reader, a collaboration in meaning making. Is it possible to reconceive rhetoric not only from the author's point of view but as a collaboration desired and initiated by the author, consented to and completed by the reader, with the "purpose" mutually defined?

Can the structure of this three-dimensional text be clear enough (even though open) to keep the user from getting lost? Perhaps readers will be able to keep track of their way through alternate forms of representing the text, such as *Storyspace's* maps or *Hypercard's* summary of the last thirty-or-so screens. But will the richness of depth available through hypertext interfere with the reader's ability to form an overview? Is hypertext an instantiation of Iser's wandering viewpoint, to such an extent that "consistency building" causes readers, especially inexperienced readers, to flounder? Would a hypertext story with electronic margins of reader response enrich an unsophisticated reader's response or simply increase demands on memory—perhaps delaying inappropriate closure, or perhaps making closure or interpretation impossible to achieve?

How will readers be able to talk to each other about a text, if the "text" becomes radically indeterminate? How will readers be able to form an interpretive community? I'm reminded of Woody Allen's short story "The Kugelmass Episode," in which Professor Kugelmass transports himself to the fictional world of *Madame Bovary* where he has an affair with Emma. According to the inexorable conventions of time (and fiction) travel, it follows that in college discussion sections everywhere, students question professors about the Kugelmass episode, citing chapter and page number. With interactive hypertext, every reader will be a Kugelmass. Readers may miss episodes because they are yet to be written by subsequent readers or because the reader can choose some story lines and not others. Teachers have always claimed that great literature forever holds new experiences in store for us. That platitude may be open to new interpretation with interactive fictions.

A final question for this new potential prosthesis: Who makes the links? Is the power to link equivalent to the power of authorship? Is linking the structuring, rhetorical feature of hypertext, whereas adding or accessing text is only information processing? If a reader never makes a link that has not already been arranged, is that a well-written hypertext in which the author has correctly anticipated reader response? Or perhaps such an experience reflects the open quality an author has adopted to "kill" himself or herself—to stay out of the way of the reader's construction.

As hypertext programs are designed, we need to be aware of the theories of literacy that they embody. I suspect that hypertext also represents more than the translation of theory to a new medium. Hypertext promises and threatens to redefine the experience of literacy, changing our theories because it changes our experience of literacy. Even with a critical perspective, it can be difficult to examine culturally induced aspects of culture because they seem so natural, so much a given. If Stevens's jar organizes the environment, then computer-supported literacy represents an importantly different jar. As we switch from the old jar to the new, we have a chance to observe how it imposes its "dominion everywhere" and what the changes are. During a time of change, we have the opportunity to question our world anew.

Discussion

TUMAN. Large-scale computer systems like Intermedia seem destined to give our students the ability to carry on much of the conversation with their instructors and their classmates online, from their dorms and other scattered sites. What fundamental changes, if any, do you see happening to traditional classes when larger amounts of important verbal exchanges take place electronically?

LANDOW. This frequently encountered question, which has begun to generate considerable literature among social scientists and educational psychologists, generally produces two different responses. Those who fear what they see as the potentially atomizing tendencies of computing, worry that students and other computer users will increasingly avoid human contact as, squirreled away in their rooms, they commune with their video screens. Others respond that studies show students and workers too shy or otherwise reluctant to contribute orally to group discussions often find computer billboards, conferences, and networks liberating and empowering. One response points to the fact that taking part in an electronically linked community hardly isolates people. Characterizing electronic communities as not *true* communities represents a political, rather than an intellectual, decision.

As Derrida might point out, many charges that computing promotes the isolation of individuals derive from unexamined notions of presence and the primacy of the spoken word. Many who fear the effects of electronic information technology, of which hypertext represents but one form, assume that the only *real* human contact is contact that entails people speaking to each other in the same space at the same time. Despite counterevidence provided by thousands of years of literature and painting, they assume that all other forms of communication represent a diminishment, a falling away from the supposedly truly adequate communication of presence.

Contrary to the expectations of those who fear the isolating effect of computing, our experience with Intermedia has revealed two possibly surprising effects. First, a three-year in-depth survey of classes, before and after the use of Intermedia, demonstrated a 300 percent increase in student participation in class discussion — that is, three times as many students took part in class discussion, and they did so three times as often after using hypertext as they did before using it. This result, I suggest, derives directly from the fact that students using hypertext had acquired more information and more techniques for using that information.

The second result, which probably has even more fundamental educational significance, was equally unexpected: by creating a new form of group (or course) memory, hypertext radically reconfigures the nature and composition of student contributions to class. Electronic linking, which makes educational and other materials usable in different contexts, also provides them with a different kind of lifespan. Specifically, students in one course (say, the 1991 version of the survey) read and react to documents created by students in an earlier iteration of the same course or by students from other courses. Therefore, a student remains a part of the electronic class discussion (and also indirectly enters oral class discussion) after he or she has completed the course — and even after he or she has received a degree and left the university. Students, who frequently comment that they have encountered texts by friends and acquaintances, experience a particular course as a kind of community with an ongoing history and culture.

Probably the most important point about these two results lies in the fact that no one anticipated them. One can conclude that if hypertext presents us with new and unique powers (as it promises), it will offer many other surprises, not all of them pleasant, to be sure. But we can never fully anticipate them. The only way to learn about the effect of hypertext and hypermedia on education and the rest of our culture is by trying it.

TUMAN.   One unflattering analogy to hypertext is the constant channel-surfing using the now-ubiquitous TV remote controls — those of us with adolescents know how difficult it is to get them to stay focused on any television program longer than a five-minute rock video. How are these same students going to get through *Middlemarch* when reading it in a medium that allows them, with two clicks on a button, to access an electronic version of Cliff Notes?

LANDOW. As long as students (and anyone else) read *Middle-march* in ways that make reading electronic versions of Cliff Notes seem a good idea, they will do so. But if they read *Middlemarch* for the reasons we say we do — because making our way through Eliot's text is a more intense pleasure and a more enriching experience than reading a trot — print or electronic versions of Cliff Notes will have little appeal. After all, students rely upon Cliff Notes and similar trots because teachers think Cliff Notes are more valuable to them than *Middle-march*. The teachers convince students to rely on these trots because they employ conceptions of education, assignments, and evaluative methods that make the use of trots a good bet for students who have little interest in the primary text itself or who have little time or little knowledge of how to approach the primary text.

Therefore, if one wishes to make students confront the text and not some pathetically reduced simulacrum of it, one must convince them that the text offers qualities and experiences unobtainable in any other way. Inspiring, wonderful teaching (such as always and undoubtedly characterizes our classroom performance) helps, to be sure; but assign-ments demanding that students make detailed, individual contact with specific passages of text play an even more important role.

A second response to this question involves the unique qualities of educational hypertext materials, specifically the fact that their almost infinitely expandable, open-ended nature surrounds the student with an enormous body of texts and images. Such hypertext corpora, even the comparatively small ones we have employed at Brown, offer more material than one encounters in conventional study guides, and that material comes from many different disciplines. Much of this material makes sense only if one already has some grasp of the primary text, so it seems unlikely to attract students who want to save time and energy by avoiding "Ode on a Grecian Urn," *Middlemarch,* or *Midnight's Children.* Moreover, since our hypermedia materials supplement and expand the kind of approaches usually encountered in classrooms, they offer little to the student who wishes to avoid choice, active learning, and independent thought. The chief principle here, as everywhere in education, is that students only read supplementary materials — whether Cliff Notes, cutting-edge scholarly publications, or manuscript and other primary evidence — when they have a reason to do so. Hypertext, book technology, and pencil and paper all have potentially great educational effects, but teachers and students have to use them in ways that release this potential. My experience of hypertext educational materials thus developed or proposed suggests that few teachers as yet wish to do more than decant old wine into new bottles.

McCorduck.   My own experience with hypertext hasn't been at all like channel-surfing. On the contrary, I'm arrested by each screen in a way a full page of text doesn't catch me. It's more like reading poetry than reading prose. I introduced Hortense Calisher, a distinguished writer of prose fiction, to hypertext using "Afternoon" (this was also her debut at a computer screen and at using a mouse, I should add), and she had the same reaction. But that might just be Michael Joyce's prose. Other writing might not be so arresting. It might just be Calisher and me. Anecdotal evidence isn't worth too much.

However, George Landow is exactly on target: people read what and how they will because that's what suits them best. An amateur reader doesn't read text the way a professor of English does, and a professor of English doesn't read the way a professional author does. But hypertext seems to me to be a way of deepening, not narrowing, a reader's experience.

TUMAN.   *Collaboration* seems to be widely touted now as a universal good in language education, when only a few years ago the notion of producing good writing collectively (especially by committee) was a standing joke. What has changed?

SCHWARTZ.   In *Keywords*, Raymond Williams talks about how words alter their meanings as cultural values change. For example, *innovation* is a buzzword for us, a word that automatically calls up a positive response—an intellectual's synonym for "new and improved" on a box of soap; an academic's analogue for the patriot's "freedom and justice for all." Yet in Shakespeare's day, *innovation* was seen as "giddy," tending toward subversion and chaos. Such buzzwords and the views they represent serve as warrants—values that underlie decisions, values that are so fully accepted it requires an effort to examine them critically unless the cultural glacier brings them to the moving edge of change and exposes them freshly to our view.

Collaborative and *individual* are two warrant terms that we can now see in the process of change. Computers enter the drama because they help us picture collaboration and its consequences differently, not as a metaphor or theory but as a new and tangible thing. When we look at a book, we see that it is the product of one person (or two or three if there are coauthors). Sure, it has ties to other people: that's what the footnotes are for. And a library has an organization (LC or Dewey decimal) that shows the place of the book in a system of knowledge. Just as the growth metaphors in *Macbeth* become more forceful when we see the witches' vision of a child holding a tree and then see Birnam Wood moving to Dunsinane, so the notion of *individual* learning becomes tangible when we see the form of the book, bound with its cover, separate from (though near) the works of others. But when the Intermedia system links texts from a literature course and a biology course, when the border between one part and another is transparent, such a conjunction instantiates *collaborative* learning, makes it tangible and more than a philosophical idea. Ted Nelson's Xanadu says one thing about the relation of the individual mind to its culture; the British Museum or Library of Congress or the lost library at Alexandria signifies a different relationship.

Individual used to be wholly good, in opposition to the dehumanization of *mass*. But with the Me Generation and a sense that individual striving may not lead to the global good, the concept has become more ambivalent in meaning. In contrast, *collaboration* used to be a euphemism for cheating (in a school setting) or for moral accommodation to evil (in Nazi-occupied countries). Now it highlights the social nature of the construction of meaning in the individual and in societies. Vygotsky hypothesizes that children learn to think by internalizing the conversations they hear; Kuhn proposes knowledge is not the discovery of an individual (or individuals) but a community's adoption of a paradigm. My point here is that learning is both individual and collaborative; it always has been and it always will be. However, the way we theorize the learning process will sharpen the focus on one aspect of learning. There is much to be said for emphasizing collaboration over our previous focus on individual learning. Education has always responded to the needs of the society for which it works. It is a commonplace now that modern American education evolved to meet the needs of an industrial society, teaching regularity (by marking tardiness, attendance, and citizenship, as well as math and social studies) and demanding memorization. In an Information Age, the emphasis on conformity and hierarchy are counterproductive when workers need judgment (even in line jobs) to function in a flatter organizational structure. The need for critical thinking replaces memorization. The need for collaboration replaces the isolation of the modular task. Yet it behooves us to look critically at the notion of collaboration, even as the computer medium makes it as real as the book made individuation. It behooves us to look at this warrant while we still can see it.

TUMAN.   One senses that as English educators we have long praised collaborative learning without being clear as to its true purpose. At times it seems to refer to coauthorship; at other times, to the more widespread practice of peer editing; and at other times, to the more pervasive sense that all writing is an inherently social, hence cooperative, endeavor. What is your sense of the differing role hypertext and computers are likely to play in facilitating these different kinds of collaboration?

SCHWARTZ.   The first two kinds of collaboration are by choice; the third is inevitable and varies only in our ability to notice it (as I have argued above). Yet the educational values are different, I would argue, for each of the three kinds. And computers can support all three, as well as calling for new software and hardware to make such support most useful.

Peer reviewing is probably the most widespread form of collaboration now practiced in higher education. The fresh eye of another critic can point out what a writer may be insensitive to. The act of criticism helps the student learn to objectify, not only to review the work of others, but to receive and act on criticism. The conversation helps the student see and internalize standards. Simple word processing, with the need to retype only what is being revised, makes revision bearable for many students. Yet the ease of doing a revision does not automatically make it easier for a student to diagnose a problem and carry out the revision conceptually. Peer review is the pedagogy that makes the technology of word processing valuable to developing writers. Hypertext is a perfect concept for keeping the integrity of the writer's text while inserting the critic's comments or responses at the point of best use.

Coauthoring requires substantial input from different minds. It allows greater knowledge to be represented, assuming that the authors are experts. Such collaboration also teaches the need for consistency of argument and style, clarity of organization, and reliability of data. Several projects, like Writing Environment (WE) at the University of North Carolina, are underway to facilitate group writing. However, even existing computer facilities support coauthoring. The ease of merging or cannibalizing textfiles supports such tasks. Access to electronic mail makes it possible to envision coauthoring in intercampus courses—such as those supported by BESTNET (Binational English and Spanish Telecommunication Network) that include American and Mexican students speaking English and Spanish and participating in courses electronically. And hypertext becomes a three-dimensional organizer for coauthoring. The early outlining programs, pretentiously called idea processors, have become three-dimensional in hypertext. I prefer to think of such systems as organizers and linkers, rather than processors. However, features that give overviews, as with *Storyspace,* do help the author to conceptualize the writing task.

And at IUPUI, urban commuter students, in a project called the Twenty-First Century Citizen Scholars, were able to converse beyond classroom bounds through the use of loaner computers and an electronic bulletin board for the class. Students discovered their diversity and had a chance to teach and support each other while integrating their study of sociolinguistics. Starting with a comment about black bean soup, their conversation wove together their diverse experiences: as a student switching codes from Black English to Standard English; as a Cuban refugee; as the mother of a deaf student; as a teacher of non-native speakers of English who attended a pep rally, and so on (Schwartz, "Twenty-first Century").

Access to electronic mail involves students in a life-or-death epistemological experiment. During the Beijing students' uprising, Chinese students in China sent news to compatriots studying in the United States and learned from them about events they were cut off from within China—via electronic mail. The computer lines could not be shut down; the computer communication could not be screened from surveillance and now serves as evidence in student trials. On PeaceNet, individuals report what they have actually seen, as a foil to official news reports. Are such reports reliable? (Which reports do you think I was referring to in the previous sentence—those on PeaceNet or those in the mass media?) Biologist and activist Marti

Crouch argues that the openness of PeaceNet (to friend and foe) problematizes the issue of reliability while also democratizing access to verifying sources.

In the postmodern world, we leave certainty behind us. As individuals we must act and accept responsibility for our actions, and so the ability to read and write the world we must act in becomes even more important. Two images come to my mind as I write: Milton's Adam and Eve leaving the Garden of Eden—"The World was all before them, where to choose / Thir place of rest, and Providence thir guide." The second image is of Gibson's computer jockey in *Neuromancer* traversing time and space, connecting and acting and deciding. Computer hypertexts and electronic mail bring exciting opportunities for authentic learning in English classrooms.

> 3 <
COMPUTERS
and New Forms of Critical Thought

Looking Out:
The Impact of Computers on
the Lives of Professionals

Stanley Aronowitz

Looking Back

I am a volunteer at a small alternative public elementary school on Brooklyn that is using Apple computers and several instructional programs to assist fifth and sixth graders to learn typing and to improve their language skills. My job is to insert the disks and load the software, observe that the programs are being properly used, and help with any problems the kids may have. Four kids at a time come to the computer room, which is a small, atticlike space on the top floor of this old building. With the exception of beginners, the kids are required only to follow the program's commands, complete a sequence of operations, and either do it all again or return to their classrooms.

The typing program is a multicolored updated version of the one I used in the seventh grade, on an old Underwood manual typewriter provided us in Junior High School 118 by the New York City Board of Education some forty years ago. Although the typing is now very quiet, the routine is identical—FRF [space] JUJ [space] . . . and so on. The feedback from the program is cuter than my typing teacher's watchful eye and disapproving, correcting words, but it is no more exciting. The programs are indexed to the kids' improvement with the higher levels of proficiency needed to copy business letters and disembodied, abstract texts geared to training modern secretaries.

Learning the old skill of typing is undoubtedly useful, and there may be no reason to forsake tried-and-true methods. It also makes sense to learn typing on a soft keyboard since most writers now use word processors, but there is nothing special about this computer exercise.

The programs for language skills are not examples of alternative ways of learning either. The old supply-the-missing-word and practice drills for vocabulary building that I experienced in my time are replicated by the programs. And like most kids back then, the kids today are appropriately bored—they dutifully perform the commands appearing on the screen with more or less difficulty, but all seem anxious to finish their assignment and leave. While their haste may have something to do with the uninviting ambience, it is caused also by a kind of learning that feels more like work than play.

These exercises are comparable to the early days of any new medium—of cinema, for example, where people filmed stage plays or the early TV where people televised radio shows. In other words, while the programmers of these learning tools seem to recognize that display graphics can enhance what would otherwise be routine operations and dull images, they seem to have no sense of the contexts within which their programs are to be used. The cute graphics serve only to underline the degree to which the capacities of the medium are under-utilized and, most significantly in this concern with display, how the users and their specific needs and interests disappear.

This example may be criticized as an extreme case, where the computer takes on the function of a rote teacher (minus the disciplinarian's disdain). The computer can be used to help students learn physics and math, subjects where operational competence seems to presuppose (at least in part) familiarity with procedures and categories that resist efforts to eliminate drills. Students can learn at their own pace the aspects of those relatively decontextualized disciplines (such as math and physics) that require a certain amount of rote learning at the outset. And, in programs developed by sophisticated computer scientists and educators such as Seymour Papert and Joseph Weizenbaum, play is combined with rigorous, rule-driven algorithms. Under these conditions, learning becomes challenging, an enjoyable activity that helps the student to master traditional analytic skills. Nevertheless, as I shall show below, the possibilities for playful *self-development* inherent in the technology remain to a large degree unexplored in schools as well as in the workplace.

The ubiquity and power of computers in the contemporary world has provoked considerable debate. For enthusiasts like Papert, Shoshana Zuboff, and many others, the computer is a *tool*, a term that suggests a neutral social and political content. The versatility of the computer can provide the key to the historic dream that all work (including schoolwork) can become a vehicle of human creativity, that is, a form of play. According to this claim, the computer provides one of the keys to the kingdom of delineated culture. Meanwhile, critics of computers (people like Weizenbaum, Hubert and Stuart Dreyfus, and Edmund Sullivan) have warned that such claims — especially those of theorists such as Herbert Simon, that artificial intelligence represents a new stage in human dominion over nature and humankind — are excessive, even dangerous.

These critics, or "humanists," advance the thesis that human agency is irreplaceable, that computers can do neither more nor less than those who create, program, and operate them. Some of these humanists agree with the enthusiasts that computers can be useful; where they disagree is with regard to the social and cultural implications. These humanists want to preserve the traditional idea that technological advances can become a tool of freedom from onerous work, but they too share the pessimism of more determined critics of computers, the belief that technology is now the predominant form of life, penetrating not only our social relations but our personalities and culture as well.

A third perspective reverses this sweeping notion that we now live in what may be termed a technoculture. While it may be true that we have all become "pluggies" — in that we are now surrounded by various forms of computer-mediated work, communications, arts, education — it is as if technology has penetrated, metaphorically, our very being. In contrast to earlier judgments of critics like Herbert Marcuse, Jacques Ellul, and Lewis Mumford — thinkers spawned in the last bourgeois era for whom the advance of electronic media spelled the doom of critical thought and democratic politics (since most of us have been deprived of the capacity for independent judgment by the new communications technologies) — the new theorists of technoculture are postcritical.[1] They believe that just as it is futile to mourn the passing of the horse and carriage, there are really no alternatives to computer and electronic mediations in everyday life. Technology has become the new form of life; the only issue is how to harness it for playful, erotic, and otherwise self-fulfilling purposes.

This essay is an exploration of the position of professionals in light of postcritical attitudes about computers. It is to be developed in three sections: first, a model of the professional life is embedded in my brief description of computer-aided instruction; second, three accounts of the ways in which computer technology is being integrated into the prevailing regime of management-directed production of goods and services; and last, a reconsideration of the problems of educating students for the computer-mediated, literate culture of the future.

On Being a Professional

The cornerstone of the ideology of professionalism is the belief that some professionals in various categories of labor possess skills or knowledge that entitle them to considerable autonomy in the performance of their work.[2] Thus there is a contrast between the capacity to make independent decisions based upon specialized knowledge and the close supervision of most labor, called for by Taylorism, presumably because the jobs require little or no training. Even skilled labor forms a relatively small part of the total labor process. Meanwhile, the extent of autonomy enjoyed by a given profession is relative to its status within the larger culture. For example, at least until recently, physicians in the United States were ordinarily subject only to peer review similar to the self-policing of natural scientists. In the Soviet Union as well as many countries of both eastern and western Europe, the state bureaucracy under the control of political managers oversees the work of physicians and others who work in the natural and health sciences.

In fact, the rapidly changing knowledge needed to perform professional work limits the ability of those physicians, scientists, and engineers (traditionally the most professional of our professions) who occupy high administrative positions in their respective bureaucracies from directing professional work. In a climate marked by such rapid change, professionals who can no longer practice their trade are often made managers, where their link to emerging knowledge is extremely fragile and, in time, may disappear entirely. One response to this recent trend is the replacement of such specialist managers by professional managers.

Even in the United States, where state bureaucracy is weakest among industrial societies, this transformation may be traced, in broad outlines, to the increased stratification of most professional services—that is, to the close integration of public and private investment in both goods and services. For example, nearly all basic research in the natural sciences is publicly supported, even if administered by nongovernmental organizations. The complexity of the relations between public and private agencies has led to the creation of a new profession of decision-making managers, especially those in the health, education, and other public services, who must now concern themselves with budgets and other specialized financial issues as well as issues involving the unionization of workers.[3] In such an environment, the administrative task of making decisions is often abstracted from the concrete labor to which they refer.

While it would be a mistake to overemphasize the degree of collegiality in the older institutions concerned with the production and dissemination of knowledge, the appearance of the knowledge factory at the turn of the twentieth century and its maturation during World War II signaled an important change in the history of science and technology, a change that can be traced in the movement from Pasteur's laboratory to General Electric's research facility in Schenectady, New York, and Bell Labs in New Jersey, and to the Lawrence-Livermore Labs and comparable facilities in Brookhaven and Oakridge, and finally to the massive biotech labs of the University of California at San Diego.[4]

It is perhaps too easy to forget how such large organizations are often inimical to invention and even innovation. Bureaucracies, like other social forms, regularly take on a life of their own, outliving their original purpose. Consequently, even giant electronic corporations such as IBM, ITT, and ATT finally grasped the wisdom of financing independent entrepreneurs to develop both hardware and software. Bankrolled by wealthy corporate sponsors, a plethora of tiny companies of two to six employees sprung up headed by former IBM, Microsoft, or DEC hackers. After developing a new wrinkle on a calculating or word-processing program, they are typically reintegrated by the corporation as a new division or "team" charged with providing technical assistance to customers using the new product or heading up a new development group. This shift toward allowing hackers (at least temporarily) the greater flexibility of small business operators has been decisive, not just in software development, but in business systems generally. Yet even in this trend, there is no indication that real control has ever passed from the hands of the traditional players.

What is at work here is a system that has developed largely since the end of World War II. Within the regime of the corporate/state bureaucracy, ruled by a professional manager rather than a specialized practitioner, the traditional professions have been increasingly proletarianized, if not with respect to income then certainly with respect to their subordination—that is, they have tended to lose their right to control the conditions of their own labor, especially to make autonomous decisions based upon judgments linked to their credentials and knowledge.[5]

The computerization of whole categories of industrial work has attracted intellectual labor mainly because it seems to provide a scientific and technical, rather than a political, basis for reintegrating design and execution. The widespread introduction of computers into industrial production, administration, and various services seems to reverse the tendency, associated with the old mechanical/industrial regime, to reproduce the "mass worker," that creation of the prolonged period of capitalist regulation following World War I (Negri 9). This mass worker represents the triumph of Fordism, the industrial movement within which production and consumption were integrated even as workers were deprived of the smallest vestiges of control that they had formerly enjoyed within the labor process before the full implementation of mass, mechanical, industrial production (Davis).

The new post-Fordist labor process seems marked by the integration, not the separation, of intellectual and manual labor. The logical and temporal sequences within design itself and between design and production have been dramatically foreshortened in those plants that employ Computer-Aided Design and Manufacture (CAD/CAM). Instantaneous communication between once distinct sectors of a plant means that different parties must adapt to and assimilate each other's specific characteristics and problems. At a minimum, the traditional bottlenecks to industrial production are more rapidly widened; at best, CAD/CAM blurs the lines of demarcation between design and execution so that the shop floor can "participate" in the design process, to the extent that management is able or willing to broaden and even democratize power over decision making so as to include "manual" labor.[6]

In fact, such distinctions today are often blurred (but not entirely obliterated) in most technologically advanced plants. Corporate-sponsored "quality circles," for example, provide an opportunity for nearly the entire work force to give views on such matters as the labor process, the conditions of work, the characteristics of management, and other shop issues. Yet such "quality circles" also provide enlight-ened management with the opportunity to coopt union-sponsored protest as well as to train workers under changing conditions that require their participation and, to a certain extent, their independent judgment regarding production decisions (Kochan, Katz, and McKer-sie). In the United States and Britain, there still remain many efforts to impose the old managerial regime on newly "socialized" workers, who are themselves capable of managing the entire labor process — that is, among workers whose grasp of the new integrated computer-mediated manufacturing process has been gained through their mas-tery of CAD/CAM.

Narrative 1: A Hopeful Look

In 1986-1989, for example, I was part of a group of social investiga-tors who observed what happened when CAD was introduced into two large New York public agencies that employed hundreds of engineers and into a similarly large New Jersey state agency.[7] What were the effects of this innovation on a group of professional and technical workers, as well as on those who, even without conventional credentials, perform professional and technical labor? We wanted specifically to know how the character of the work was changed, and whether power relations between managers and employees were signif-icantly altered. How did these groups compare with industrial and clerical labor, workers that had experienced computerization mainly as an extension of the old industrial culture? Were new work relation-ships forged among these more highly qualified groups?

Civil, electrical, and mechanical engineers employed by public agencies design a variety of infrastructure installations such as water systems, pumping stations, switch signals for subways, and bridges for trains and autos. Traditionally, nearly all the design work was per-formed by hand and brain, employing no mechanical equipment other than drafting tools, many of which were as old as engineering itself.

CAD and its counterpart CAM marked a revolution in the work of these engineers. Now almost all the painstaking labor of preparing blueprints—a process that used to mean weeks of work before matters of design innovation could even be considered—is reduced to several hours of work on a computer. After the basic model has been generated on the screen, adjustments and variations can be quickly made online.

Where, in the old design process, mathematical calculations had to be performed one at a time, now the engineer can call up a menu of mathematical options from the CAD program merely by pressing a key, and, since much of the design work of civil engineering is based on standard dimensions, only a small percentage of the work involves special problems of calculation. In the old regime, nearly 90 percent of an engineer's time was spent on drafting and on math—more or less routine activities that were the necessary preconditions for innovations required as a result of the special conditions of a project, for example, the limitations of space and terrain of a waste disposal system. CAD sharply reduces the time necessary to generate these routine preconditions and thus allows more time to be spent on these limiting special conditions. But CAD can do much more: some CAD programs developed in the past decade are equipped with three dimensions, a feature that obviates one of the most crucial components of engineering design, the engineer's ability to visualize the end product. Now the relative literalization of the image removes another major obstacle to the time taken in design.

The engineers at one of the agencies were initially delighted to have CAD, because it made their work not only less tedious (mainly by removing drawing) but more precise as well, without their having to produce a seemingly endless series of distinct drawings. The introduction of computer terminals throughout this agency enhanced the solidarity of the engineers by providing them with knowledge that managers did not necessarily possess. In addition, they learned CAD together, and its application, unlike that of drafting, became a collective effort. The managers and engineers, eager to expand CAD so that everyone had access to a terminal, hoped that the new technology would bolster their long-standing complaint against contracting out design work. Here, they felt, was a technology that made them more versatile and more productive. Many of the agency's managers shared a vision of restoring the reality of a fully competent *public sector* that might use private contractors for specialized jobs, but that would take full responsibility for all aspects of the design process.

For these employees, the dream of merging work with play seemed to be within their grasp. The actual work process began to resemble a basic science laboratory that facilitated experimenting with different approaches to a given problem; what had formerly been considered routine manual labor now became truly intellectual work. We observed engineers who delighted in the work regardless of the routine nature of the design problem itself. What counted here was, in the first place, the possibility of gaining, through technology, an edge in their never-ending quest for greater job control. They were learning something new, and it was this learning itself that excited them, as much as the possibilities for gaining greater autonomy from managerial bureaucracies whose responsibilities in the past often constrained creative work.

It is still too soon to know whether these hopes can be fully realized in what remain hierarchical organizations, even for qualified professionals and even with the support of creative managers. The work process, after all, is finally subject to the economic and political exigencies and struggles of larger organizations. Even if these engineers are being transformed from relatively highly paid workers to hackers (the term denotes people who dedicated themselves to exploring the full potential of personal computers), they are finally not free to determine the product of their labor. In this, they are like the important group of systems analysts and programmers described by Steven Levy, who were completely oblivious of or indifferent to the larger context of their work—the extensive defense operations at MIT. These engineers mirrored the complicity of those scientists who, without reservation, worked for the defense establishment because the Department of Defense was virtually the only source of funds for basic research. Civil engineers are historically also free of such considerations, and thus free to turn their relatively routine labor into creative work.

Narrative 2: A Troubling Look

What happened to the engineers in the other two public agencies provides a fruitful contrast to this one relatively optimistic case. In the other two agencies, the management selected a less versatile CAD program, one lacking the capability of three dimensions. Training was not provided for the entire engineering work force. The introduction of CAD was seen by the management to be strictly a question of productivity gain: its chief function was to reduce and eventually eliminate drafting and to facilitate the rapid completion of routine tasks. The engineers in turn did not respond enthusiastically to the introduction of this limited CAD program or to the prospects of computer technologies in general. They were suspicious of the management's exclusive preoccupation with productivity at their expense, and issues of job security rose to the fore.

As with the first agency, engineers in the other two agencies had also been long concerned with the issue of contracting out. Management, they charged, had reserved the more interesting and complex work for outside contractors; to which management responded that inside employees lacked the necessary expertise. Over the years the amount of work that was farmed out grew steadily, with inside employees relegated to routine assignments and to inspecting the finished work of others. These engineers complained that they were really correcting the mistakes of the contractors while being prevented by political and bureaucratic authorities from fully utilizing the potential of CAD. Interviews with the engineers in these two agencies reveal the extent to which the panopticon remains in place, even as technology with truly revolutionary potential is directed to the task of reproducing power, indeed, of further proletarianizing the labor of engineers.

Narrative 3: A Realistic Look

General Electric's aircraft engine plant in Cincinnati, Ohio, employs some 2,000 design engineers, divided into several categories: a fairly large number employed in CAD/CAM with the job of working with managers and workers in the production end while assuring quality control of the end product; a smaller section employed exclusively on the designs of engine parts using CAD for routine tasks; and finally a small elite corps engaged in basic and applied research on CAD software itself, of which General Electric (GE) is a major producer both for its own operations and commercially. The employment-relations manager of the plant told me that much of this research was dedicated to finding ways to cut even further the labor force of engineers and manual workers. He acknowledged that the productivity savings in drafting made possible by CAD would reduce the number of engineers to one-sixth, a number that could be balanced only by a sixfold increase in defense and commercial orders. When I visited the plant in 1986, half the orders were for civilian aircraft and the other half for military; with pressures mounting in Congress for cuts in the military budget, the company anticipated considerable reductions in drafters and engineers.

Also clear was a severe reduction in the ratio between manual and professional employees. Thousands of square feet of space stood relatively empty of living labor, inhabited by computer-driven numerical controls sitting inconspicuously atop most of the machine tools and computer-mediated lasers used for boring holes. Where, in the old regime, the floor had been crammed with people, there was now only the haunting presence of robots. The few live workers, who seemed marginal to the production process, were in fact knowledgeable workers who served not merely as watchers, in the sense that Marx used the term in the *Grundrisse;* they were constantly making adjustments in the programs—in part by continual communication with the CAD/CAM engineers in which they offered valuable input that was used in making design changes. These machinists may have lost some of their older skills, but they were now programmers. They may have missed some of the features of the old industrial regime, but they also enjoyed a considerable range of activity offered in their new work.

While some machinists and toolmakers said they had always interacted with engineers, they also admitted that the quality of this interaction had been improved by the new knowledge base resulting from the introduction of CAD/CAM. The manufacturing side now seemed less subordinate. The distinction between socially constructed manual and intellectual sectors ("socially constructed" because all work entails judgment and planning), was preserved, however, in part by corporate labor relations and union contracts. The managerial and engineering staffs, as part of the company's commitment to preserving the hierarchy of knowledge, shared only a limited quantity of power with the machinists. Although the integration of design and execution had become the official discourse of company managers with whom I talked, ultimately hierarchical relations remained in force, especially in the face of any lurking disagreement. There was no mechanism for resolving differences, and the machinists were invariably obliged to back down—despite their considerable experience in the technical aspects of design, their newly won familiarity with computer programming, and their understanding of production problems.

This GE plant is only one of several that I visited in which the introduction of CAD/CAM revealed the janus-faced character of technology. The company employed computer-mediated processes to upgrade the qualification of some workers and thus to enable these workers to participate in some decisions; but the company used the technology also to cut costs by reducing labor forces at all levels while retaining operational control, as well as ultimate authority, at the level of top management. Despite the partial breakdown of the pure form of managerial authority characteristic of older assembly and parts plants, the panopticon remained alive and well at GE.

Looking Forward

Proponents of computer-aided education have advanced several central arguments. Computers, they argue, can individualize instruction in a way that traditional teaching modes cannot. Computers are also versatile; they can be tutors, as seen in the opening of this essay, or tools, as they are here in providing an array of editing features even as I compose. They can even be tutees—that is, agents that students themselves (playing the role Seymour Papert calls epistemologist) instruct by writing programs. As Papert contends, the discipline of writing instructions helps the student learn a metaskill, although his insight is partially vitiated by his adherence to an information-processing model of human thought, one that equates insight into how a computer operates with insight into human intelligence.

Hubert and Stuart Dreyfus, John Broughton, and Edward Sullivan, among others, have provided powerful critiques of such thinking. For the Dreyfuses, for example, the computer has a valuable, but limited, role to play as a classroom tutor for those subjects that require considerable rote learning. They reject, however, the notion that the human mind really follows rules analogous to that of the computer and thus reject attempts to apply computers in areas involving context-bound thinking. Here knowledge of the terrain must be obtained more by intuition, memory, and specific knowledge of actors or geography than by mastering logical rules. In learning to program we learn only certain Aristotelian rules of thought; we do not learn much about those processes of thinking that are entwined with indeterminate situations in which the governing rules are, likely as not, invented by the actors themselves, modified in the course of interaction and negotiation, and not infrequently even violated in order to accommodate the specificity of the terrain.

Whatever its physiological and biological presuppositions, the development of thinking is profoundly shaped and frequently altered by multiple determinations, including choices made by people themselves. Even if psychological research has established that the brain is a binary organ, with each side the repository of certain functions, such an understanding would supply us with only the general preconditions of thinking. Thus, while we can design a computer that helps us address logical, analytic problems (surely an important part of education), the computer will not be able to anticipate or respond to problems that lie outside its logical ordering. While the computer may be designed to replicate the epistemological foundations of technological thinking (which is rule-driven, rather than context-driven), it cannot be taken as a model for normative thought. It is an interesting machine, beautifully designed for some, not all, purposes.

The elementary school that uses programs to replicate traditional pedagogies is, consciously or not, wasting the instructional potential of computers. Better to employ peer tutoring in cases where some students need additional assistance in mastering the rote features of some disciplines. Interacting with another person is usually a more pleasant way to learn a routine exercise, and the tutor can use insights into the nonlogical problems the tutee may be experiencing.

Papert is convincing in arguing that certain computer games can teach students problem-solving skills in math and science. Such creative employment of the discoveries of artificial intelligence has been utilized in schools all over the country. Yet the epistemological and educational claims for these programs demonstrate the severe limitations of computer-aided instruction as well. They presuppose a theory of thinking that reduces the brain to a calculating instrument, one whose characteristics may be described and measured with the same precision as a bridge or a water-distribution system.

Here in the image of the computer program is the basis for the mechanistic worldview of molecular biology. The course of an individual's life, like circuits of a computer chip, are inscribed in DNA, the substance that constitutes the genetic material of life. This determinism, which continues the great tradition of genetic science and challenges the largely indeterminate character of evolution theory, evokes the image of the body as a type of machine, an image that has dominated biological thought since the sixteenth century. Vitalism arose in the nineteenth century to oppose this reductionism and proposed, instead, a teleonomic model of the organism according to which, from the smallest level of cell to the body as a whole, *purpose* is seen as part of the process of reproduction and decay.[8] Most importantly, while the mechanists obliterated the distinction between mind and body by reducing mind to the brain and the nervous system—that is, by reducing human consciousness to the variations and combinations of atoms, molecules, cells, ganglia, and receptors—the vitalists insisted on a place for spirit, although they used biological parlance of teleonomic language to disguise the term's idealist origins.

Between mechanism and vitalism, a third group has insisted on treating thinking as a dialectically complex process involving both the internal relations of the organism to itself as well as to its environment and the external relations to the larger economic, political, and cultural milieu.[9] Such an approach holds that the life process in all its aspects bears on how we think. Each of us is an actor shaped by a biophysiological situation, and each of us is an actor who shapes the multiple aspects of our own thought—modes of communication, discourse, ideology—forms of knowledge that constitute the lifeworld in which we are all ensconced.

Learning, according to this third way, is not exclusively, or even principally, a matter of acquiring logically constructed, decontextualized systems of knowledge; instead, it is a matter of the ability to test, on a selective basis, the appropriateness of fixed knowledge in concrete situations. Only in reflecting upon such tests do we acquire new knowledge. The student working with a computer on programming or in the pursuit of traditional material is not truly participating in education, as a tutor or a tutee. In either case, as Broughton has shown, the student is obliged to surrender control over his or her education to the deterministic algorithms of the computer program. Such a student must submit to an externally determined order of knowledge, regardless of how playfully it is taught. Indeed, even the language of computer terminology, with terms such as *command* and *menu*, indicate the degree that self-management of the learning process is constrained by heteronomy. The binary structure of the computer's yes/no questions provides few opportunities for *maybe*; Turing's logic inevitably reduces choices to an Aristotelian imperative.

To be sure, there are attempts to reach beyond such limitations, as in the playfulness of computer-mediated hypertext. Logging printed texts of all kinds on the computer allows the reader to construct a text without observing any linear order. Such a practice reveals the degree to which texts can be produced, not merely imbibed, by readers. This seminal claim of reader-response theory in literary criticism is thus now given material substance in the indeterminacy of a hypertext. Armed with a bountiful hard disk upon which a "classic" novel, poem, or play has been transcribed, the reader is free to become the producer of a new text by juxtaposing words, sentences, and paragraphs, creating new narratives and images, and scrambling the symbolic order of the "original" author, revealing hidden dimensions of the work of art or treatise that had been statically enframed.

The implications of such a practice are quite revolutionary. We seem to be entering an era when irony and its companion skepticism are no longer incidental rhetorical devices. Hypertext may become a form of *techne*, in Heidegger's usage, but beneath this new kind of text lies a larger will to playfulness. In a time when we generally admit that the past can be recaptured only from the perspective of a present that is characterized by its own doubts concerning the possibility of any form of self-knowledge, the invocation on the computer monitor of the sacred texts of Western culture no longer enframes our culture. The enframing that does occur makes the opposite point, that what we had thought of as permanent is really only contingent, that high and popular cultures are ineluctably entwined with technology. The assertions that the reader is the author and that the text is a system of signs whose meaning possesses no fixed center have moved beyond the pretty formulations of a literary critic to become, at least tendentially, our new historical situation.

Some claim that when reading becomes nearly identical with writing—that is, when reading is no longer a putatively passive activity but instead an intervention, an act of transformation—the problem of literacy may no longer possess existential significance. Just as work can become play for those empowered to remain at the controls, so art will no longer be, properly speaking, the work of specialists (artists) but will be broadly dispersed throughout the technoculture. This transformation applies not only to language but also to images that can now be reproduced without the painstaking preparation of art school or its equivalent in endless years of practice. Such computer-generated images bear the same relation to painting that the mass-produced automobile bears to the hand-built car.

In this regard, Benjamin's meditation on the fate of art work after lithography and photography applies to the age of the computerized text as well. The auratic has by no means disappeared; throngs of people crowd into museums to view authentic paintings in the latest Picasso or Van Gogh retrospective, and dealers and collectors offer millions of dollars to possess just one work of art. Yet too often the significance of going to a museum is encapsulated in being there rather than in our relation to the meaning of the work of art, in any of the possible connotations of that phrase. Museum statistics have become a sociological category that has little to do with the aesthetics of presence.[10]

So too with technoculture's appropriation of the literary work. The reader can now deconstruct the work even before reading it in a continuous manner, a practice some would recoil at, not only on grounds of bourgeois taste but as an educational and a political issue. After all, might it not be the case that those who ignore history, literary or otherwise, are doomed to relive it—or worse, just plain doomed?

Under such circumstances, some believe that books will become objets d'art, museum pieces whose survival is a measure only of the reluctance of a conservative publishing industry to develop new markets. As repositories of fixed knowledge, even if subject to interpretations and variations, books do act as cultural gatekeepers. The unfulfilled promise of hypertext is that it will abolish all forms of authority, revealing in the process that standards are socially produced, usually in behalf of the claims of the powerful to act as legatees of culture. What hypertext promises to expose, in other words, is the authoritarian character of taste; it is a weapon of the powerless in the struggle for control over the signifiers of culture.

In this context, hypertext is at once a reading of the past and a production of the future in the present. The question is, By whom and for what? For those who object to Benjamin's withering critique of high culture, it is enough to recall that he was among its most dazzling products. Given his understanding of culture as a discourse on power, Benjamin saw the mechanical reproduction of art as an important element in the effort to transform power relations. In effect, he felt that capitalism's development of the means of mass reproduction of art, a corollary of its compulsion to revolutionize the means of production, also signaled its loss of control.

Technoculture (notwithstanding its appropriation by capital as the condition of its growth) is, in all its forms, inherently destabilizing to the regime that gave it birth—the result of dispersal of knowledge by the technology that separates it, at least in part, from power. Or, to be more optimistic, power and knowledge shift away from centers where the new technologies can be easily assimilated into the old cultural and industrial order. The judgment of such writers as Andre Gorz, that the technical experts are merely an adjunct to the capitalist order (largely because they have lost their critical capacity), needs to be reversed. Although the traditional intellectual had a wide ideological influence in dominating ethical and cultural discourses, even when politically at the margins of power, the manager nevertheless remained the key intellectual of the industrial order. To the degree that scientific and technical intelligence was merged with management through its final separation from manual labor in the nineteenth and early twentieth centuries, capital could regard resistance in the workplace as a large, albeit manageable, problem existing within rather than outside the social order.

Since World War II, we have witnessed a massive growth of the technical intelligentsia far beyond the traditional professions. The real work of this stratum in the labor system has been to eliminate labor, a development that has produced such massive disruptions in the social and political order that capitalism has had to devise artificial ways of maintaining social discipline through all sorts of useless employment and education. Many capitalist economies today can offer only part-time work for tens of millions of workers, many of whom have experienced sharp reductions in their standard of living.

Technoculture, meanwhile, has transformed the nature of information and knowledge beyond the workplace. The growing skepticism of the underlying populations of all countries concerning their economic and political systems is not the result of ignorance but of the counter-surveillance techniques of mass communications and computerization. Even though such events as the Iran-Contra investigation in the mid-1980s were "botched" by a political system lacking political will, and even though the Reagan and Bush administrations succeeded in concealing the Savings and Loan scandal for months, their eventual exposure have accelerated the antipolitical tendency of the majority. To understand electoral politics profoundly is to despise and shun them, even where there is no alternative. One of the hallmarks of the panopticon, the one-way mirror, has been smashed, but the result is not to strengthen the democratic tendencies of liberal culture. Rather, we can observe in the steadily diminishing voter-participation rates in elections, the formation of a new oligarchy of the involved, who in turn fear the entropic effects of what is commonly called political apathy.

Thus, despite herculean efforts to quarantine technoculture in trivial pursuits and to confine its applications to entirely conventional areas, its corrosive, antiauthoritarian effects persist. Technological determinists are wrong in thinking that industrial societies can safely contain these effects. One of the inherent features of the microchip is presaged in Marshall McLuhan's nimble phrase *the global village*. Prevailing powers have always been able to evoke and reproduce the exotic, the esoteric. In a computer-mediated world, even the subaltern has lost the aura of otherness. With the emergence of dialogics and the philosophy of difference there is now the promise that communication can overcome all barriers, even though the spurious quest for universal truth seems today as common as ever.

Notes

1. For example, see *Technoculture*, edited by Penley and Ross, and Lanham's *Literacy and the Survival of Humanism*. These texts are postcritical, insofar as they take

technology as a given that sets boundary conditions for culture and in whose terms "humanists" are obliged to work.

2. For a sophisticated and succinct treatment, from a sociological perspective, of the social relations of professionals, see Larson's *The Rise of Professionalism.*

3. For a debate about the rise of the professional/managerial class, see *Between Labor and Capital,* edited by Walker.

4. For a powerful treatment of the growth of the laboratory as a knowledge factory that may be taken as a model for the new world, see Latour's *Science in Action.*

5. For some of the recent literature that addresses the erosion of professions, see Hoffman's *The Politics of Knowledge* and Derber's *Power in the Highest Degree.*

6. The term *post-Fordist* in this context means the end of the capitalist regulation according to which workers, in exchange for high levels of consumption and social welfare benefits, negotiated away or otherwise surrendered their claim to control the labor process, a regime commonly called Fordism. In the post-Fordist period, the inversion seems to be that workers are invited to participate in managing the labor process but are no longer beneficiaries of a secure union contract or a welfare state, whether this is provided by government or by the employer.

7. This section is a compressed survey of three studies of CAD performed by the Technology Research Group at the Graduate Center, City University of New York, between 1986 and 1988. The studies are available from the author.

8. For a concise and authoritative discussion of the use of telenomic processes in contemporary biology, see Mayr's *The Growth of Biological Thought.* The relationship between the idea that organisms act according to a program that simulates a purposive end is only a distant cousin to the more popular version proposed by Henri Bergson in, for instance, his *Creative Evolution.* Nevertheless, the degree to which biological science has been converted to a more dynamic version of organic development can be seen in virtually any major work on evolution. In contrast many biologists, influenced by the physical model of organism-molecular biology, see the world in older mechanistic terms.

9. For an attempt to develop this complex view, see Levin and Lewontin's *Dialectical Biologist.*

10. For a scathing attack on contemporary museum culture, see Crimp's "The Museum in Ruins."

Grammatology (in the Stacks) of Hypermedia, a Simulation: Or, when does a pile become a heap?

Gregory L. Ulmer

Introduction

This article is an experiment based on my original symposium talk, which placed the current developments in artificial intelligence and hypermedia programs in the context of the concept of the "apparatus" used in cinema studies to mount a critique of cinema as an institution, as a social "machine" that is as much ideological as it is technological. The same drive of realism that led in cinema to the "invisible style" of Hollywood narrative films—and to the occultation of the production process in favor of a consumption of the product as if it were "natural"—is at work again in computing. It was clear that the efforts of critique to expose the oppressive effects of "the suture" in cinema (the effect binding the spectator to the illusion of a complete reality) had made no impression on the computer industry, whose professionals (including many academics) are in the process of designing "seamless" information environments for hypermedia applications. The twin peaks of American ideology—realism and individualism— are built into the computing machine (the computer as institution).

The very concept of the "apparatus" indicates that ideology is a necessary, irreducible component of any "machine." Left critique and cognitive science agree on this point, although their attitudes toward the inherence of stereotypes in knowledge are opposed. Critique is right to condemn the acceptance of or reconciliation with the given assumptions implicit in cognitive science, but its response to the problem, relying on the enlightenment model of absolute separation between episteme and *doxa*, knowledge and opinion, is too limited. This spat is replicated in the institutionalization of critique in aca-

demic print publication resulting in a specialized commentary separated from practice.

Grammatology provides one possible theoretical frame for an alternative approach to the operation of stereotypes in research, being free
of the absolute commitment to the book apparatus (ideology of the
humanist subject and writing practices, as well as print technology)
that constrains research conducted within the frame of critique. The
challenge of grammatology, against all technological determinism, is
to accept responsibility for inventing the practices for institutionaliz-
ing electronic technologies. We may accept the values of critique
(critical analysis motivated by the grand metanarrative of emancipation) without reifying one particular model of "critical thinking." In
the experiment that follows this introduction, I attempt to write *with*
the stereotypes of Western thought, using them and showing them at
work at the same time.

The experiment concerns the mode of "immanent critique," a
reasoning capable of operating within the machines of television and
computing, in which the old categories (produced in the book
apparatus) separating fiction and truth break down. Rhetoric has
always been concerned with separating the true from the false, and it
will continue to function in these terms in the electronic apparatus, as
it did in oral and alphabetic cultures. The terms of this sorting will be
transformed, however, to treat an electronic culture that will be as
different from the culture of the book as the latter is different from an
oral culture. It is important to remember that all three dimensions of
discourse exist together interactively. Hence, one goal of this experiment is to provide a model for an alphabetic assignment, as a form for a
paper applying hypermedia—logic, if not technology—to a research
project.

I am particularly interested in the figure of the *mise en abyme*, as
elaborated in Jacques Derrida's theories, in this context. The *mise en
abyme* is a reflexive structuration, by means of which a text shows
what it is telling, does what it says, displays its own making, reflects its
own action. My hypothesis is that a discourse of immanent critique
may be constructed for an electronic rhetoric (for use in video,
computer, and interactive practice) by combining the *mise en abyme*
with the two compositional modes that have dominated audiovisual
texts—montage and mise-en-scene. The result would be a deconstruc-

tive writing, deconstruction as an invention (rather than as a style of book criticism). "Grammatology (in the Stacks) of Hypermedia" is an experiment in immanent criticism, attempting to use the *mise en abyme* figure to organize an "analysis" of the current thinking about hypermedia. The strategy was to imitate in alphabetic style the experience of hypermedia (really only hypertext) practice—navigating through a database, producing a trail of linked items of information. I adopted the stack format of hypercard, confining myself largely to citations from a diverse bibliography of materials relevant to hypermedia. These materials were extended to include not only texts about hypermedia, from academic as well as journalistic sources, but also texts representing the domains used in these sources as metaphors for hypermedia design. Two basic semantic domains, then, provided most of the materials for the database: the index cards organized in stacks, to be linked up in both logical and associative ways; and the figure of travel used to characterize the retrieval of the information thus stored.

The critical point I want to make has to do with a further metaphor that emerged from juxtaposing the other two—an analogy between the mastery of a database and the colonization of a foreign land. The idea was to expose the ideological quality of the research drive, the will to power in knowledge, by calling attention to the implications of designing hypermedia programs in terms of the *frontiers* of knowledge, knowledge as a territory to be scouted, where outposts were to be established, even while the emotions evoked by this scenario are tapped for their motivating power. The goal is not to suppress this metaphorical element in design and research, but to include it more explicitly, to unpack it within the research and teaching activities. In this way stereotypes may become self-conscious, used and mentioned at once in the learning process, and ultimately transformed (or educated).

My version of a hypermedia essay consists of some twenty-nine cards, simulating one trail blazed through a domain of information about hypermedia—concerned, that is, with a subdomain holding data on the semantic fields of the terminology of program design for hypermedia environments. In hypermedia, the cards could be accessed in any order, but in the alphabetic simulation, which is an enunciation or utterance within the system, the sequence does develop according to an associative logic (it is precisely an experiment with the capacity of association for creating learning effects). In hypermedia, the scholar does not provide a specific line of argument, an enunciation, but constructs a whole paradigm of possibilities, a set of statements, leaving the act of utterance, specific selections and combinations, to the reader/user. Or rather, the scholar's "argument" exists at the level of the ideology/theory directing the system of the paradigm, determining the boundaries of inclusion/exclusion.

A final word might be in order concerning the "conventions" of simulation. As a simulation of a trail through a database, the text consists mostly of citations, suggesting that hypermedia may be the technological realization of Walter Benjamin's dream—a book composed entirely of quotations. As in Benjamin's Arcades project, the simulation is a collage, relying upon the remotivation of preexisting fragments in a new context for the production of its own significance. The passage from scholarship to "free writing" with the database is gradual, using typographical conventions to distinguish my "own" prose from that of my "sources." Indeed, part of the effect of montage writing depends upon the visibility of the original context as a remainder within the new setting. Perhaps the one real liberty taken is in not marking the ellipses. Rather, a manner of hyper-elision takes over at certain points, providing a pleasure of composition transforming a semantic domain into the Elysian Fields. The full possibilities of this citational writing remain to be developed elsewhere, such as in the new online journal *Postmodern Culture* from North Carolina State University.

1. As his epigraph for *Literary Machines, the report on, and of, Project Xanadu concerning word processing, electronic publishing, hypertext, thinkertoys, tomorrow's intellectual revolution, and certain other topics including knowledge, education, and freedom,* Ted Nelson cites Annie Dillard: "Whenever a work's structure is intentionally one of its own themes, another of its themes is art." I was reminded of Gregory Bateson's *metalogue*—"a metalogue is a conversation about some problematic subject. This conversation should be such that not only do the participants discuss the problem but the structure of the conversation as a whole is also relevant to the same subject" (Bateson 1). Question:

could I make a text that would tell about hypermedia by doing it? Assignment: compose an essay imitating the concept of hypertext.

2. I went to a conference on computers and literacy held in Alabama. A comment I heard frequently was that hypermedia makes French poststructuralist theory seem obvious, perhaps even superfluous. "There is a theory of hypermedia writing, and it is French." A librarian from Mississippi bought a copy of *Applied Grammatology*. "The kids who come to see me are interested in electronic things."

3. The *Whole Earth Review* has become a *hyperlog* (Apple used a HyperCard version of the catalog as the demo for the new utility at its premiere in the MacWorld Expo).
"The model for HyperCard is the 3-by-5 card. A card is represented by a Macintosh screen. As you flip through screens (cards) you read them one after another, as if they were in a stack. Cards can hold any kind of information you want, in any format you want, including pictures. Rather than rest inertly, as on a Rolodex, information can be actively linked to any other point on any other card. Another way to imagine it would be to think of a book that had footnotes that appear only when you clicked on a passage you wanted to know more about. It would carry you to interesting details, which might themselves have footnotes which are footnoted, and so on" (*Whole Earth Review* 57, 1987: 102).

4. *Stack:* "A pile, heap, or group of things, esp. such a pile or heap with its constituents arranged in an orderly fashion."
"A *sorites* is a chain of linked syllogisms — the form of argument in which the predicate of each statement is the subject of the next. "All ravens are crows; all crows are birds: all birds are animals: all animals need oxygen." The premises of sorites join up and lead to an obvious conclusion ("all ravens need oxygen"). Recognizing sorites is the key to many logic puzzles. The sorites is named for the Greek word for heap, since it is the form of reasoning used (fallaciously) in the paradox of the heap. . . . Sorites paradoxes derive from the way the slight inaccuracy of a premise can accumulate when the premise is applied over and over. . . . Most of what we know or believe is through sorites" (Poundstone 95).

5. "Conceived in this way, allegory becomes the model of all commentary, all critique, insofar as these are involved in rewriting a

primary text in terms of its figural meaning. Allegorical imagery is appropriated imagery: the allegorist does not invent images but confiscates them. Allegory is not hermeneutics. Rather, another meaning is added to the image: the allegorical meaning supplants an antecedent one: it is a supplement. This is why allegory is condemned, but it is also the source of its theoretical significance. Here we encounter a link between allegory and contemporary art: in strategies of accumulation, the paratactic work composed by the simple place-ment of 'one thing after another.' One paradigm for the allegorical work is the mathematical progression. 'What would be a random sequence to an inexperienced person appears to the mathematician a meaningful sequence. Notice that the progression can go on *ad infinitum*.'' (Owens 205, 207).

6. "Perhaps the most fragile component of the future lies in the immediate vicinity of the terminal screen. We must recognize the fundamental incapacity of capitalism ever to rationalize the circuit between body and computer keyboard, and realize that this circuit is the site of a latent but potentially volatile disequilibrium. The disciplinary apparatus of digital culture poses as a self-sufficient, self-enclosed structure without avenues of escape, with no outside. Its myths of necessity, ubiquity, efficiency, of instantaneity require dismantling: in part by disrupting the separation of cellularity, by refusing productivist injunctions, by inducing slow speeds and inhab-iting silences" (Crary 294).

7. "The desktop metaphor allowed you to manipulate data intu-itively. It made using a computer much easier than it had ever been before. The people who developed the Macintosh made a very basic realization about personal computing. The way a user interacts with a computer is as important as the computation itself: In other words, the human interface, as it has come to be called, is as fundamental to computing as any processor configuration, operating system, or pro-gramming environment. This philosophy further postulates that the ultimate goal of computer technology is, in a sense, to make the computer disappear, that the technology should be so transparent, so invisible to the user, that for practical purposes the computer does not exist. In its perfect form, the computer and its application stand outside data content so that the user may be completely absorbed in

the subject matter—it allows a person to interact with the computer just as if the computer were itself human" (*MacUser*, March 1989: 89).

8. "In essence, a hypertext system allows authors or groups of authors to link information together, create paths through a body of related material, annotate existing texts, and create notes that direct readers to either bibliographic data or the body of the referenced text. Using a computer-based hypertext system, students and researchers can quickly follow trails of footnotes and related materials without losing their original context: thus they are not obliged to search through library stacks to look up referenced books and articles. Explicit connections—links—allow readers to travel from one document to another, effectively automating the process of following references in an encyclopedia. Hypermedia is simply an extension of hypertext that incorporates other media in addition to text—static graphics, animated graphics, video, and sound. Intermedia is both an author's tool and a reader's tool. The system, in fact, makes no distinction between types of users, provided they have appropriate access rights. Creating new materials and making and following links are all integrated into a single SEAMLESS, multiuser environment" (Yankelovich, Haan, Meyrowitz, and Drucker 81-82).

9. The frustration of critique, concentrating on the cinematic apparatus (the human-camera interface)—that the production machine disappears, erases itself in favor of its effects, promoting a dominant ideology, that is then mistaken for reality. Viewers not only forget the work of the machine, but forget their own work binding them to the images, accepting the invisible style of Hollywood cinema as the only possible world, not a style at all but life. Having labored to bring the cinema machine—which is first of all a social organization—into appearance, at least for specialists, critique had at least one excuse: that the cinematic apparatus had a head start. At the time Hollywood established the invisible style, critique had not yet found its way to film as an object of study. And now it is all happening again, this fading of the work of production.

"Hence the necessity to engage not a history of the technology of [the computer], but a history of the computer-machine that can include its developments, adaptations, transformations, realignments, the practices it derives, holding together the instrumental and the symbolic, the technological and the ideological, the current ambiguity of the term *apparatus*. Hence the necessity also to conceive that history is a political understanding, to imagine that it can be grasped critically from aspects of contemporary avant-garde practice, or that it might be radically envisaged and recast by the questions posed by women to the machine in place" (Heath 7).

10. "The 'self' was a Socratic discovery or, perhaps we should say, an invention of the Socratic vocabulary. The linguistic method used to identify it and examine it was originally oral, so far as Socrates was concerned. Later it was 'textualized' as we say by Plato. But though oral, the Socratic dialectic depended upon the previous isolation of language in its written form as something separate from the person who uttered it. The person who used the language but was now separated from it became the 'personality' who could now discover its existence. The language so discovered became that level of theoretic discourse denoted by *logos*. Aside from the reflexive pronouns (my-self, your-self, him-self) the chosen symbol of selfhood became *psyche*, often erroneously rendered as 'the soul.' The choice betrays an instinctive fidelity, on the part of those who exploited the word, to the continuing partnership between orality and literacy. For here was the symbol of the speechless thoughtless 'ghost' of oral epic, able in Greek orality to discourse (and so 'think') only after being revived by the warm blood of temporary human life, but now given a new dimension in the guise of the 'ghost in me' which as it speaks also thinks and, through the new life of the intellect, achieves the only complete life of man" (Havelock 114).

11. "Cinema, like dream, would seem to correspond to a temporary form of regression, but whereas dream, according to Freud, is merely a 'normal hallucinatory psychosis,' cinema offers an artificial psychosis without offering the dreamer the possibility of exercising any kind of immediate control. The wish is remarkably precise, and consists in obtaining from reality a position, a condition in which what is perceived would no longer be distinguished from representations. It can be assumed that it is this wish which prepares the long history of cinema: the wish to construct a simulation machine capable to offer the subject perceptions which are really representations mistaken for perceptions. Cinema offers a simulation of regressive movement

which is characteristic of dream—the transformation of thoughts by means of figuration. In other words, without his always suspecting it, the subject is induced to produce machines which would not only complement or supplement the workings of the secondary process, but which could represent his own overall functioning to him: he is led to produce mechanisms mimicking, simulating the apparatus which is no other than himself. The presence of the unconscious also makes itself felt through the pressure it exerts in seeking to get itself represented by a subject who is still unaware of the fact that he is representing to himself the very scene of the unconscious where he is" (Baudry 59, 61).

12. "'Cheshire Puss,' Alice went on. 'Would you tell me, please, which way I ought to go from here?'

'That depends a good deal on where you want to get to,' said the Cat.

'I don't much care where—' said Alice. 'But I don't want to go among mad people.'

'Oh, you can't help that,' said the Cat: 'we're all mad here. I'm mad. You're mad.'

'How do you know I'm mad?' said Alice.

'You must be,' said the Cat, 'or you wouldn't have come here.'

Alice didn't think that proved it at all: however, she went on. 'And how do you know that you're mad?'

'To begin with,' said the Cat, 'a dog's not mad. You grant that?'

'I suppose so.' said Alice.

'Well then,' the Cat went on, 'you see a dog growls when it's angry, and wags its tail when it's pleased. Now I growl when I'm pleased, and wag my tail when I'm angry. Therefore I'm mad.'

'I call it purring, not growling,' said Alice.

'Call it what you like,' said the Cat.

'I wish you wouldn't keep appearing and vanishing so suddenly: you make one quite giddy.'

'All right,' said the Cat; and this time it vanished quite slowly, beginning with the end of the tail, and ending with the grin, which remained some time after the rest of it had gone" (Carroll 62-64).

13. "The components of an augmentation system are the bundle of all the things that can be added to what a human is genetically endowed with, the purpose of which is to augment human capabilities

in order to maximize the capabilities that a human or human organization can apply to the problems and goals of human society. What seems necessary to me is the development of a completely new discipline that embraces the whole augmentation system. What are the practical strategies that will allow our society to pursue high-performance augmentation? My strategy is to begin with small groups, which give greater 'cultural mobility.' Small groups are preferable to individuals because exploring augmented collaboration is at the center of opportunity. These small groups would be the 'SCOUTING PARTIES' sent ahead to map the pathways for the organizational groups to follow. I have come to call these exploratory groups 'high-performance teams.' You also need 'OUTPOSTS' for these teams. There's just an overwhelming amount to do, and we're just getting started. And it is going to be, I think, the most exciting intellectual thing that anybody's ever been able to participate in historically. The early emergence of language itself was very, very exciting, but it took a long, long time. But here things are just going to catapult" (Engelbart 28-30).

14. "I asked myself why I was so fascinated by the trails that led our westering ancestors toward the sunset. I knew that, for some time, the number of people they carried was small. Between 1840 and the California gold rush, fewer than 20,000 men, women, and children followed those roads westward—the Santa Fe Trail, the Oregon Trail, the Bozeman Trail. . . . Yet the story of the overland trails was told a thousand times for every one telling of the peopling of the Midwest. Why? Excitement was there, of course: Indian attacks and desert hardship and even cannibalism. But I suspected that the greatest appeal of the trails lay in the role they played as avenues of progress for the enterprising. The men and women who followed them exemplified— and exaggerated—the hopes and dreams of all Americans for a better life. These were no cautious stay-at-homes content to endure fate's buffeting. The roads that the pioneers followed symbolized the spirit of enterprise that sustained the American dream" (Billington 5).

15. "We conventionally characterize memory in terms of storing information in some place. The process of retrieval has thus been characterized as 'finding the right place in memory.' The connectionist model, however, offers a completely different conception, in which

information is not stored anywhere in particular. Rather it is stored everywhere. Information is better thought of as 'evoked' than 'found.' Information is stored in the relationships among the units and each unit participates in the encoding of many, many memories. To an intuition tutored on the spatial metaphor this is a strikingly nonintuitive proposal. How can a simple memory unit reasonably participate in the encoding of a large number of memories? These distributed memories can retrieve individual memory traces from a complex of memory traces in much the same way that a filter can extract individual frequency components from a complex acoustic waveform. The most interesting aspect involves what happens when memories are not independent of one another. In these cases they do interact. Storing one memory can affect another. But herein lies the great strength of the system. Information that is related to, but different from, previously stored information tends to evoke the original pattern of activity—even though the inputs may differ in many details. Similar items of information interact with one another in such a way as to reinforce those aspects they have in common and cancel out those aspects on which they differ—this can lead to the building of a prototype representation that is most sensitive to information falling about the central tendency of the highly similar inputs" (Hinton and Anderson 3-4).

16. "The mind is a bundle of paradoxes. It has insight, but at the cost of frequent errors. It harnesses the 'vice' of prejudice in order to make new discoveries about the world. And whereas it might be thought that having a perfectly open mind is an asset, a desirable and attainable goal, it turns out that such a mind does not exist, and if it did, it would be a liability. A curious feature of a mind that uses Baker Street [Sherlock Holmes] reasoning to create elaborate scenarios out of incomplete data is that its most deplorable biases often arise in a natural way out of the very same processes that produce the workmanlike, all-purpose, commonsense intelligence that is the Holy Grail of computer scientists who try to model human rationality. A completely open mind would be unintelligent. It could be argued that stereotypes are not ignorance structures at all, but knowledge structures. From this point of view, stereotypes cannot be understood chiefly in terms of attitudes and motives, or emotions like fear and

jealousy. They are a device for predicting other people's behavior. One result of the revival of the connectionist models in the new class of artificial intelligence machines is to downgrade the importance of logic and upgrade the role of knowledge, and of memory, which is the vehicle of knowledge. In a distributed memory, the address of an item is another item, which is related to the first item by its content. For this reason such a memory is called 'content addressable.' The words *Richard Nixon* set off a pattern of activity in the network, turning on some units. Since similar memories interact, due to the multiple role of single units, the *Richard Nixon* activity sets off a *Watergate* pattern and pretty soon a memory of the entire Watergate scandal is brought to consciousness" (Campbell 35, 151, 158).

17. "Originally, *theoria* meant seeing the sights, seeing for yourself, and getting a worldview. The first theorists were 'tourists'—the wise men who traveled to inspect the obvious world. Solon, the Greek sage whose political reforms around 590 B.C. renewed the city of Athens, is the first 'theorist' in Western history. Herodotus is called the father of geography and ethnography as well as history, but because his book also explores the whole nature of places in Greece, Asia, and Egypt, I claim him as the father of topistics as well. *Theoria* did not mean the kind of vision that is restricted to the sense of sight, but implied a complex but organic mode of active observation—a perceptual system that included asking questions, listening to stories and local myths, and feeling as well as hearing and seeing. It encouraged an open reception to every kind of emotional, cognitive, symbolic, imaginative, and sensory experience—a holistic practice of thoughtful awareness that engaged all the senses and feelings. The world theorists who traveled around 600 B.C. were spectators who responded to the expressive energies of places, stopping to contemplate what the guides called 'the things worth seeing.' Local guides—the men who knew the stories of a place—helped visiting theorists to 'see'" (Walter 18-19).

18. "Vannevar Bush's classic article of more than 40 years ago describes an ambitious vision for information researchers—one that is only now being realized. The problem then was an increasingly specialized growing mountain of research, that, ironically, might hinder further scientific progress because of difficulties in sifting through this mass of material. Bush's proposed Memex would have

been a library-in-a-desk: more than an extensive storage medium, it would also have provided powerful ways to consult and modify the human record. Information would be accessible through association as well as through indexing. The user could join any two items, including the user's own materials and notes. Chains of these associations would form a 'trail,' with many possible side trails. Trails could be named and shared with other information explorers. 'Wholly new forms of encyclopedias will appear, ready-made with a mesh of associative trails running through them, ready to be dropped into the Memex and there amplified,' Bush predicted. 'There is a new profession of trailblazers, those who find delight in the task of establishing useful trails through the enormous mass of the common record. The inheritance from the master becomes not only his additions to the world's record, but for his disciples the entire scaffolding by which they were erected.' As we build and experiment with such information systems, it's important to look beyond Memex, and beyond browsing, because the importance of a trail often relates to educational purpose; instead of hypertext systems, we need to consider 'hyperknowledge assistants.' We need fundamentally new organizing principles for knowledge, and we need new navigation and manipulation tools for the learner. Instead of regarding an intelligent system as a human replacement, we can consider the system as a helpful assistant or partner. This means improving the organization of information — conveying knowledge as part of a neighborhood of concepts. Intelligence in filtering or guiding means taking advantage of the relationships between concepts, to prescribe a preferred path" (Weyer 89, 90).

19. "The two recognized, contemporary authorities on Columbus are his son Ferdinand and the traveling monk Bartolome de las Casas. Both cite the reason why Columbus believed he could discover the Indies as threefold: 'natural reasons, the authority of writers, and the testimony of sailors.' As to the natural reasons, 'first, philosophical authority supports the fact that the earth is round . . . therefore Columbus thought it possible to circumnavigate it from East to West.' As to the ancient authorities, Columbus' son cites Aristotle, Seneca, Strabo, Pliny, and Captilonius. None of these ancient writers gave a route plan — it had to come from another source. Las Casas says of the Spanish committees, 'they met often. Columbus would present his

proposal, giving reasons and authoritative support to prove it feasible, *but keeping the most urgent ones to himself.*' During the ensuing discussion, it is stated 'Sailing straight West, as Columbus planned. . . .' But Columbus did not sail 'straight west' and here we have evidence of *what* was omitted—the route plan. The source for that plan had to be St. Brendan, the Navigator. Brendan lived in the 6th century A.D. when many Celts, feeling the pressure of the overflowing Angles and Saxons, sought refuge over the sea, colonizing the Orkney Islands, Shetland Islands, the Inner and Outer Hebrides. . . . The Irish clergy had a second reason for overseas travel. They were a devout group and practiced a form of wandering in the wilderness. Not having a desert nearby, they did their wandering at sea. The principal source of information on Brendan is a book entitled *Navigatio Sancti Brendani,* available to Columbus in Latin and vernacular translations. In the *Navigatio* the manner and style of navigational reports are as excerpts relating the interesting events, taken from a monk's diary, or a seafarer's logbook. The subsequent versions of the *Navagatio* were penned by monks in monasteries. These contain religious matter of a mythical nature which has obviously been added to the original" (Chapman 23, 28, 30, 172).

20. "Removed from the tangible environment of their culture, travelers came to rely on this most portable and most personal of cultural orders as a means of symbolic linkage with their homes. More than any other emblem of identity, language seemed capable of domesticating the strangeness of America. It could do so both by the spreading of Old World names over New World places, people, and objects, and by the less literal act of domestication which the telling of an American tale involved. Moreover, it could provide voyagers just departing for America with a set of articulated goals and designs by which the course of Western events actually might be organized beforehand. This ability to 'plot' New World experience in advance was, in fact, the single most important attribute of European Language.

Francis Bacon, primary theorist of a new epistemology and staunch opponent of medieval scholasticism, extrapolated Columbus himself into a symbol of bold modernity. His voyager was decidedly not the man of terminal doubt and despair whom we encounter in the Jamaica letter of 1503. He was instead a figure of hopeful departures, a man whose discovery of a 'new world' suggested the possibility that 'the remoter and more hidden parts of nature' also might be explored with success. The function of Bacon's *Novum Organum* was to provide for the scientific investigator the kind of encouragement which the argument of Columbus prior to 1492 had provided for a Europe too closely bound to traditional assumptions" (Franklin 7-8).

21. "The *schadchen* jokes are almost all of two types. In one type, the matchmaker attempts to convince the prospective bridegroom of the attractiveness of his match, but in his unrestrained praise of the woman and her family, he simultaneously reveals the existence of some fundamental flaw.

> A *Schadchen* had brought an assistant with him to the discussion about the proposed bride, to bear out what he had to say. 'She is straight as a pine tree,' said the *Schadchen*. — 'As a pine tree!', repeated the echo. — 'And she has eyes that ought to be seen!' — 'What eyes she has!' confirmed the echo. — 'And she is better educated than anyone!' — 'What an education!' — 'It's true there is one thing,' admitted the broker, 'she has a small hump.' — 'And *what* a hump!' the echo confirmed once more.

In the other type of *schadchen* joke, the flaw is already obvious, and the schadchen employs sophistic arguments in an attempt to mitigate the flaw or turn it into a virtue" (Oring 27).

22. "Of all the affairs we participate in, with or without interest, the groping search for a new way of life is the only aspect still impassioning. We should therefore delineate some provisional terrains of observation, including the observation of certain processes of chance and predictability in the streets. The word *pyschogeography*, suggested by an illiterate Kabyle as a general term for the phenomena a few of us were investigating around the summer of 1953, is not too inappropriate. Psychogeography could set for itself the study of the precise laws and specific effects of the geographical environment, consciously organized or not, on the emotions and behavior of individuals. The research that we are thus led to undertake of the arrangement of the elements of the urban setting, in close relation with the sensations they provoke, entails bold hypotheses that must

constantly be corrected in the light of experience, by critique and self-critique. Among various more difficult means of intervention, a renovated cartography seems appropriate for immediate utilization. The production of psychogeographic maps, or even the introduction of alterations such as more or less arbitrarily transposing maps of two different regions, can contribute to clarifying certain wanderings that express not subordination to randomness but complete *insubordination* to habitual influences (influences generally categorized as tourism, that popular drug as repugnant as sports or buying on credit). A friend recently told me that he had just wandered through the Hartz region of Germany while blindly following the directions of a map of London. This sort of game is obviously only a mediocre beginning in comparison to the complete construction of architecture and urbanism that will someday be within the power of everyone. We need to work toward flooding the market—even if for the moment merely the intellectual market—with a mass of desires" (Knabb 6, 7).

23. "Can the hypermedia author realize the enormous potential of the medium to change our relation to language and text simply by linking one passage or image to others? No, linking by itself is not enough. Working within this new medium, authors must make use of new techniques that will enable the reader to process the information presented by this new kind of information technology. One begins any discussion of the new rhetoric needed for hypermedia with the recognition that authors of hypertext and hypermedia materials confront three related problems: First, what must they do to orient readers and help them read efficiently and with pleasure? Second, how can they inform those reading a document where the links in that document lead? Third, how can they assist readers who have just entered a new document to feel at home there? Drawing upon the analogy of travel, we can say that the first problem concerns *navigation* information necessary for making one's way through the materials. The second concerns *exit* or *departure* information and the third *arrival* or *entrance* information" (Landow, "Rhetoric," 40-41).

24. "The walking of passers-by offers a series of turns (*tours*) and detours that can be compared to 'turns of phrase' or 'stylistic figures.' In introducing the notion of a 'residing rhetoric' we assume that the 'tropes' catalogued by rhetoric furnish models and hypotheses for the

analysis of ways of appropriating places. Two postulates seem to me to underlie the validity of this application: 1) it is assumed that practices of space also correspond to manipulations of the basic elements of a constructed order; 2) it is assumed that they are, like the tropes in rhetoric, deviations relative to a sort of 'literal meaning' defined by the urbanistic system. There would thus be a homology between verbal figures and the figures of walking (a stylized selection among the latter is already found in the figures of dancing) insofar as both consist in 'treatments' or operations bearing on isolatable units, and in 'ambiguous dispositions' that divert and displace meaning in the direction of equivocalness in the way a tremulous image confuses and multiplies the photographed objects" (de Certeau 100).

25. "'Where do you come from?' said the Red Queen. 'And where are you going? Look up, speak nicely, and don't twiddle your fingers all the time.'

Alice attended to all these directions, and explained, as well as she could, that she had lost her way.

'I don't know what you mean by *your* way,' said the Queen: 'all the ways about here belong to *me*.'

Alice didn't dare to argue the point, but went on: '—and I thought I'd try and find my way to the top of that hill—'

'When you say "hill,"' the Queen interrupted, 'I could show you hills, in comparison with which you'd call that a valley.'

'No, I shouldn't,' said Alice, surprised into contradicting her at last: 'a hill *can't* be a valley, you know. That would be nonsense—'

The Red Queen shook her head. 'You may call it "nonsense" if you like,' she said, 'but *I've* heard nonsense, compared with which that would be as sensible as a dictionary!'

For some minutes Alice stood without speaking, looking out in all directions over the country—and a most curious country it was. 'I declare it's marked out just like a large chess-board!' Alice said at last. 'There ought to be some men moving about somewhere—and so there are!' she added in a tone of delight. 'It's a great game of chess that's being played—all over the world—if this *is* the world at all, you know"' (Carroll 145-46).

26. "It has been said that the history of cinematic discourse could be written in terms of the invention of two devices: montage and mise-

en-scene. *Montage*—a term derived from the French word for hoisting, getting up, mounting, or assembling—hence, staging in theater usage and editing in film terminology. It is associated with the work of Sergei Eisenstein, in which it came to represent the rhetorical arrangement of shots in juxtaposition so that the clash between two adjoining images creates a third, independent entity and a whole new meaning. *Mise-en-scene*—French, literally the placing of a scene—for the act of staging or directing a play or a film. In cinema, Andre Bazin and other theoreticians and critics have used it to describe a style of film directing emphasizing the content of the individual frame. Its proponents see montage as disruptive to the psychological unity of man with his environment" (Katz 813, 820).

In the rhetoric of hypermedia a third device will be added to these two cinematic devices, to organize the digitalized convergence of media into a theoretical diegesis. The name of that device is also French—*mise en abyme*—associated with the theorist Jacques Derrida. *Mise en abyme* (literally, placing in the abyss) refers to the heraldic "device" of representing the whole field in one of its parts; the term is used in art criticism to refer to a work that displays its own formal properties. As developed in poststructuralist theory, the *mise en abyme* does *not* involve a formalist separation of art from its historical and sociopolitical contexts. On the contrary, it is a transformation of the concept of "place" (topos) in rhetoric. The topics and commonplaces were a body of material common to orators and poets alike, forming an important part of the general cultural tradition. Curtius has shown how the topics persisted as "cliches," which can be used in any form of literature, and how they spread to all spheres of life with which literature deals and to which it gives form. This tradition now faces the challenge of artificial intelligence, and hypermedia, in which the stereotype functions as knowledge: how to make the stereotype self-conscious. The name for the device replacing the "places/tool" of argument is *chora*, whose stylistic realization is the *mise en abyme*.

27. "The authors of the alphabetic Popol Vuh do not identify themselves directly, but they give enough clues to permit a hypothesis that they were the officials named in their own text as the 'Great Toastmasters' or 'Great Conveners of Banquets,' matchmakers who

presided over the feasts where marriage arrangements were negotiated between patrilineages. They were also known as 'Mothers of the Word, Fathers of the Word.' The emphasis on the 'Word' suggests the contemporary matchmakers called 'road guides,' who are recruited from the ranks of motherfathers (metaphorical parents to everyone in their patrilineages) and whose way with words is unsurpassed. The Great Toastmasters made a record of what a reader would say when he fleshed out the notes, lists, plot outlines, and charts given in the ancient writing, to the point where they came to life as narrative. Interwoven with the narrative proper is an interpretive discourse addressed to the reader. This is often metasemantic, explaining how particular places, plants, animals, peoples, and persons received their names. At other times the interpretive discourse is metapragmatic, treating past events as 'examples' of what should (or should not) happen when similar situations recur in later times" (Tedlock 61).

28. "If there is indeed a chasm in the middle of the *Timaeus*, a sort of abyss 'in' which there is an attempt to think or to say this abyssal chasm which would be *chora*, the opening of a place 'in' which everything would come both to take place and to be reflected (for these are the images which are inscribed there), is it significant that a *mise en abyme* regulates a certain order of composition of the discourse? And that it goes so far as to regulate even this mode of thinking or of saying which must be similar without being identical to the one which is practiced around the edges of the chasm? Is it significant that this *mise en abyme* affects the forms of a discourse on places, notably political places, a politics of places entirely commanded by the consideration of sites (jobs in the society, region, territory, country), as places assigned to types or forms of discourse? At the opening of the *Timeaus*, there are considerations on the guardians of the city, the cultivators and the artisans, the division of labor and education. Those who are raised as guardians of the city will not have anything that is properly their own. To have nothing that is one's own, isn't this also the situation of the site, the condition of *chora*? One can say the same thing about the remark which follows immediately and touches on the education of women, on marriage and above all on the community of children. In procreation any attribution or natural or legitimate property must be excluded by the very

milieu of the city. We are perhaps already in a site where the law of the proper no longer has any meaning. Let us consider even the political strategy of marriages. It manifests a relation of abyssal and analogous reflexivity with what will be said later about *chora*, about the 'riddles' or sieves shaken in order to sort or select the 'grain' and the 'seed.' The law of the better is crossed with a certain chance. Let us explain it at once. These formal analogies or these *mises en abyme*, refined, subtle, are not considered here as the art of Plato the writer. This art interests us but what is important in this very place, and first of all, independently of the supposed intentions of a composer, are the constraints which produce these analogies. Shall we say that they constitute a program? A logic whose authority was imposed on Plato? Yes, up to a point, and this limit appears in the abyss itself: the being-program of the program, its structure of pre-inscription and of typographic prescription forms the explicit theme of the discourse *en abyme* of *chora*. The latter figures the place of inscription of all that is marked on the world" (Derrida).

29. "The card index marks the conquest of three-dimensional writing, and so presents an astonishing counterpoint to the three-dimensionality of script in its original form as rune or knot notation. (And today the book is already, as the present mode of scholarly production demonstrates, an outdated mediation between two different filing systems. For everything that matters is to be found in the card box of the researcher who wrote it, and the scholar studying it assimilates it into his own card index.) But it is quite beyond doubt that the development of writing will not indefinitely be bound by the claims to power of a chaotic academic and commercial activity; rather, quantity is approaching the moment of a qualitative leap when writing, advancing ever more deeply into the graphic regions of its new eccentric figurativeness, will take sudden possession of an adequate factual content. In this picture writing, poets, who will now as in earliest times be first and foremost experts in writing, will be able to participate only by mastering the fields in which it is being constructed: the statistical and technical diagram" (Benjamin, "Reflections," 78).

Discussion

TUMAN.   Part of the success of your piece, I suspect, comes from the fact that we are trained as traditional readers to work hard at discerning overarching themes and connections between different sections. We still see reading (and the act of writing about reading) as an imaginative act of re-creating a whole. Could you speculate on the differences we might expect in an electronic (or video) age when writings like yours are the norm, not the exception?

ULMER.   My reply necessarily will be superficial, or conversational, partly to comply with the spirit of dialogue motivating this part of the collection and partly to avoid writing another article, which would be needed to do justice to the question. I might recast the question somewhat, to articulate one of its implications: How should we teach reading and writing in a way that takes into account the electronic apparatus?

I want to frame my remarks too, keeping in mind Stanley Aronowitz's article, which makes clear several points about the electronic apparatus relevant to my argument. The first point is that collectivities (institutions such as the agencies and businesses Aronowitz studied) and individuals are in the process of adapting to an electronic environment: they are learning to live in an electronic machine that is social as well as technological. Some institutions and individuals make the least adjustment possible, while others make fuller commitments. The rule for such change demonstrated by Brian Winston is the "law" of the suppression of radical results. *Law* is in quotation marks, because this phenomenon is not necessary or determined but is the result of certain ideological considerations and practices that could be changed.

The second point of overlap between my article and Aronowitz's article is the idea that human cognition and different modes of logic are profoundly involved in the apparatus issue. My comments are meant in part to elaborate Aronowitz's point that "we are entering an era when irony and its companion skepticism are no longer incidental rhetorical devices"—meaning, in my terms, that these and other literary or artistic devices, while not specific to one medium, are especially favored by the features inherent in electronic technology (its facility with juxtaposition). The two points come together in the question of the role of the school in preparing individuals to live in the electronic machine. The crucial issue here is to realize that the electronic machine includes invention of social and personal practices as well as of technical and technological inventions. The school could—if it would—provide significant leadership in the design of the human-computer interface at collective and cognitive levels alike.

The school, in short, may have as big an impact on the electronic apparatus as do hardware and software producers, both in terms of what it demands from these producers (what it expects of a mind tool oriented toward learning and creativity) and what we ourselves contribute to the invention process. The scientific and business disciplines have responded well to this opportunity. The same cannot be said of the humanities. To return to the initial question, for example, How might we teach an introductory writing course considering the possibilities of composition made available by hypermedia? It is not a matter of the equipment, but rather of how to adapt alphabetic reading and writing to the design of an institutional interface bringing together the cultures of print and electronics.

To pose the question at a practical level, consider what kind of alphabetic assignments teachers of composition might pose to explore electronic cognition—without needing any computer equipment. (In answering the question at this level I will make a number of assertions that would need to be demonstrated if this were an article.) The principal assertion is that, at a basic level, there are three ways to organize the release of information, which are used across all media: narrative, exposition, and pattern. The three modes are not mutually exclusive; on the contrary, all three are present in any work, with one dominant, and the other two subordinate. Thus narrative predominates in story, exposition predominates in documentary, and pattern dominates in collage. One way to construe what is happening as we pass from print apparatus to electronics apparatus would be to say that the dominant forms for organizing information in print have been narrative and exposition—splitting the functions of imagination and fact between them—with pattern predominating only in the arts, at the bottom of the hierarchy of knowledge in the relations among science, social science, and the humanities. The dominant form organizing the release of information in the new apparatus, however, is pattern, whose essential form is collage (in the way that mystery is the essential form of narrative, and propaganda is the essential form of exposition). Story and document are still operating in collage, but they are subordinated to and manipulated by the operations of pattern, which transform their signifying effects.

One immediate implication of this observation is that we should be teaching the reading and composing of collage in our general education writing courses, along with instruction in the other modes. In all three cases, the instruction must not confine itself to study *about* the mode but should include exercises using the mode in question. Each mode, it is important to note, has its own logic in the same way that it has an essential form. Narrative, that is, reasons abductively, exposition reasons inductively and deductively, and pattern reasons conductively (Ulmer). Since collage has been seriously neglected in general composition courses, this latter point is not widely appreciated. Conduction, as the name for the logic of pattern, has been most thoroughly worked out thus far within the institution of psychoanalysis, in terms of dream-work.

A typical assignment, then, for teaching writing and thinking as pattern primarily, rather than as story or argument primarily, includes an introduction to conductive (dream-work) logic (displacement, condensation, dramatization, secondary elaboration) as well as to the representational devices of collage (citation or appropriation, juxtaposition, fragmentation). In this context, Freud's *On Dreams* (his own popularization of the *Interpretation of Dreams*) may be taught as a rhetoric, rather than as an essay in psychology. This logic like each of the others, has its own aims and purposes — specifically, discovery and invention.

To give just one example of an exercise in collage conduction, I have based an assignment on Freud's statement in *On Dreams* that analysis and dream-work are dialectically related, with each one being a reversal of the other: what the dream-work weaves, analysis unravels. A common analytical assignment is to read a work of literature as if it were a dream (to interpret the literary devices by translating them into the terms of psychoanalytic theory). Much less common is the corollary task of reading an analytical essay as if it were a dream. The collage conduction exercise would push the latter project a step further by asking the student to select a critical essay (in any field) and translate it into a dream style, making systematic application of the rhetoric of dreams to the analytical material.

Such an exercise has several learning effects, not least of which is an experience of creativity, since the results of the translation tend to be surprising. The translation has a critical effect—it often exposes some unnoticed aspect of the original to new scrutiny, and it provides insight into the cognitive capacities of the poetic and artistic devices exploited in dream-work. To return to the basic point of the initial question, there is a new attitude toward gap filling promoted in collage conduction.

One insight into the whole problem of "suture" in critical theory in the past several decades was to show that, within the context of a semiotic epistemology (in which language exchanges are conceived in terms of "communication," with messages encoded by senders and decoded by receivers), readers or viewers tended to be unaware of their active participation in constructing the meaning of a work. The rhetoric of the real (realism) rendered as invisible or transparent as possible the discursive, textual nature of language practices. An electronic rhetoric will have an opposite effect, in that it requires the most active readers/viewers possible. This active reading strategy must be actively taught, although it is being assimilated through the entertainment industry in a variety of ways. The most essential practice of print writing is argumentation—exploiting a feature (or an abuse) of expositional logic, the enthymeme, and leading readers in a linear fashion through a body of information oriented by a problem to a univocal conclusion or solution. The most essential practice of hypermedia is to provide the whole set of possibilities, the paradigm it-self, through which many different arguments or lines might be traced, or even by means of which alternative framings (other than that of "problem") might be arranged. Readers of an argument are supposed to be moved to take an action, an action that the composer had in mind, but the readers of hypermedia must take action at an earlier state of the question, taking responsibility themselves for the line traced through the database. Such a cognitive movement has to be at least in part an invention, understood in both the classical rhetorical sense of *invention* and in the avant-garde sense of *innovation*. The principles directing this inventive passage are associative, a style of reasoning that is as systematic as are the logics of story and argument.

All three modes and logics, to reiterate a point made earlier, may be practiced in any medium (voice, print, video, or hypermedia), but each one tends at the same time to predominate in a given apparatus or social machine. Narrative is the native form of oral culture, exposition is the native form of alphabetic literacy (in the sense that scientific writing is the privileged discourse of the print apparatus), and collage pattern is the native form of electronics. This suggestion has to be demonstrated, and this is a project to which much of my research, writing, and teaching is devoted.

Meanwhile, to summarize my response, teachers of composition have a direct contribution to make to the electronic problematic: to include along with exercises in narrative and exposition exercises in pattern (the three are best learned together, to observe their interactions, mutual interdependence, and relative strengths and weaknesses). The active seeking for and construction of coherence, which is part of the alphabetic reading strategy, will be enlarged and extended in electronic composition, informed by a set of expectations and a body of poetics that are still in the formative, emerging stage.

There is a political dimension to this shift in modes and logics that ought to be mentioned as well. To say that the logic of electronics is dream-work is to propose that the unconscious (what is named and gathered under that concept) be included explicitly and systematically in reasoning and writing. One implication of this proposal is that the alphabetic and modernist inclination to keep categories neatly separated will break down in an electronic environment; another implication is that there will be a rearrangement of relationships among the divisions of knowledge, with the gradual realization that the strategies of information management based on the alphabetic apparatus are inadequate for dealing with an electronic environment. Some invention at the institutional level is called for now (based in the humanities and arts disciplines) with the purpose to show the culture as a whole what electronics (hypermedia) is for, what it can do best (and what it has not yet been set to perform).

PROVENZO. A brief comment. Hypertext and hypermedia allow users to draw on the computer's strengths in "structured symbolic manipulation," while permitting them to take advantage of their ability to use semantic networks. This possibility was recognized by Douglas C. Engelbart in his essay "A Conceptual Framework for the Augmentation of Man's Intellect" (1963). What we can do is use the computer as a means of enhancing one's cognition—of augmenting one's intelligence—much like we use a screwdriver to set a screw more effectively than we can with our bare hands. Hypertext and hypermedia, if employed properly, have the potential to enhance and expand our intellects—"mind tools" if you will. The potential impact on traditional knowledge and scholarship is profound. Probably the more intelligent and creative you are, the more of an impact using the computer to augment your intelligence will have. Fully exploring this topic takes a considerable amount of space.

> 4 <
COMPUTERS
and New Forms of Administrative Control

The Electronic Panopticon: Censorship, Control, and Indoctrination in a Post-Typographic Culture

Eugene F. Provenzo, Jr.

It is the thesis of this essay that important new models of social and political control emerged in Europe at the end of the eighteenth century with profound implications for the contemporary computer revolution. The appearance of these new models brought with them the exercise of a new type of power—the power of normalization. As I will attempt to demonstrate, this normalizing power—which in the eighteenth century first manifested itself in penal institutions, hospitals, factories, and schools—has come to be realized in our own era through instrumentalities provided initially by mainframe computers and more recently microcomputers.

The analysis of the power of normalization constituted a major theme of the work of the French social theorist and historian Michel Foucault. Specifically, in his work *Discipline and Punish* Foucault was concerned with the emergence of modern forms of social regulation and control. According to Foucault, by the end of the eighteenth century, there was a movement away from a focus on the power of individual men (monarchical power)—a reversal of the "axis of individualization"—toward the collection of records and information about individuals over whom power could be exercised.

For Foucault, knowledge and power directly imply one another: "There is no power relation without the correlative constitution of a field of knowledge, nor any knowledge that does not presuppose and constitute at the same time power relations" (2). The English utilitarian philosopher Jeremy Bentham (1748-1832), according to Foucault, was the social theorist from the period who most completely understood the emergence of the new models of knowledge/power and social control. In particular, his work the *Panopticon; or the Inspection House* (as it is listed on the title page) outlined a master plan for the observation and control of individuals living and working in any of a number of institutions including: "prisons, houses of industry, work-houses, poor-houses, manufactories, mad-houses, lazarettos, hospitals and schools."

The main element in Bentham's plan was a penitentiary inspection-house, which he called a "Panopticon." As he described it:

> The building is circular.
> The apartments of the prisoners occupy the circumference.
> You may call them, if you please the *cells*.
> These *cells* are divided from one another, and the prisoners by
> that means secluded from all communication with each other, by
> *partitions* in the form of *radii* issuing from the circumference
> towards the centre, and extending as many feet as shall be
> thought necessary to form the largest dimension of the cell.
> The apartment of the inspector occupies the centre; you may
> call it if you please the *inspector's lodge*. (40)

The inspector's lodge had numerous windows that made it possible to peer into the prisoners' cells. Lighting was arranged in such a way that the inspector in the central lodge or tower of the Panopticon could keep the prisoners in their individual cells under constant observation without their being aware that they were being observed. Speaking tubes connected the inspector with the prisoners. The slightest whisper of a prisoner could be heard by the inspector in his central tower.

According to Foucault, Bentham's plan for the Panopticon reversed the principle of the dungeon, which enclosed and hid the prisoner and deprived him of light. Instead, through an ingenious use of architecture, the Panopticon enclosed and held the prisoner in what Foucault refers to as a constant trap of visibility. Foucault goes on to explain:

> [The prisoner] is seen, but he does not see; he is the object of
> information, never a subject in communication. The
> arrangement of his room, opposite the central tower, imposes on
> him an axial visibility; but the divisions of the ring, those

separated cells, imply a lateral invisibility. And this invisibility is a guarantee of order. If the inmates are convicts, there is no danger of a plot, an attempt at collective escape, the planning of new crimes for the future, bad reciprocal influences; if they are patients, there is no danger of contagion; if they are madmen there is no risk of their committing violence upon one another; if they are schoolchildren, there is no copying, no noise, no chatter, no waste of time. . . . (200)

Under Bentham's panoptic system, the individual came to believe that he was under constant observation. As long as the prisoner, inmate, or student sensed that he was potentially being observed, the automatic functioning of power/knowledge and control was assured.

In modern literature, the most chilling realization of the principles of Bentham's Panopticon is described in George Orwell's novel *1984*. In the novel, Big Brother keeps the population of Oceania under continual observation through the use of a system of two-way televisions or "telescreens." Located at a central point in one's home, the telescreen could be dimmed, but never completely turned off:

The telescreen received and transmitted simultaneously. Any sound that Winston made above the level of a very low whisper, would be picked up by it; moreover, so long as he remained within the field of vision which the metal placque commanded, he could be seen as well as heard. There was of course no way of knowing whether you were being watched at any given moment. How often, or on what system, the Thought Police plugged in on any individual wire was guesswork. It was even conceivable that they watched everybody all of the time. But at any rate they could plug in your wire whenever they wanted to. You had to live—did live from habit in the assumption that every sound you made was overheard, and, except in darkness, every movement scrutinized. (6-7)

Symbolically, posters of Big Brother inscribed "Big Brother Is Watching" stare down from every stairwell, from every corner on the street, and in every public place. The visual image of Big Brother was "so contrived that the eyes follow you about when you move" (5).

In effect, Orwell with his telescreen, Thought Police, and Big Brother created a fictional, but potentially very feasible, electronic panopticon.[1] While Orwell did not include computers in his anti-utopia—there being no indication in his work that he anticipated them as a possible technology—the mechanisms for carrying out the functions of control, censorship, and indoctrination described by Orwell are implicit in the instrumental reason or nature of computers, microcomputers, and laser disks. In the following essay, I wish to examine in detail the implications of computer technology for intellectual and personal freedom and education in our culture.

Implicit in my argument is the conviction that the technology of the computer—like any technology—is not neutral. The computer frames how we think and act.[2] In an educational context, this point is demonstrated very clearly by C. A. Bowers who, in his recent book *The Cultural Dimensions of Educational Computing,* maintains that computers establish frames that shape "patterns of communication and the structure of knowledge, mediate the individual's sensory relationship with the environment, and re-encode the vocabularies of the culture, while at the same time influencing what gets saved and what gets lost in the transmission process" (2). Bowers's recognition that computers are not a neutral technology is profoundly important. In *Beyond the Gutenberg Galaxy,* I argued that as a result of the widespread introduction of microcomputers we are seeing the emergence of what I called a "post-typographic culture." Drawing on Marshall McLuhan, I argued that the widespread proliferation and use of computers and microcomputers had the potential to create a new human environment. In this context I quoted McLuhan to the effect that "technological environments are not merely passive containers of people but are active processes that reshape people and other technologies alike" (iv). Despite this fact I was, in this study, generally optimistic about people's ability to control the new technology. I assumed that the technology of the computer and microcomputer was neutral. In the seven years since I began *Beyond the Gutenberg Galaxy,* my point of view has changed. While I believe that the computer—particularly in the form of the microcomputer—has consistently demonstrated its potential as a tool for creativity and productivity, it has also increasingly demonstrated its potential to abuse our rights of privacy, personal freedom, and liberty. This potential for abuse has particularly important implications in the area of education and intellectual inquiry. While I have not lost my enthusiasm for the positive ways computers and microcomputers can be employed in our society, I am increasingly concerned that we are liable to allow the techniques implicit in computerized systems of knowledge and control to infringe on our personal freedoms and dominate our lives.

We are faced in a post-typographic and electronic culture with a new type of literacy—one that is subject to greater control and manipulation than was the case in a typographic culture. My arguments in the rest of this essay are cautionary in nature. They suggest that literacy in a post-typographic society—our confidence in texts— demands a greater understanding and caution concerning how what we are reading can be manipulated and controlled.

Literacy in a post-typographic culture requires us to be acutely aware of the medium through which we "read" the culture and society around us. In doing so, we must understand at the most fundamental level the potential of the computer to create conditions for both good and evil—both freedom and control.

We need to be aware that because of their potential to empower people—both good and evil people—computers cannot be considered neutral. They are instrumentalities. Implicit in their use is an overwhelmingly powerful potential for censorship and control. As will be demonstrated later in this essay, the threat of the computer to violate our personal rights and freedoms, in particular the right of free inquiry, is inadequately understood, not only by the general public but by our educational and cultural leaders as well.

Post-Typographic Culture as a Digital Culture

Post-typographic culture is a digital culture. It represents a new phase of our cultural history. According to Robert McClintock in adopting digital technology "we have initiated an irreversible action in cultural history." A frontier has been crossed that "is not simply technical, but deeply cultural" (349).

For McClintock, culture is defined as a "vast store of externalized memory" (350). It is memory put into things outside the human brain—into books, architecture, paintings, and photographs, to name just a few examples. Up until now, the various means of coding information outside the brain have functioned very differently: "The codes of writing are different from those of pictorial representation, which in turn differ from those of sculpture, architecture, still photography, or film" (350). These different codes have been analog rather than digital in nature. As McClintock explains: "Analog technologies use changes in one medium, say electromagnetic waves, to represent changes in another medium, say sound waves or changes of illumination along a path back and forth, filling a phosphorent screen. The system is inexpensive and efficient, but inherently prone to error, which we experience as noise, static, interference" (347).

Analog systems have a much greater tendency toward entropy than digital systems. Digital systems "re-create" an object or thing from a binary code. As long as the binary code is preserved and not allowed to degenerate, an exact copy of original phenomenon is reproduced. With a laser audio disk, there should be no difference between the master disk and the digital copy made. Thus a recording of Glenn Gould playing Bach's *Goldberg* Variations is virtually the same on the digital master and the compact laser audio disks that are produced from it. In marked contrast, an analog recording involves an analog master, which reproduces the sounds from the recording studio as a series of variations recorded on the surface of a medium such as plastic or vinyl. A rough analog model is created by the recording, which is then used to press copies. These analog messages are then translated through a stylus and amplified.

Analog and digital represent systems subject to different physical laws. Entropy is not as serious an issue in digital systems as in analog systems. McClintock believes that the ramifications underlying analog versus digital systems are profound:

> For instance, copyright laws seem to break down in the digital environments because the familiar dynamics of reproduction do not seem to hold. Copies in the familiar analog realm are costly to make and at best approximate, leaving clear traces of what is original and what is the copy. In the digital realm, copies are nearly costless, they are often indistinguishable from the original, assuming some real meaning to "original" can in fact be attached to something substantial. (348)

The fundamental rule of digital culture is that "insofar as we can express something in binary code, we can recreate it" (348). According to McClintock, the implications of this fact are that as we learn to specify things in binary or digital code "we can recreate in digital technology the forms of intelligence so specified" (351). In doing so we have initiated ourselves, McClintock concludes, into a culture based upon *intelligence* rather than *remembrance*.

This idea of a culture based on intelligence rather than remembrance has profound implications. A culture based on remembrance is one that is stored externally in books, paintings, sculpture, and other analog forms. A culture based on intelligence is digital and processed. It is the computer's potential to process information, however (and in doing so potentially distort or reconstruct in altered form that which we wish to preserve), that is ultimately one of the most disturbing and difficult issues we must face as we proceed into a post-typographic culture. As suggested earlier, the requirements of literacy—more specifically critical literacy—are necessarily increased.

The Electronic Panopticon

As demonstrated in Foucault's work, the desire to exercise power or control is not new. Such systems date back hundreds of years. However, their effectiveness has been limited and circumscribed as a result of imperfect technologies, which have made it possible for individuals to resist and rebel. In George Orwell's *1984*, Winston Smith—the novel's main character—works in the Ministry of Truth where he rewrites newspaper articles to conform with changing political and social conditions. History is processed rather than remembered. As Smith explains:

The Party said that Oceania had never been in alliance with Eurasia. He, Winston Smith, knew that Oceania had been in alliance with Eurasia as short a time as four years ago. But where did that knowledge exist? Only in his own consciousness, which in any case must soon be annihilated. And if all others accepted the lie which the Party imposed—if all the records told the same tale—then the lie passed into history and became truth. "Who controls the past," ran the Party slogan, "controls the future:

who controls the present controls the past." And yet the past, though of its nature alterable, never had been altered. Whatever was true now was true from everlasting to everlasting. It was quite simple. All that was needed was an unending series of victories over your own memory. "Reality control," they called it; in Newspeak, "doublethink." (32)

Doublethink required Oceania, and more specifically the Ministry of Truth, to be involved in a process of constantly rewriting and republishing history. As mentioned earlier, computers were not part of Orwell's utopia. As a result, the sort of control and rewriting of history that he warned of was not really feasible and could only exist in Orwell's fictional reality. In analog culture, the economies of scale necessary to control information have been too circumscribed and limited to make such a system practical. This is no longer the case in digital culture.

Anyone who has used a word-processing system with a substitution or replacement function knows how easy it is to transform information in a digital context. One word can be automatically substituted for another, a name changed, a date altered, an idea corrupted without any record left of the original source. The past, as Orwell so correctly predicted, can be altered. Those who fall out of political favor could be eliminated from history: "People simply disappeared, always during the night. Your name was removed from the registers, every record of everything you had ever done was wiped out, your one-time existence was denied and then forgotten. You were abolished, annihilated: *vaporized* was the usual word" (20). History becomes a function of the future, of changing ideologies and political opinion.

The ability to alter the past has always been potentially possible in analog culture. It has tended, however, to be enormously time-consuming and relatively easy to detect. Stephen Jay Gould in his book *The Mismeasure of Man*, for example, demonstrates that the American psychologist William Henry Goddard deliberately altered photographs of a family of feebleminded individuals he was studying and whom he code-named the Kallikaks. As Gould explains:

My colleague Steven Selden and I were examining his copy of Goddard's volume on the Kallikaks. The frontispiece shows a

member of the kakos line, saved from depravity by confinement
in Goddard's institution at Vineland. Deborah, as Goddard calls
her, is a beautiful woman. . . . She sits calmly in a white dress,
reading a book, a cat lying comfortably on her lap. Three other
plates show members of the kakos line, living in poverty in their
rural shacks. All have a depraved look about them. . . . Their
mouths are sinister in appearance; their eyes are darkened slits.
But Goddard's books are nearly seventy years old, and the ink has
faded. It is now clear that all the photos of noninstitutionalized
kakos were phonied by inserting heavy dark lines to give eyes and
mouths their diabolical appearance. The three plates of Deborah
are unaltered. (171)[3]

Goddard, among other things, was attempting to demonstrate the bene-
ficial effects of institutionalization. His alteration of the photographs of
the Kallikak family and his use of untouched photographs of Deborah
Kallikak—his patient at Vineland—provided "visible" evidence of the
efficacy of the program and treatments that he was promoting.

A second example of the alteration of photographic material can be
seen in a series of pictures showing the Russian political leader Lenin
addressing a crowd on Sverdlov Square, May 5, 1920. In the first picture,
taken from a newsreel, the figures of Trotsky and Kamenev are clearly
visible. Another photograph taken a few seconds later—and retouched
under Stalin's regime—shows Trotsky and Kamenev (having fallen out of
political favor) literally "taken out of the picture" (Payne 263).

The alteration of digitally stored photographs in our own era is quite
practical with the necessary equipment. Companies such as Canon
and Sony are distributing cameras that no longer use film but record
information electronically on computer-type data disks. Since this
data is digital in nature, it can easily be restructured or reformatted—
it can be altered to meet the needs of the user.

Scanning photographs into computer databases and altering them
is another approach. Image Network (an architectural and design
group in Coral Gables, Florida) is described in a promotional flyer
"Visualizing Change Before It Occurs" as:

a revolutionary consulting firm dedicated to *visualization*—
helping people understand how changes in the built environment

will look. We make simulations that are quickly produced, easily modified, and television-realistic. . . . Color photos of the existing conditions are scanned into powerful computers. Using a unique combination of software, we alter the pictures to create realistic 'before and after' simulations. This technique can be used to simulate new buildings on their sites, historic preservation projects, landscaping, and much more.

Finished images can be produced in the form of 35mm slides, color thermal plots, videotapes or can be projected straight from the computer.

Victor Dover, the president of Image Network, explains that the mission of his company came out of a very real educational need on the part of the public. According to him:

When new construction is proposed everyone wants an answer to the question, "What is it going to look like? Yet all around us bad decisions are being made about design—partly because of limitations in the traditional media of handcrafted drawings, sketches, and models. . . . Crude traditional renderings tend to be so time-consuming to produce and difficult to change that they are made as seldom and as late as possible. . . . We provide images which are quickly produced, easily modified, and highly realistic." (49)

Image Network is concerned with providing architects, designers, real-estate developers, and public agencies with the means by which to make better decisions about how they will change and alter the environment in which we live and work.

An example can be seen in their simulation of a redevelopment plan for Boca Raton, Florida (Figures 1-3). According to Dover:

We made a presentation on behalf of the Redevelopment Agency in Boca Raton, Florida, which showed the city commissioners how a proposed redevelopment scheme will improve downtown streets. This project had been delayed for many months and was marred by controversy. A theatre-size public audience attended the presentation. As they watched, projected images showed the

The Image Network, 1988

Fig. 1. Before: Street scene in the redevelopment district in Boca Raton, Florida.

streets as they appear today. Next, the telephone poles and overhead wires vanished. New paving patterns replaced broken sidewalks. Rows of royal palms lined the streets. Finally, new buildings rose along the streets. The audience was looking at a picture of the future. (51)

Dover and his associates are providing a powerful and useful medium for helping people make difficult decisions in architecture and planning. Their work represents an important use of computers as tools to help us more carefully plan our environment. Image Network is also acutely aware of the potential types of abuse inherent in the new technology they are employing.

The fact remains, however, that every simulation—no matter how well conceived—nonetheless represents a specifically constructed point of view. Such simulations are not necessarily new. In typographic culture they have existed in the form of literature (the novel as a simulation of reality). However, in a post-typographic culture they

The Image Network, 1988

Fig. 2. After: The same scene with overhead wires removed via computerized retouching.

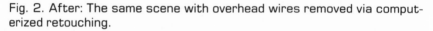

have adopted additional new forms (reconstructed photographs, gaming simulations, and so on). As Ted Nelson argues in his book *Computer Lib:* "Every simulation program, and thus every simulation, has a *point of view.* Just like a statement in words about the world, it is a *model* of how things are with its own implicit emphases: it highlights some things, omits others, and always simplifies. The future projections made by a simulation only project these views forward in time" (149). Computer simulations will have the potential to politicize and potentially misrepresent the interpretation of data more than ever before. As Nelson reasons, new meaning will be given to Francis Bacon's dictum "Knowledge is power": "In the politics of the future, all sides will have simulations, projections, charts, ostensible results. Some will be good. Most will be biased. Many will be rhetorical, like speeches, but supplying dummy numbers to their presenters, and thus looking important and factual when, like speeches, they are emptier than they seem" (Nelson 145).

Numerous examples of how data can easily be altered in the context

The Image Network, 1988

Fig. 3. After: A totally fictional scene—what redevelopment might look like.

of computer simulations are available. A recent cover of the *New York Times* Sunday magazine, using techniques like those employed by Image Network, moved and removed key pieces of architecture from a wide-angle photograph of the city taken from Brooklyn. Downtown buildings were transplanted uptown. The Trans-America building from San Francisco was incorporated into the landscape. The *National Geographic* used similar techniques to move the Giza pyramid sideways so it would fit better on the cover of their February 1982 issue (Brand 220). The cover of a 1985 issue of the *Whole Earth Review* shows a photograph of three flying saucers flying over downtown San Francisco. Night can literally be turned to day. A color slide of a downtown building can be reprogrammed to show how it might look lit up at night (Figures 4 and 5).

The alteration of photographic data by digital techniques represents a major problem in terms of the integrity of historical documents, and the extent to which we can trust the information from such sources in the future. As argued earlier, the potential to alter photographic

The Image Network, 1987

Fig. 4. Before: Renovated historic building in Toronto, Canada.

sources has existed since the invention of photography as a medium. What is new is the potential to alter data so easily and effectively—a situation made possible by advanced computer systems. Assuming that we increasingly convert to digital storage mediums for both text and pictures, Orwell's vision of *1984* becomes more and more likely. Trotsky—or any other individual deemed undesirable by the state or by a large corporation with control of the appropriate database—can indeed be removed from history and our culture's consciousness. The critically literate interpreter of such documents will have to be, even more than with traditional photographs, sensitive to the potential for electronic or digital photographs to be altered.

The Computer as a Surveillance Machine

"The Machine is a myth," exclaims Ted Nelson. "The bad things in our society are the products of bad systems, bad decisions and conceivably bad people, in various combinations" (31). Nelson, in

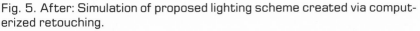

The Image Network, 1987

Fig. 5. After: Simulation of proposed lighting scheme created via computerized retouching.

arguing here that "machines per se are essentially neutral," is attempting to counter another myth that surround machines—the myth of omnipotence, and thus of the powerlessness that we as individuals often feel to alter the state of things. But Nelson likely also knows that (as I am arguing here) a machine like a computer is an instrumentality. It is not neutral, because it gives an individual, or a group of people, means by which to act that would otherwise not be possible. Computers are increasingly interfering with our freedom to engage in the process of inquiry, as well as to act without interference or manipulation as private citizens. Legal safeguards that are supposedly in place are inadequate. As Theodore Roszak argues, most of these laws are "broad spectrum legislation" and are filled with so many loopholes and exceptions that they cannot effectively be enforced (181).

Because effective laws are not in place does not mean that such laws are not necessary or cannot be implemented. In fact, such legislation must be systematically implemented, particularly as the power of the computer becomes more widespread with the extension of its use. An interesting example of why this is important can be seen in the case of Robert Bork's nomination to the Supreme Court. During the review process for Bork's appointment to the court, a reporter for the *City Paper* (a weekly newspaper in Washington, D.C.), Michael Dolan, got access to computer records showing what videotapes Bork and his family had rented from their local video store over an eighteen-month period.[4] Wire service articles picking up the story were subsequently published in newspapers across the country. In an interview with National Public Radio, Dolan was asked about the ethics of reporting on the Bork family's private viewing habits. He replied sarcastically that what he had done was "scabrous."

Dolan's article revealed nothing of particular interest. Undoubtedly, he was concerned with whether the Borks might be viewing pornography, or something else of interest to Bork's critics or to the public in general. It is inconceivable to imagine tolerating the public presentation and examination of what Judge Bork and his family check out of the library, or buy at the local bookstore. Yet this was precisely what occurred by looking at Bork's video rental records.

Whether they are a public broadcast documentary, a concert by a rock group, a classic movie, or a pornographic film, videotapes represent sources of information in our culture. As in the case of print sources where it is no one's business what you read, it is no one's business what you view. This is true whether you are a factory worker in Detroit or a nominee for the Supreme Court.

While on the surface, the culprit in the invasion of the Bork family's privacy was the computer that kept the records of what they rented from the video store, the computer was only an instrumentality. The real culprits were Dolan and the individual in the computer store who gave him access to Bork's records. Also culpable was the newspaper that published his article and the legal system that allowed Dolan to get away with abusing the privacy of the Bork family.

Unexpected types of microsurveillance, such as the record of the Bork family's videotape rentals, are pervading virtually every aspect of our society. For example, a recent *Miami Herald* article reports on how Domino's Pizza Inc. recently tested a pilot computer system that tracks not only how often you buy a pizza from them, but how many of them you buy and which toppings you order (Chardak). The company rationalizes its use of the system by saying it foils pranksters who order pizzas for addresses that don't exist or individuals who shortchange the delivery people or who harass them. There are other benefits, however, to the system. As Moira McDermott, a Domino's Pizza spokesperson, explains in the *Herald* article: "If you can pull up one year's worth of information about a customer, that can tell you a lot."

Now, whether one eats anchovies or sausage on one's pizza may not seem important. Yet by tracking and quantifying the consumption patterns of an individual, it becomes relatively easy to reconstruct in detail when an individual is at home, when he or she has been traveling, and so on. Combined with other types of digital information sources, it is possible to process a remarkable amount of data into a coherent and meaningful pattern.

Domino's seemingly mundane data collection process in fact does have the potential to impose itself on an individual's day-to-day experience. With computer records on consumption habits, it suddenly becomes possible for a customer to become the target of a specific advertising campaign, for example. Coupons can be distributed that focus on a customer's particular affection for anchovies. The consumer is encouraged to buy a particular type of pizza based on their previous consumer history.

In fact, this situation is not a new one. The proliferation of junk mail and computerized mailing lists demonstrates clearly how the process operates. But the question arises, What right does a catalogue company have to sell an individual's name and address to another catalogue company, simply because a person has ordered something through them? What right do they have to track a consumer? Why should a consumer be compelled to release data to a company when completing a warranty form or guarantee?

The potential for our videotape rentals to be monitored, our pizza toppings to recorded and analyzed, our test scores to be reviewed, our credit to be checked, our reading and viewing habits to be recorded, and so on represents an ultimate extension of Bentham's model of the Panopticon. Using Foucault's terminology, we are watching being set in place, through the widespread use of the microcomputer, a system of hierarchical observations that has the potential to keep us under nearly perpetual observation and control.

Education and Panopticonism

In a recent series of interviews on teacher attitudes that I conducted with my colleagues Marilyn Cohn, Robert Kottkamp, and Gary McCloskey, an elementary-school teacher described to us how she kept the children in her classroom under control by telling them there was a giant computer "downtown" that kept a record on everything they did, and that if they did not do well in their studies or if they misbehaved their records would follow them. Stories such as these may not be far from the truth as computerized record keeping and instructional systems become more and more widespread in our schools.[5] C. A. Bowers cites Roszak to the effect that we are confronting increasingly widespread use of a surveillance technology that harks back to the social vision of utilitarian philosophers such as Bentham. According to Bowers: "In this increasingly panopticon society, individuals internalize the new technology of social control by adjusting their behaviors and thoughts in accordance with the categories and logic that will constitute a positive personal data profile, and in the process become, like the prisoners, self-monitoring" (19).

Panoptic principles have been built into the very foundations of European and American education. Foucault notes, for example, how schools such as the Ecole Militaire in France became elaborate pedagogical machines designed for observation and control.

The very building of the ecole was to be an apparatus for observation; the rooms were distributed along a corridor like a series of small cells; at regular intervals, an officer's quarters were situated, so that "every ten pupils had an officer on each side"; the pupils were confined to their cells throughout the night; and Paris ["the director"] had insisted that a "window be placed on the corridor wall of each room from chest-level to within one or two feet of the ceiling." . . . In the dining room was "a slightly raised platform for the tables of the inspectors of studies, so that they [might] see all the tables of the pupils of their divisions during meals"; latrines had been installed with half doors, so that the supervisor on duty could see the heads and legs of the pupils, and also with side walls sufficiently high "that those inside [could not] see one another." (177-78)

Foucault noted that subtle features were introduced into the design of the Ecole Militaire that made possible the "progressive objectification and the ever more subtle partitioning of individual behavior."[6]

This desire to partition individual student behavior into ever more subtle units—to systematically collect data—is built into the structure of many computer education programs. In fact, it provides their main source of appeal for many educators. Bowers cites, for example, a school instructional management program implemented in Utah known as AIM (Achieving Instructional Mastery), which demonstrates clearly "how far the technology (and human will) has evolved in bringing all aspects of school-life under the data-recording gaze of the computer" (Bowers 18). Under the AIM system, students' progress is monitored in order to direct them toward "teacher-defined objectives." In addition, the system records assignments, tests, and grades in an electronic gradebook, it keeps data on school attendance and lunch-period activities and is able to provide for the analysis of all recorded data. As part of the system's surveillance system, through an elaborate classification system, AIM can correlate academic performance with behavior.

According to Bowers, the system is interesting because it requires the core curriculum to be organized in terms of objectives that fit the evaluation format of the management program (that is, true/false multiple-choice responses) and objectives that are specified in advance. Significantly, the management system provides surveillance not only of students but of teachers as well, since precise data on student performance is seen as a means by which the school district can report on the supposed efficiency of the teacher. This last idea recalls Foucault's argument that in systems of hierarchical observation everyone is being observed, including the supervisors such as jail wardens, nurses, or teachers.

The AIM system is also of interest, according to Bowers, because students learn that surveillance is part of their education. Mastering the new computer literacy implies the acceptance that information will be automatically collected and that in turn control will be exercised. The acceptance of such a system is to be perceived as "essential to the development of the socially responsible citizen, and thus it could be expected to view it as a normal, even necessary, aspect of adult life" (Bowers 19).

Bowers points out that the use of the computer to collect data on all aspects of schooling is not unique to the AIM system in Utah but is found to a greater or lesser extent in school systems across the country. In a search through the ERIC database for information on this topic for the period January 1983 to October 1989, I found a total of 629 articles dealing with "Computer Assisted Management." Representative articles included a piece by Richard Kern entitled "Individualizing Educational Strategies: An Apple Computer Managed System for the Diagnosis and Evaluation of Reading, Math and Behavior," a computer-based management system with "criterion referenced-testing," an instructional management system, and a behavior evaluation tool developed by the author" (Bowers, 20). Other titles include "Using Computers for Instructional Delivery and Diagnosis of Student Learning in Elementary Schools," and "Data-Based Program Modification: A Continuous Evaluation System with Computer Software to Facilitate Implementation." Hundreds more articles could be cited, but these should be sufficient to make the case.

The movement toward "Computer Assisted Management" is only just beginning. Its increasing potential to dominate education is obvious and deeply disturbing. As Bowers argues, it is a movement that is "turning the school into a model of the panopticon society" (19). In doing so, there is the potential of the new post-typographic electronic literacy to circumscribe and limit the freedoms assumed under the older typographic tradition. As a result, schools have the potential to become even more controlled and to have their freedom more limited than has been the case up until now.

Conclusion

This essay barely touches the surface of how the instrumentality of the computer—its potential to operate as a tool of surveillance and control—is creating an increasingly panoptic society. In doing so we are also creating a new culture which, to use Foucault's terminology, represents a reversal of the "axis of individualization" toward the collection of records and information about individuals over whom power can be exercised. In this context, literacy has the potential to become increasingly circumscribed and controlled. The computer— like its physical predecessor the Panopticon—has in its various forms and combinations the potential to capture the individual in a trap of constant visibility. A private literacy—the ability to read, reflect, and write—in the context of computer-mediated surveillance becomes more problematic in a post-typographic culture. Using Foucault's terminology, the literate individual increasingly becomes an "object of information, never a subject in communication."

We must fight against the instrumentality of the computer. I am not calling for us to abandon the use of the machine. It is a powerful tool for creativity and productivity. But it is a tool that, if we do not control its use, will allow others to control us, and in doing so destroy the foundations of our democratic society.

Notes

1. The idea of the computer as providing the basis around which an electronic panopticon can develop was an original idea to me when I wrote the first draft of this essay. Its power as an idea is indicated by the fact that the image is also picked up independently by other authors. See, for example: Zuboff, chapter 9 "The Information Panopticon" (315-61), chapter 10 "Panopticon Power and the Social Text" (362-86), and Bowers, "Computers and the Panopticon Society" (14-19).

2. My use of the term *frame* is based on the work of the British sociologist Erving Goffman and more specifically his work *Frame Analysis*. Bowers (24-27) draws on Goffman and frame analysis as part of his analysis of the cultural dimensions of educational computing. Among Bowers's most compelling arguments: that the supporters of educational computing, "by providing the metaphorical language considered appropriate for thinking about the educational uses of the microcomputer . . . controlled the frame that governed the discourse and thus the context for thinking about the educational potential of this new technology" (25).

3. Confirmation of the altering of Goddard's photographs is cited by Gould in a letter from James H. Wallace, Jr., the director of photographic services at the Smithsonian Institution, to Steven Selden.

4. For more information on Judge Bork and the invasion of privacy, see my article in the editorial section of the *Miami News*, "Bar Access to Computer Data on Individuals" (October 22, 1987, 15a).

5. Such scenarios are not far from the truth in other segments of our culture. Theodore Roszak notes that five major federal agencies handle somewhere between

two and four billion overlapping files on the public. Information from these files is integrated through "matching programs" with other agencies: "Thus, a driver pulled over for a faulty break light may soon have his whole life run through a battery of integrated data banks that will contain anything anybody ever cared to put on file: alimony and child support, delinquent loans, welfare violations, etc." (Roszak 182-83).

6. Together with my wife and coauthor Asterie Baker Provenzo, I have been working on a book-length study on the influence of disciplinary power (Panopticonism, hierarchical observation, normalizing judgment, and so on) on the evolution and development of British and American education. Our paper on British schools, "Andrew Bell and Joseph Lancaster: An Examination of the Emergence of the Theme of Knowledge and Power" (presented at the November 1988 History of Education Society meeting) is the first chapter of a larger study tentatively entitled *Knowledge/ Power/Control and Education: A Foucaultian Interpretation of the History of American Education*.

Naturalizing the Computer:
English Online

Victor Raskin

Introduction

This paper consists of two parts. The first part deals with natural language interfaces (NLIs) placing an emphasis on semantic scripts as their basis. The second part deals with computers and cultural literacy, focusing on whether the computers are good or bad. The scripts provide rather a close link between the two parts (as they always do). I know too much for my own good about the first part and too little about the second, so the average should be about right.

1. Meaning Online

Natural Language Interface

As computer hardware prices go down and computers become more available to large numbers of users—most of whom, especially in the humanities, lack any solid foundation in computer science—the problem of friendly interfaces becomes more important. A friendly interface can be roughly represented as shown in Figure 1. The computer system block can be thought of as a word-processing system, an information-retrieval system, an expert system, a database-management system, or any other currently existing or future system that has a function, a useful job to perform.

The alternatives to the development of friendly human-computer interfaces are untenable. One of them is doing without the information made available by the computer. However, the use of large databases for the decision-making process by mid- and high-level managers is essential for business, government, and defense. Many other varieties of useful software have penetrated not only research in

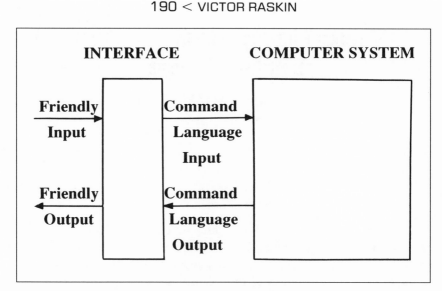

Fig. 1. A user-friendly interface to a computer system.

the humanities and social sciences but also the personal needs of the citizenry. The other alternative is to teach all the users the formal machine languages—and this is unfeasible and prohibitively expensive. The third alternative, which is still practiced in the industry and academe, is to make decision makers dependent on programmers. This is becoming increasingly less affordable as the number of computer users grows, so this alternative is being phased out. It is clear, in other words, that the computer terminal, which has been a necessary part of office (and home office) decoration, and a status symbol, for the better part of the last decade, is in fact being used by the tenant on a more regular basis.

At the same time, the manufacturers of expert systems are becoming seriously concerned about the low acceptance rate of their products by the consumers unless the friendly interface is part of the package. Thus, at a recent conference on AI applications for defense (Erdman), all the presentations concerning the products marketed or about to be marketed dealt with the necessity of providing a friendly interface (see especially Reibling). In an independent development, a conference organized in Detroit in 1987 by the Society for Machine Intelligence, an affiliate of IEEE, featured "gaining user acceptance" of expert systems among the principal topics. It is well known that even such relatively simple computer systems as word processors, editors, or formatters are doing well only if users find them friendly. It should be added here, however, that word processors, while they can be unfriendly, are not the prime candidates for natural language interfaces for two main reasons: first, most of them are not complex enough and take only a few hours to learn and, second, they do not call for many nontrivial inquiries in natural language about them. Both of these reasons will become clearer in a while.

The friendly interface is a roundabout designation of a simple concept, namely, allowing the user to communicate with and control the computer in a natural language such as English. As we will see below, such interfaces can range from an insignificant improvement over the use of formal languages all the way to a natural and easy way for an untrained user to operate the computer. Everybody who has struggled with the acquisition of new software, with yet another menu, set of commands, and its own quirks and idiosyncrasies, all of which have to be memorized and stored right along with dozens of similar sets for other pieces of software, can appreciate the problem. Would it not be just swell to forget all those different systems and programs and access them all by simply stating your needs and queries?

In a recent paper, Carbonell speculated interestingly on the aspects of a viable user model, in view of which interfaces should be developed. According to him, these aspects include "the familiarity of the user with the functionality of the underlying system, . . . the long-term commitment of the user, . . . the range of sophistication of the expected user population," the potential role of "the user as an interface designer," and the possibilities for "mixed-initiative capabilities" (Carbonell 216-17). In other words (to take the extreme positions on all these aspects), the user who is familiar with the intricacies of a computer system, who is going to use it for a long time, and who is sophisticated in the use of computer systems does not need a friendly interface, especially if he or she is not going to modify the system (in the process of using it) and if no interaction between the user and the computer is built into the system. Any departure from these extreme points will necessitate the development of an interface, which becomes absolutely essential in the increasingly widespread case of the user who is not familiar with the system and who does not need to be, who is likely to be an occasional or short-term user, who is not generally sophisticated in computer science, and who does need to modify the system in the process of using it and to interact with it effectively in other ways as well. Figure 2 summarizes these claims.

Standard menus make an appearance of friendliness, and they do use English words. However, the necessary commands posing as words should be used precisely as stated in the menu, and no synonym or reasonable substitution will do. Who has never forgotten that this particular program requires "quit" and has not tried desperately to get out by feverishly printing "exit," "bye," "stop," "out," or "logout"—a present-day version of the Magic Pot nightmare? Or, generally greatly assisted by helpful icons, does one always remember what each stands for, even after not having used a program for a while? Menus and graphic aids in interfaces are a common feature but only an NLI gives users confidence and frees them from the necessity to memorize anything. But then, not all interfaces billed as NLI are created equal.

Figure 3 introduces a chart representing twenty-one possible combinations of seven important features and three values for each of them. Figure 4 lists those types linearly and more descriptively.

Systems 1 are those "user-friendly" software packages (such as standard word-processing software), which substitute English words

REASONS FOR A FRIENDLY INTERFACE:

- To increase availability of computers
- To use large databases in decision making
- To minimize the cost of training
- To minimize the cost of programming
- To enhance customer acceptance of computer products

BASIC KINDS OF FRIENDLY INTERFACE:

- Pseudo-Natural Language (menus)
- Direct Manipulation (graphics, icons, mice)
- NL

Fig. 2.

	Yes	Somewhat	No
Constrained Input	1	2	3
Meaning Extraction	4	5	6
World Model	7	8	9
Limited to I/O	10	11	12
Goals/Beliefs	13	14	15
Domain-Specific	16	17	18
Oral Input	19	20	21

Fig. 3. Possible types of interfaces.

for code designations on a one-to-one basis, for example, "print" for the "lpr" or "xyz123" that the software requires in its native BASIC, FORTRAN, C, or other programming language. The commands in such interfaces have a better mnemonic value, but they have to be learned in exactly the same fashion as the corresponding commands in code, and no synonymous substitution (such as "delete" for "erase" or vice versa) will do.

Systems 2 represent what is predominantly billed as NLI for expert systems or knowledge-engineering shells and environments. The minimal ones allow for some cases of synonymy, such as mentioned above, and feature a vocabulary of a few hundred words at the most. Considerable effort is still required to learn to use the interfaced computer systems.

Systems 3 allow the user to communicate with the computer system in an unconstrained fashion, just as he or she would with a colleague. The only requirement is to stay within the domain served by the system and, therefore, to use the corresponding sublanguage of English—a requirement that will be satisfied automatically by any pertinent communication. Systems of this kind can translate any paraphrase of a command or a chain of commands into the machine code.

Systems 1: "user friendly" software packages, English menus
Systems 2: so-called NL interfaces for expert systems or shells
Systems 3: unconstrained, full-fledged NLI of the future
Systems 4: meaning or knowledge-based NLI
Systems 5: minimum, non-semantic NLI
Systems 6: non-semantic, mechanical, keyword-based NLI
Systems 7: knowledge-based NLI
Systems 8: popular partially knowledge-based NLI
Systems 9: non-knowledge-based, most commercially available NLI
Systems 10: non-interactive NLI
Systems 11: partially interactive, often billed as interactive NLI
Systems 12: fully interactive NLI, explanatory models and learning
          models
Systems 13: NLI, accounting for the beliefs, goals, plans, and intentions
          of all the active agents
Systems 14: NLI, accounting for some beliefs, goals, etc.
Systems 15: dominant NLI, not accounting for beliefs, goals, etc.
Systems 16: NLI dedicated to a certain constrained domain
Systems 17: NLI dedicated to a type of domain
Systems 18: unlimited NLI of the future
Systems 19: oral-input NLI of the future
Systems 20: combo key-board, limited voice recognition NLI
Systems 21: dominant keyboard-input NLI

Fig. 4. Properties of interface types.

Systems 4 analyze the NL input semantically, extract the extended meaning, and act on it accordingly. While it seems to be the only reasonable way to proceed, there are no NLIs in existence that do it to the full extent because the methodologies of meaning processing in NL processing (NLP) are not developed enough—partly because of the "mortal fear of meaning" that infected the field after a spectacular collapse of the first incarnation of machine translation some twenty-five years ago and that has led to the expenditure of an enormous amount of funds and talent on the largely futile attempts to bypass meaning with the help of purely syntactic parsers, even when sophisticated and accurate.[1]

On the other hand, in the last decade and a half, there has been a definite movement toward semantic parsing in NLP.[2] This results primarily in Systems 5, tending toward the lower end of meaning processing. In Systems 6, interfacing is based on the system's recognition, not understanding, of certain words (keywords), word combinations, or, more sophisticatedly, words combined in a certain syntactic way. Most NLIs and, more generally, NLP systems do not go beyond this stage.

Systems 7 are based on the knowledge of the world of the domain in which the interfaced computer system operates. Systems 9, on the other hand, do not have such a knowledge base. Many NLP systems and, therefore, some NLIs have some elements of world knowledge and thus belong to Systems 8.

Systems 10 have the interface serving only the input and/or output of the computer system without any interaction between the user and the system. Contrary to that, Systems 12 are fully interactive — and that includes explanatory models and learning models. Systems 11 allow for a limited amount of interaction, usually for troubleshooting.

Systems 13 analyze the beliefs, goals, plans, and intentions of all the active agents in the world of interfaced computer systems. There are only a few research groups attempting the development of such NLP systems, and no NLIs of that kind seem to be in existence. Systems 14 are likely to emerge from these research efforts in the 1990s, but most NLIs are still doomed to fall within Systems 15.

Most NLIs and NLP systems are committedly Systems 16; that is, they are dedicated to a certain constrained domain. While by and in itself it seems to be inevitable and harmless, unfortunately what follows is that vastly ad hoc methods of semantic analysis are practiced in such systems. As a result, the meaning processing within one system cannot be extrapolated or transported to another, and the work in the latter has to begin from scratch. It is essential that Systems 17 and, later, Systems 18 replace Systems 16, and this is dependent on the development and implementation in NLP practice of the applied theory of linguistic semantics for NLP, which makes it possible to combine significant generalizations and common approaches in meaning processing with the advantages of domain-specific constraints.[3]

Systems 19 allow the user to introduce data by voice just as a science-fiction hero communicates with his or her robot. Voice recognition presents a difficult technological and conceptual problem, and, although a considerable research effort is expended in this direction, only partial and costly solutions are still available. Most existing computer systems belong to Systems 21, that is, keyboard-input.

Obviously, an NLI that belongs simultaneously to Systems 3, 4, 7, 12, 13, 18, and 19 would let the user communicate with a computer system absolutely freely and without any preparation. There is basically one reason why such NLIs are not easily available—and will not be for quite some time—and that is semantic analysis.

Semantic Analysis and Scripts

Linguistic meaning is hard to represent and to analyze. There is no comprehensive theory of meaning. All this creates a serious bottleneck in NLP and partly explains the seemingly absurd attempts to bypass meanings with the help of increasingly artful syntactic parsing.

In order for the computer to fully understand an input in natural language, it should recognize all the words, figure out all their meanings, select the one actually intended for each word, combine all these meanings together correctly, and augment the whole, if necessary, with pertinent elements of world knowledge. A powerful way to do all that is provided by script-based semantics (Raskin, "Script-based Semantics"). Scripts (also known as frames or schemata) are structured chunks of information we store in association with words and wordlike items. Figure 5 contains an informally represented script for *physician*. Script-based semantics consists then of three main knowledge resources as shown on Figure 6.

A script-based approach to NLIs constitutes the so-called opportune (or opportunistic) method of comprehensive meaning analysis,[4] and it defines the closest feasible approximation to the ideal NLI of the future described at the close of the previous section (see Fig. 7).

The approximation belongs to Systems 3, 4, 7, 12, 14, 17, and 21. It allows the user to communicate with the system in an unconstrained fashion within the sublanguage of the domain served by the interfaced computer system. The approach is based on the principle of complete multilevel meaning extraction, which is, however, scaled down in accordance with the semantic complexity of the sublanguage and the actual needs of the computer system. In other words, only as much meaning is processed as is necessary for the successful interaction of the computer system.

The development of such an NLI is preceded by a knowledge-engineering effort aimed at the creation of the world model, ontology, or "theory" of the domain served by the computer system. This results in

Subject: Human, Adult
Patient: Human
Activity: (Past) Study medicine
   (Present) Receive patients
     Diagnose disease
     Cure disease
Location: (Past) Medical School
   (Present) Office or Hospital
Time: (Past) Several Years
   (Present) Daily
Condition: Doctor Patient Physical Contact

Fig. 5. Script for *physician*.

- Script-based Semantics

- Scripts in Lexicon

- Combinatorial Rules for Compositional Semantics

- World Knowledge Management for Supracompositional Semantics

Fig. 6. Script semantics: Knowledge resources.

the creation of a concept lexicon of the domain that provides a basis for the analysis and generation lexicons of the sublanguage. The former relates the words and phrases of the sublanguage to the concepts in the world of the domain, and the latter provides the opposite correlation.[5]

OPPORTUNE SEMANTIC APPROACH TO NLI:
- Constrained Input
- World Knowledge Based
- Interactive
- Partially accounting for beliefs, goals, etc.
- Domain-Type Specific
- Keyboard Input

THREE-LEXICON APPROACH:
- Concept Lexicon
- Analysis Lexicon
- Generation Lexicon

PRINCIPLES OF MEANING ANALYSIS:
- All levels
- Semantics and Pragmatics
- Variable Depth (Grain Size)

Fig. 7. Comprehensive semantic analysis in natural language processing.

The approach is highly interactive both for its own needs and to serve as much interaction as provided by the computer system interfaced with its help. The approach tries to handle some obvious goals and plans, but it is designed primarily to serve domains with a limited number of agents, often just the user and the computer, so the goal or belief aspect of the interface does not need to be developed too much, in strict accordance with the needs-oriented principle described above. The approach is based on the applied theory of lexical semantics for NLP and thus renders the interface as transportable into another domain as possible.

Before discussing what an ideal or a feasible NLI can do for computer technology and its user, we will look briefly into a metaphorical extension of script-based semantics, which provides a clue into the nature of cultural literacy.

Semantic Nature of Literacy: Scripts, Scripts, Scripts

This section stands out of this paper because it does not bear directly either on NLIs as a way to ease access to computer technology or on the possible perils and promises this technology generates. Rather, it demonstrates that the same semantic theory that enables the development of NLIs can be extended to shed some light on the semantic nature of cultural literacy.

The concentric circles on Figure 8 represent the kinds of script-encoded knowledge we have internalized in our minds. The smallest inner circle includes the language scripts, roughly the lexicon as it is understood in script-based semantics. This is the most shared layer of scripts, even though there is a difference among the various dialects and idiolects of the same language. The scripts of this kind are known by virtue of knowing one's native tongue.

Close to the language scripts lie the scripts of common sense. These include the simple and not so simple things that people know about the world. Some of these are universal and, therefore, language-independent; others are culturally bound—in fact, a more detailed chart would probably have a culture-scripts circle as the next-larger one after the commonsense one.

From common sense on, the outer circles add constraints and restrictions—they are shared by fewer people. The cultural-literacy scripts are available only to those who are indeed culturally literate—that is, a relatively small minority in a culture or speech community. The restricted scripts are those that are contingent on the knowledge of certain non-universal events and circumstance. A typical example would be the scripts of institutional history (read "gossip") available to those associated with a company or campus. The private scripts are available only to individuals.[6]

The anthropological, sociological, and cultural aspect of the cultural-literacy scripts goes far beyond the scope of this paper written by a mere linguist. The essential aspect for this discussion is that cultural literacy is a bunch of interrelated scripts considered important and prestigious by the elite of the society. Interestingly, it is an intellectual elite; that is, not the most powerful or popular people: thus, it is probably still true that the phrase "to be or not to be" has a more secure place among the cultural literacy scripts than "the Trump Tower" or Madonna's "like a virgin." But then, maybe it is not true

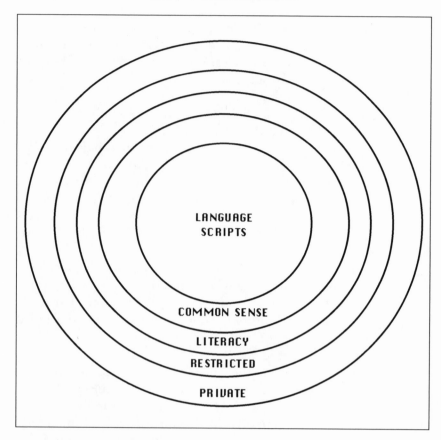

Fig. 8. Types of internalized scripts.

anymore. The number of cultural-literacy scripts seems to be finite and limited, but few would be willing to "hirsch" out a guess about what is and what is not included. Many cultural-literacy scripts are short-lived and transient—others stay for a long time. Either way, they are scripts, structured chunks of information, much like language meanings—just acquired differently and for a different reason and by a smaller number of people.

2. On Promises and Perils—From the Neutral Perch

The Neutrality Stand

NLIs are one step away from the issue of computers and cultural literacy. They only provide an easier access to computer systems. Whatever a computer system is designed to do, an NLI will allow an untrained user to get the system to do it. If the system does something to enhance cultural literacy, the NLI makes it easier to do so. If the system imperils cultural literacy, the NLI will facilitate that as well. In other words (in computerese), an NLI is a throughput device, neutral, indifferent, "objective." Even those NLIs that are supposed to guess the user's intentions and beliefs are interested only in figuring out what the user wants the system to do when the instruction is camouflaged by inept, imprecise, inarticulate language the user put in—the intended meaning and its implementation in the computer meaning is all an NLI is interested in. An NLI is, therefore, an automatic translation machine between the natural language, say English, used by the system operator and the command language of the computer system.

It can be argued that the neutrality stand is an exaggeration, actually a cop-out. An NLI does create a new reality in which a computer system is placed in the hands of a person who would otherwise have no access to it. This leads to a wider use of computer technology and, on the face of it, the enhancement of whatever effect it has on life, society, or history. The difference—between this newly admitted clientele and those who could use the computer system before it was equipped with a friendly interface—lies in the necessary computer skills. What effect does the introduction of an NLI have on cultural literacy? Are computer skills part of it? If so, then the introduction of an NLI makes it unnecessary to work hard to acquire computer skills as part of cultural literacy and thus seems to weaken the cause of cultural literacy. While the concept of cultural literacy as to its exact script composition will vary from person to person, group to group, and society to society (see the preceding section), it is probably safe to assert that computer literacy is not yet included in cultural literacy. Then, if all an NLI does is to let one bypass computer literacy, it is still neutral with regard to cultural literacy.

But what follows from making computer technology more accessible, as NLIs definitely do? Will this enhance or imperil cultural literacy? Before answering these questions, we will have to look briefly at the promises and perils of computer technology regardless of the interfaces.

Overstated Promise?

The word processor, the most widely used computer application, lets one edit, cut, and paste much more efficiently than ever before. Augmented by spelling checkers, grammar checkers, style checkers, such programs provide significant help in making the output look better. No help is available, however, as to what to say—that still comes from the author. The ingenious ways of using the computer to teach writing, as in Helen Schwartz's presentation in this volume, lets one learn the correct discursive practices but still not the substance, not the contents, of what one wants to say. It will help to express one's thoughts, but it will not create those thoughts for one.

Cultural literacy on the other hand, at least if taken seriously, is a property of that substance, those contents, rather than of the form of expression. Let us assume, for the sake of the argument (pace Tuman 9-34), that cultural literacy is precisely the 5,000 items Hirsch wants us to believe it is. A computer database can be easily created with the phrases and names corresponding to those items and descriptions of some length explaining each item. Such a database would make it easy for an uncultured person encountering one of the expressions to look it up in the database and get the general picture. Is this good or bad?

First, such a database would be good only for the limited purpose described above. Any slight paraphrase or an allusion would throw the system off. The explanations will be limited and no substitute to the real knowledge the 5,000 items seem to imply. Besides, dictionaries and encyclopedias are available to do the same now, so all the computer system does is make it faster. Users must still find themselves in a situation when it is possible to encounter a cultural-literacy item and necessary to look it up. This is most likely to happen in the process of doing something pertaining to cultural literacy in the first place (for instance, acquiring it). That seems to contradict the scenario of an uncultured user trying to bypass the acquisition of culture through the use of computers.

The strong suggestion is that the most significant effect of computer systems is on the life and work of those who are already doing what the computer systems facilitate, and this means that it is a quantitative, not a qualitative, leap—and then it is all good. It should be noted in this connection, however, that an average computer user is currently in possession of much more technology than he or she is actually using or will ever use. Thus, many word-processor users see the computer as a slightly enhanced typewriter only and act accordingly.

Similarly, a colleague in technical writing here at Purdue University, herself a pioneer of computerized teaching, reports that a class in journalism scheduled to use the fully networked computer lab after her own class there, was given an assignment: to develop a theme on the word processor, print it out, and hand it over to the instructor. Virtually no benefit provided by state-of-the-art smarts and conveniences was either reaped or acknowledged in that class.

It is also universally true that few computer users suffer from a shortage of computer power. On the contrary, underused computers abound in businesses, on campuses, and in the government. The amount of untouched software is likely to be comparable with the number of books never requested in the libraries; and that as I recall from the statistics of the Lenin Library in Moscow, U.S.S.R., amounted in the late 1960s to about 85 percent of the holdings (and not all of that unloved literature was Brezhnev's speeches). Also similar to the underused library holdings is the problem of the users' not knowing about the existence of a program answering their needs exactly.

An enormously powerful tool is thus being underused, which moderates the promise. The amount of training for a gigantic number of users in order to overcome computer underuse is prohibitive, so the situation is not likely to change for the better without a significant progress with unrestricted, meaning-based interfaces, especially if there is a breakthrough with voice recognition.

Overstated Peril?

Large networks of computers, exchanging data from enormous databases all over the world in no time whatsoever, feed one's paranoia very effectively. Provenzo's pizza nightmare (in this volume) provides a plausible empirical reinforcement to the unpleasant feeling that everything there is to know about me is available to virtually anybody for a nominal price. This paranoia is already costing me $35 a year in membership dues to some strange outfit that reports to me on every case they report on me to somebody else. (For a mere $5 a year, I will gladly report to anybody else whenever that happens.)

Another nightmare is the computers' making decisions about me (if I am loanworthy or not, for example). They calculate points on the basis of the figures I make available to them and/or the figures they verify in order to determine whether I am a good risk for a mortgage or a credit line. The impersonality and pseudo-objectivity of these deliberations, and especially of negative decisions, is an offense on my humanity and dignity, isn't it? A human loan officer would look into my honest unblinking eyes and reverse his verdict even in spite of the shameful assets-versus-liabilities ratio, or wouldn't he? Okay, even if he didn't, I would at least have an opportunity to suggest to him what he and his bank could do with all their money!

Somewhat similarly, computerized instruction robs the student of the warm human guiding hand, thus dehumanizing the process of education and cognitive development—possibly with unimaginably monstrous long-range consequences. (Aren't the yuppies the first computer generation?) Besides, the emphasis in this sort of education is necessarily on the techniques rather than on creativity, on deceptive certainty and solvability rather than on the fuzziness and messiness of human thought.

Futuristic digital photography (see Provenzo in this volume again), which is capable of projecting with spectacular precision what a building from the architect's blueprints will look like on this particular spot, can falsify reality and—of all the unspeakable horrors—put Oprah Winfrey's head on Ann-Margaret's body on a *TV Guide* cover. (Provenzo, that incorrigible highbrow, overlooked this one!)

With their powers of surveillance and control over human lives, the computers can become powerful tools of oppression. Just imagine Orwell's *1984* written after the computer revolution—surely, the TV surveillance in the novel would have been powerfully augmented by computer power, and the main hero would have been rewriting history on the word processor (in fact, he would have probably lost his job because fewer people would have done that faster on a computer).

Aren't these real and serious perils? They surely are; except that they aren't, not really. They are real, all right, but there is nothing new about them; and that makes them much less scary and much more manageable. Some people like to get excited about new things, to ignore things of the past, and to perceive the problems of today as new as the world such people inhabit. This world is often referred to as the New World, and its inhabitants are known as Americans.

The others, from the Old World, try to substitute cynical wisdom for youthful energy, They have seen it all and heard it all, and no problem has a solution, which has been solidly proven by our sordid history. An American knows that the world was not born yesterday. For him, history begins around the time grandpa came here from the old country, but it was sort of on hold till about a couple of years ago.

A European lives on top of the enormously long history, just a tiny speck, there for a minute or so, compared to history's prohibitive length, so he tries to prolong this minute and stop the time by endlessly lingering over his Perrier at a street cafe.

True, it is the naive romanticists of the New World who often solve the unsolvable problems—however, the fact that Alexander the Great cut the Gordian knot does not mean he could untie it or that the cut knot is the same as the knot untied. All I can offer by way of apology for party pooping is that I refuse to get excited by or scared of the computer revolution because I do believe that the problems are old and, therefore, proven manageable, and I felt that way even as I was watching Stanley Kubrick's *2001* back in the 1960s.

Let me explain what I mean to those few who are still with me even after they read the previous paragraph. A sergeant and a rookie from the local police department could gather all the information Provenzo's pizza parlor had amassed on him and his wife in, say, a day and a half. Their labor costs considerably less than the total cost of acquiring, setting up, and maintaining the computer database for parlor customers. Society measures access to commodities in cost, not time. So the human information-gathering effort is just as accessible. Another point on the monster of global computer surveillance for my liberal friends: surveillance has become more democratic with computers. Before, the police, the investigative reporters, and the private investigators did the human surveilling. All of them represent various branches of the ruling establishment, the government, and/or the capital. Computers make it easier for everybody to gather large databases on everybody else—this makes it a quantitative version of millennia-old gossip. It can hurt, but so what else is new?

Computer decision making can hurt, but so can decision by flipping the coin. It is humans who authorize the computer to make a decision. This act of authorization is as rash as deciding the outcome of a dilemma by flipping the coin. What makes the situation dangerous and unacceptable is the human power of attorney granted to an artifact while removing the humans' own judgment and responsibility for the decision. The now-proverbial computer error is the good old clerical error of the past.

Entrusting to the computer those aspects of education that require human participation is another rash authorizing decision made by humans. If the result of that are recent high-school-graduate nincompoops whose hungover minds are incapable of extending themselves beyond the small computer operation they perform, they and their unfortunate customers should sue those people who gave them the deficient education, not the computer. Besides, a generation or so ago, their parents' or cousins' minds possibly did not extend itself beyond the one type of entry they made in a log in longhand.

Futuristic photography is a more serious matter. But before photography, drawings played the same role. Surely, we associate photography with stark reality, but photographic trickery followed the invention of the medium by less than a decade. Before that, history had been falsified in writings and folklore.

It does not require a lot of imagination to see what a powerful tool of oppression the computer can be. (It makes one pause for a second, however, that the most oppressive regimes in the world are usually so much behind economically that they cannot afford computers and do all the oppression the old-fashioned, precomputational way.) The real question is, What cannot be used as a tool of oppression? Any commodity, be it a consumer product or an implement, can be distributed in a highly restricted way in exchange for services required by an oppressive ruling class. In fact, an oppressive ruling class will attempt and usually succeed in controlling all distribution this way.

What presents a real problem, and an old one, is that people want to spy on each other and invade each other's privacy, and that access to unpublished information has always been a source of power. And people often shy away from decisions and flip the coin — that may take the form of an arbitrary decision (if I see six bicycles between now and the next turn, I'll call Julie tonight); of asking for and getting incompetent advice; or going to the function of one's support group consisting of equally shy and incompetent people. Letting a program written by another person decide for you is not different from all of those three, and it is virtually indistinct from the middle one.

And we don't really know, schools of education notwithstanding, how to educate people most effectively. One thing we do know is that we have not been sending our best to educate. It is only fair to qualify this by adding that we have definitely not educated educators well.

By and of itself, the computer is neither good nor bad, but it can be either in the hands of the user. And it shares this with any machine, any tool, any artifact, actually any thing. A screwdriver can be used to poke an eye, break into a house, and kill a man. The manufacturing machinery of the industrial revolution caused casualties, and so did the railroads. There are always Luddites and those romancing the machine (see Bolter, *Turing's Man,* for an excellent historical perspective).

And people will lie, falsify, mystify, self-aggrandize. They will use all forms of perjury to do that. They will use futuristic photography or quotes from senior officials. And as long as it is there, they will grab any tool to achieve this goal. The same goes for oppression. Computers are wonderful for all of that, so they will naturally be used this way, along with many good ways of using them.

These problems are an inalienable part of human existence. They are not solvable perhaps but the advent of computers did not introduce them, nor did it change the ratio of good to evil in the world. The preachers of computer revolution, the optimists and doomsayers alike, should be taken seriously but understood correctly: what they are saying amounts to an assessment of what form the age-old problems and conflicts will take with this new and powerful tool around.

Hypertext

Little remains to be said in this part of the paper, and I would like to say it in connection with hypertext. My co-contributors to this volume will have said virtually all there is to say on this interesting facility. They will have commented on the powerful apparatus of cross-references enabled by hypertext, on the nonlinearity of hypertext as opposed to the linearity of print, on the reader's ability to rewrite hypertext by clicking on some links, ignoring others, and creating their own. They will have raised legal questions of copyright and authorship considerably complicated by hypertext. They will not have forgotten the role of hypertext as a powerful tool of oppression—imposing links set by somebody else on you clearly violates your human and civil rights.

Some may object—and if they don't I will—that powerful appara- tuses of cross-references have been known since the Talmud, that natural language is linear while a good thoughtful reading of the text is not (because of associations, diversions, the need to check on a quotation or compare an account), that copyright and authorship are moot issues without and before hypertext (are jokes copyrightable?), and that having clearly presented hypertext links sure beats the links being imposed on one by an inarticulate (or highly articulate) classroom instructor or article writer who cannot display those links on request, and who may share ignorance of them with his or her audience.

What is much more significant, however, is that hypertext as a computational facility does not help one discover those links and connections, or determine the substance of the hypertext stacks, which still need to be written. All hypertext does is to present a format, a methodology, a tool for recording the already-established links. The substance for that comes from beyond the computer, and judging by the hype about hypertext, quite a few people are not making this distinction between the contents and the technology. They seem to think that hypertext is cognition itself. They are mistaken—but, in the meantime, they are romantically involved with hypertext and are having a good time. How dull is it not to be able to be with them! Once a nerd, always a nerd, I guess.

Conclusion

Whatever computers are used for, good things, bad things, neither-good-nor-bad things, the NLIs will make it easier, faster, and cheaper. An NLI is no more promising or perilous than the computer system for which it serves as front end. It was argued in Part 1 that the NLIs do not even seem to change the demographic aspect of cultural literacy. In other words, they do not devalue it by putting it in the hands of the uncultured. If, as argued in Part 2, the computer in general is not particularly promising or perilous, at least not in any new or especially alarming way, the NLIs are doubly neutral. And the big question remains, What am I doing among the excited people writing about such exciting things as the end of one cultural era and the beginning of another brought upon by the computer and hypertext?

Notes

1. See, however, Sergei Nirenburg, *Proceedings of the Conference on Theoretical and Methodological Issues in Machine Translation of Natural Languages* and *Machine Translation: Theoretical and Methodological Issues*; also Gazdar, Woods, Aho and Ullman, Joshi et al., Winograd, and references therein.

2. See, for instance: Graeme Hirst, *Semantic Interpretation Against Ambiguity* and *Semantic Interpretation and the Resolution of Ambiguity*; Roger C. Schank, "Identification of Conceptualizations Underlying Natural Language," *Conceptual Information Processing,* and "Reminding and Memory Organization"; also Birnbaum and Selfridge, Bobrow and Winograd, Brachman, Cullingford and Onyshkevych, Fass, Schank and Abelson, Wilensky, and Wilks and Fass.

3. See Victor Raskin, "Linguistics and Natural Language Processing," "What Is There in Linguistic Semantics for Natural Language Processing?" and Sergei Nirenburg and Victor Raskin, "A Metric for Computational Analysis of Meaning."

4. See Sergei Nirenburg and Victor Raskin, "The Subworld Concept Lexicon," for further discussion of this point.

5. See Nirenburg and Raskin, "A Metric for Computational Analysis"; Roger C. Schank and S. P. Shwartz, "The Role of Knowledge Engineering," 193-94; and Jerry R. Hobbs, "Overview of the Tacitus Project," 220.

6. See Victor Raskin, *Semantic Mechanisms of Humor,* 135, for a related discussion.

Discussion

TUMAN.   Neither of you seems to see important cultural changes as the unavoidable result of our increased reliance upon computers in manipulating texts: Provenzo sees new dangers that we are warned to avoid; Raskin sees only more of the same age-old problems. Yet should we not expect that widespread technological changes analogous to the industrial revolution will necessarily alter certain aspects of our collective life? Do you not see certain changes for better or worse as inevitable?

PROVENZO.   While I agree to a certain extent that the debate between Victor Raskin and myself may be whether the glass is half-empty or half-full, my concern over computers and their capacity to intervene in our lives and limit our freedom remains undiminished. Raskin assumes that it is not worth the bother and that the cost will be prohibitive for a McCarthy-type agency to sift through mountains of data to find potentially incriminating evidence concerning an individual. Unlike Raskin, I am convinced that this is neither too expensive nor too difficult a process to be undertaken with an individual who has been marked for surveillance. I am in complete agreement with Raskin about the potential of computers to act as vehicles to liberate individuals and groups. This belief is largely responsible for much of my enthusiasm for the machine.

I cannot avoid the more sinister aspects of computerization however. Perhaps it is simply my nature to be more negative and skeptical—as Raskin's nature is to be optimistic. In *Video Kids*, I look in detail at the corporate organization and future plans of the Nintendo Corporation.

Plans are in the works, for example, at Nintendo to unveil by the end of 1991 an interactive video game and information-system network for the United States. Under the proposed plan, Nintendo Entertainment System video games would function as terminals that would allow long-distance game playing as well as access to financial and news-information services. The project will probably be conducted in collaboration with American Telephone and Telegraph (AT&T). The proposed network is modeled after one that is already available in Japan. Nintendo is confident that AT&T will eventually cooperate in the joint venture. According to Nintendo CEO and President Hiroshi Yamauchi: "AT&T is quite rational and ultimately will cooperate." Nintendo has no intention of remaining just a video-game company—its purpose is nothing less than to establish itself as a global electronics communications giant. As Yamauchi explains: "We learned our lessons well from Atari. We are able to understand very clearly why Atari failed. No toy company ever became a big company successfully by remaining a toy company." I find comments and plans such as these chilling. It will be interesting to see what comes of it all.

Researching and writing *Video Kids* convinced me even more of the non-neutrality of the computer. Because of the limitations of cost, equipment, and programming protocols, video games, which are essentially simulations, present very limited points of view. Think for a minute about how most video games are designed with a godlike overview or sideview. Except for something like an auto-race game, it is too difficult to program the machine from the perspective of an individual engaged in the action of a game. As we turn more to simulated environments for our experience, this built-in or non-neutral perspective of the machines will become more of an issue.

In summary, there is an old maxim: if a technology or scientific discovery is available, it will almost inevitably be used. Computers have a potential for expanding the possibilities of surveillance and control. I suspect that their potential in this context will be well tried and tested in the future.

RASKIN. I do not think it was any more naive on my part to suggest that the current situation with computers versus privacy, decision making, or education "is somehow not different from the past" than it was for Provenzo to suggest that it was totally new. We are definitely dealing here with the half-full–half-empty controversy.

I applaud Provenzo's efforts to alert us to the perils of the computer. The result of this educational effort will be social and legal defenses against computer abuse. What I protest is the apocalyptical dimensions these perils can take in the minds of some of his readers. And this is where I say, "Come on, we've been here before!"—and we have. Cataclysms following the introduction of new technology are not new to humanity, and we have developed natural ways of dealing with them, which include Provenzo-like alarmism, Raskin-like unperturbability, and the finally enlightened society's mature response to the challenge.

One thing I refuse to be scared by is the purely quantitative aspect of the computer revolution. Provenzo thinks it would be a lot easier for the McCarthy committee to do much more harm if they had "access to computer records of the type discussed in [his] essay." Yes and no. And my No is much more resounding. Yes, McCarthy's clerks could have amassed gigabytes of computer data on each subject of their investigation within a short period of time (they would still have had to figure out first where to go for those records, and no metacomputer would have helped them with that). But what would they do with that mass of information? Speaking of naivete, if I may, Provenzo does not seem to realize that browsing through these computer records would incur prohibitive costs, either in terms of human effort to assimilate computer-generated information or in terms of research costs for attempts to automate the procedure. If, however, the clerk knew what he was looking for and just needed a record confirming his suspicion, then my sergeant-and-rookie example comes back into the picture — they could have found that record too, easily.

Besides, many computer records are too "flat," as in "flat database software," and uninformative. Yes, you can go to my video store and collect all the movies I have checked out since they first opened (you would probably have to pay them for the list, and they may already be legally prohibited from giving it to you). Can you easily figure out my political convictions from that list? Not with the help of a computer, anyway.

Oh, but record-keeping has become more thorough and efficient, Provenzo would object. True enough. If, however, a detailed record is kept by all businesses for all customers for all times, the cost is enormous — in computer hardware (no cheap Commodore or Tandy will do), costly software, and expensive human operators. This cost is my protection against global surveillance.

My best protection, however, is my own anonymity or inconspicuousness. If I am singled out for surveillance by the government, organized crime, or a disgruntled spouse or business associate, they may succeed with or without computers. If, on the contrary, I am one of the anonymous crowd, I will be surveilled only if everybody is surveilled, and that is cost-prohibitive.

This is my passive defense against computer surveillance. I can defend myself actively as well because I also have access to computers. In this week's *Newsweek*, the availability of the census data on a disk for a personal computer is touted as a powerful weapon in gerrymandering. It is certainly true, but this disk is available to both parties.

Besides my passive defense and active defense, I want to be protected from computer surveillance by society. This is where Provenzo's position is useful and mine is not. He informs and alarms; I soothe and lull to oblivion. The computer has not, however, won everybody over—there is a pocket of resistance against using it in research and teaching and against allocating resources to computerization even in my own department. And how about a newly liberated third-world country like the U.S.S.R. deciding whether to self-computerize and weighing Provenzo's alarm against Raskin's complacency? This is where my position is useful and Provenzo's is not (I know he is not against computers, but he can scare an uninformed individual, group, or society away from them), because both my department and Russia must computerize (my department is actually a century ahead of Russia in that).

I have a Solomon's decision on this half-full–half-empty issue: when weighing the perils of the computer against its promise, hire both Provenzo and Raskin as consultants!

McCorduck.   Much of my spare time has been taken up this year with matters of computer privacy and freedom of expression. Yes, we have been here before, and yes, it is somewhat different. I've written elsewhere that computer perils can only be met by the strong interaction of three kinds of sanctions: legal, technological, and social. None by itself will work at all, and the three together can only work to a degree. Anybody *can* mug a frail senior citizen or abuse a child, but we have laws against it, we try to protect such citizens with (rather primitive) technology, and we abhor it as a society. These will be our safeguards against computer abuses too.

Tuman.   I am fascinated by the idea of an interface capable of responding to our intentions, not our words—as if we are moving beyond the notion of an amanuensis (capable of producing a grammatically correct transcription of what we dictate) to that of an executive assistant who can generate the text for us ("Write a thank-you note to . . ." or, perhaps someday, "Write a critical article synthesizing . . . "). In such a world, one wonders, what becomes of the nuances and subtle shadings of meaning, of just those aspects of reading and writing texts on which we have traditionally placed such great emphasis in our English composition and literature classes?

RASKIN. The natural language interfaces (NLIs) of the future will have to be capable of analyzing the meaning of the user's input to a variable predetermined degree, from a crude guess to subtle nuances. The principles of such an approach have already been set up in Sergei Nirenburg and Victor Raskin, "A Metric for Computational Analysis of Meaning," and developed further in *Computational Linguistic Semantics*. The degree of analysis, or the depth of it, depends on the nature of the job required of the interface, and that is determined by the computer system it serves.

Let me first give you an example of a crude analysis. We have implemented here a fairly simple NLI, Smearr, for a lexical database. The database is an enriched dictionary of English, which consists of individual entries in a specified format and rich, hypertext-type links among the entries. (First implemented in the Framekit environment of the Texas Instruments Explorer II in Common Lisp, the whole system is being transposed now into the 2.0 Hypercard on Macintosh and Interface Builder on the NeXT station.)

Users unfamiliar with the Smearr system can place inquiries with it in plain English. They can ask to see an entry in isolation or in conjunction with the entries for related words. Altogether, there are twenty-odd functions that the system can perform for users. The interface is capable of recognizing dozens of paraphrases of the same request, such as "Show me the entry for X," and respond to it correctly. All the paraphrases are the same for the interface, and the nuances among them do not matter.

In other words, the subworld of the computer system Smearr is divided into, say, twenty categories, and the NLI is designed to recognize English phrases and fragments that belong to each of them. The NLI assigns all the input it cannot handle to the twenty-first, none-of-the-above, category, and such an occurrence triggers a powerful help subsystem, as the ultimate attempt to assign unrecognized input to one of the twenty categories and thus recognize it.

This system has a large granularity, and meaning analysis is done to a large grain size. On the other hand, a computer system analyzing relationships would need to recognize hundreds if not thousands of complex and interrelating categories. In such a system, "I love you," "I care for you," "I like you a lot," "I like you," and so on should all represent different degrees of attachment and intimacy, for the picture to be accurate and for the system to be useful. (Such a system could, for instance, replace Ann Landers—I almost said "And maybe it already has"—except that, repetitious as "her" answers are in recommending therapy, they are often too erratic and humanly silly, otherwise. Still, Ann Landers would be my first choice for computer emulation.) Such a system will require fine granularity and subtle meaning analysis. In fact, in a 1971 book on sublanguages, I distinguished between nonsubtle and subtle sublanguages on the basis of the granularity required by the subworlds served by them.

When we teach people to express themselves in writing, they have to deal with the whole world, and this is why we insist on nuances. To use the evaluative scale as an example, we want college freshmen to master all the gradations from superb, sublime, exquisite, excellent, and so on at the top of the scale to awful, hideous, disgusting, revolting, and so on at the bottom, and to use this fine granularity— instead of their native large-grain-size system with only two categories of evaluation, "kind of, like, cool, you know" and "gro-o-o-ss!"

Obviously, nonsubtle, large-grain-size NLIs are easier to implement, and there are more of them around. Moreover, the large-grain-size worlds are easier to represent and serve in a computer system. Nevertheless, even in such NLIs, meaning analysis is not trivial. Thus, in the Smearr NLI, an input sentence such as "Give me something like *say*" may evoke the synonym function (which will produce the entry for *say* and its synonyms, such as *utter*) or, alternatively, the sibling function (which will show the entry for *say* and similar verbs like *talk*, *speak*, and *tell*, which all have significantly different meanings in the subtle fine-grain-size "whole" world).

MCCORDUCK. The interface—I might almost say the 'entity'— suggested here, which responds to our intentions instead of our explicit instructions, will be wondrously complex to do such a job. Most humans can't even do it for one another without long habituation—spouses speaking for one another, an assistant speaking for a supervisor—and even so that sometimes fails.

But let's suppose you can train your personal electronic agent to become your alter ego. It acquires a detailed cognitive map of your cognitive map and can anticipate how you'd respond in any situation. It even knows when it doesn't know, and when to ask for guidance. Why would you settle for anything less?

The marvel is when your agent can do better than you—or any other human. Those chess programs edging up to world championship level (as I write, they play better than most humans in the world save a small handful of grand masters) are at their most interesting when they dream up moves no human has ever produced: they're beginning to do just that. How will I feel when my electronic alter ego does better than I do? Me, I'll be tickled pink.

Because what actually happens in such a case is coevolution. I get smarter as it gets smarter (or more subtle, or more imaginative, or whatever). I know of two humans who've built electronic alter egos (one a chess grand master, one an artist, and each alter ego a twenty-year project), and this has been their enviable reward.

> 5 <
COMPUTERS
and New Forms of Knowledge

Digital Rhetoric:
Theory, Practice, and Property

Richard A. Lanham

We have always, from Pascal to the present, thought of computers, especially digital computers, as logic machines. Whether they helped us with our weaving, our business tabulations, our artillery trajectories, or our atomic bombs, we have always located them where we locate logic, at the familiar Platonic center of human reason. It was a Monster of Pure Reason that threatened to fold, spindle, and mutilate the riotous Berkeley students of the 1960s. It was the same monster that prompted Hubert Dreyfus to write his equally riotous satire of artificial intelligence, *What Computers Can't Do,* a modern *Dunciad* from which neither satirist nor satirized have yet to recover. Two distinguished chroniclers of this "logical" history have contributed essays to this collection: Jay David Bolter, whose acute discussion of *Turing's Man* develops the logic-machine case from a deep knowledge of both Western philosophical tradition and computer science; and Pamela McCorduck, whose broad-ranging and sympathetic account of the AI world and its Dreyfus confrontation, *Machines Who Think,* comes from a personal acquaintance with the major players.

I would like, as a supplement and complement to this view from philosophy and theory, to suggest that in *practice* the computer often turns out to be a *rhetorical* device as well as a logical one, that it derives its aesthetic from philosophy's great historical opposite in Western thought and education, the world of rhetoric. And I would like to suggest that the computer galvanizes the arts as effectively as it crunches the numbers of science. I shall argue that the aesthetics of computer display were worked out in the visual arts long before the dominance of the computer itself. This prophetic reincarnation allows me to develop my argument largely through illustrations from this pre-electronic visual history.

Let me begin by summarizing the transformations practiced on words and images by a digital display and suggesting some of the rhetorical forebears of these transformations. Finally, I'll sketch briefly a larger context within which to comprehend them.

First, a text moving from print to digital electronic display becomes unfixed and interactive. The reader can change it, become writer. The center of Western culture since the Renaissance (really since the great Alexandrine editors of the Homeric text), the fixed, authoritative, canonical text, simply explodes into the ether, as we can see in Filippo Tommaso Marinetti's 1919 collage, *SCRABrrRrraaNNG*.

Italian Futurism, which began with Marinetti's famous *Futurist Manifesto* in 1909, was a complex (and as things turned out prophetic) movement that combined theatrical evenings like the happenings of fifty years later with political outpourings of an apocalyptically fascist sort; it took an interest in a new nonharmonic kind of music that used both silence and noise in ways foreshadowing John Cage, and it argued for the primacy of vision over print in ways that point toward Marshall McLuhan. The final aim of all this was, at least sometimes, the conflation of the arts into a single theatrical whole, something Marinetti called "Il Teatro di Varietà," a theater that seemed, at least for him, to find its most natural future home not in live theater but in cinema. (Cinema was then *the* new technology. He would locate it now, I think, in the digitally driven "theme parks" being designed by LucasFilm and built by Disney and MCA. The perfect example of "Il Teatro di Varietà" would be the new Disneyland space-travel attraction called "Star Tours.")

I want to single out from this prophetic melange of violent theater and political rant only one of its dominant interests, the attack on the printed codex book and its typographical conventions, an attack symbolized by the *esplosione* at the center of Marinetti's typographic bomb. In a tract called *La cinematografia futurista*, Marinetti and some of his pals target the book as the main villain of the old order:

> The book, the most traditional means of preserving and
> communicating thought, has been for a long time destined to
> disappear, just like cathedrals, walled battlements, museums, and
> the ideal of pacifism. . . . The Futurist Cinema will . . .
> collaborate in a general renewal, substituting for the magazine —
> always pedantic —, for the drama — always stale —, and killing

Fig. 1. Filippo Tommaso Marinett, "SCRABrrRrraaNNG," from *8 anime in una bomba—romanzo esplosivo*, 1919.

the book—always tedious and oppressive [*sempre tedioso e opprimente*]." [*Marinetti e il Futurismo*, 189-90. My translation.]

The book is seen as static, inelastic, linear, sluggish; the new cine-matographic form is seen as dynamic, interactive, simultaneous, swift. This war on the book chose typographical convention as its main point of attack, with results like *SCRABrrRraaNNG*. Here we see the book and all it represents in the act of deconstructing itself (all unawares the little children played, even as early as 1919), an *esplosione* at its center literally shattering typographical convention into dis-tended fragments. Subsequent collage techniques from Dada to the present day have diffused the force and direction of this attack, but Marinetti was taking aim at the fundamental convention of a literate society. Eric Havelock, in his brilliant pioneering work on Greek literacy, argued that a culture, to be truly literate, must possess an alphabet simple enough to be learned thoroughly in early youth and unobtrusive enough in its calligraphy so that a reader simply forgets about its physical aspects and reads right through it to the meaning beneath. The written surface must be transparent—transparent and unselfconscious. We must not notice the size and shape of the letters. We may, in some subconscious way, *register* the chirographic or typographic conventions but we must not *see* them. Havelock points to those early Greek vase paintings—where letters of the alphabet are used as decorative motifs, noticed for their size and shape only—as registering the preliterate, still oral, use of the alphabet.

It is to this stage that Marinetti—and, I would argue, electronic text—would return us. He seeks to make us aware of the enormous act of simplification that an ordinary printed text represents; he wants to make us self-conscious about a register of expressivity that we as literate people have abjured. It is common to call experiments of this sort "outrageous," but surely they aim more at didacticism? In a literate culture our whole conception of meaning—whether of logical argu-ment or magical narrative—depends on this radical act of typographi-cal simplification. No pictures; no color; strict order of left to right, then down one line; no type changes; no interaction; no revision. In attacking this convention, Marinetti attacks the whole literate con-ception of humankind—the central self, a nondramatic society out there just waiting for us to observe it—and the purposive idea of language that rests upon it. He would urge us to notice that all this reality-apparatus is as conventional as the typography we are trained *not* to notice. There was a time, in fact, when it did not exist: in the *oral* culture from which Greek rhetoric originally came. Marinetti's techniques have often been employed since then—most notably in discussing digital text, I suppose, in Ted Nelson's *Computer Lib*— where we can see more clearly than with Marinetti the native didacticism of the genre. Here, oddly enough, the self-conscious typography advocates a theory of prose style—a campaign against Cybercrud and for an unselfconscious CBS (clarity, brevity, sincerity) prose style which the self-conscious typography contradicts at every point.

Concomitantly with the explosion of the authoritative text, electronic writing brings with it a complete renegotiation of the alphabet/icon ratio upon which print-based thought is built. We can see this foregrounding of images over written words most clearly nowadays in the world of business and government communications, but it is happening everywhere. When the rich vocal and gestural language of oral rhetoric was constricted into writing and then print, the whole effort to preserve it was concentrated into something usually called *ecphrasis*, dynamic speaking pictures in words. Through the infinite resources of digital-image recall and manipulation, *ecphrasis* is once again coming into its own, and the pictures and sounds suppressed into verbal rhetorical figures are now reassuming their native places in the human sensorium. The complex icon/word interaction of oral rhetoric is returning, albeit *per ambages*.

We can see this happening in another prophetic pre-electronic instance, one of Kenneth Burke's proverbial doodles, or "Flowerishes," from the *Collected Poems* (88). The "text" of this typographical game is a series of comic apothegms: "In a world full of problems he sat doing puzzles"; "One must learn to be just morbid enough"; "They liked to sit around and chew the phatic communion." The center of Burke's philosophy of rhetoric has been his discussion of "Orientation," the self-conscious perception of the fundamental paradigms for apprehending reality that we customarily push to the side, to our peripheral vision. Here he uses the conventions of typography to pun on orientation. To "orient" ourselves to this self-conscious form of proverbial wisdom, we must, like an illiterate pretending to read, turn the book round and round in an effort to make sense of it. We are made

CYBERCRUD

A number of people have gotten mad at me for coining the term "cybercrud," which I define as "putting things over on people using computers." But as long as it goes on we'll need the word. At every corner of our society, people are issuing pronouncements and making other people do things and saying it's *because of the computer*. The function of cybercrud is thus to confuse, intimidate or pressure. We have all got to get wise to this if it is going to be curtailed.

Cybercrud takes numerous forms. All of them, however, share the patina of "science" that computers have for the layman.

1a) COMPUTER AS MAGIC WORD

The most delicate, and seemingly innocent, technique is the practice of naming things so as spuriously to suggest that they involve computers. Thus there is a manufacturer of pot-pipes with "Data" in its name, and apparently a pornography house with "Cyber-".

1b) COMPUTER AS MAGIC INGREDIENT

The above seems silly, but it is no less silly than talking about "computer predictions" and "computer studies" of things. *The mere fact that a computer is involved in something has no bearing on its character or validity.* The *way* things are done with computers affects their character and validity, just like the way things are done without computers. (Indeed, merely using a computer often has no bearing on the way things are done.)

This same technique is easily magnified to suggest, not merely that something *involves* computers, but is wholly done by computers. The word "computerize" performs this fatal function. When used specifically, as in *computerize the billing operation*, it can be fairly clear; but make it vague, as in *computerize the office*, and it can mean anything.

"Fully computerize" is worse. Thus we hear about a "fully computerized" print shop, which turns out to be one whose computers do the typesetting; but they could also run the presses, pay the bills and work the coffee machine. For practical purposes, there is no such thing

as "fully" computerized. There is always one more thing computers could do.

2) WHITE LIES: THE COMPUTER MADE ME DO IT

Next come all the leetle white lies about how such-and-such is the computer's fault and not your decision. Thus the computer is made a General Scapegoat at the same time it's covering up for what somebody wants to do anyway.

"It has to be this way."

"There's nothing we can do; this is all handled by computer."

"The computer will not allow this."

"The computer won't let us."

The translation is, of course, THE STINKY LOUSY PROGRAM DOES NOT PERMIT IT. Which means in turn: WE DO NOT CHOOSE TO PROVIDE, IN OUR PROGRAMS AND EQUIPMENT, ANY ALTERNATIVES.

Now, it is often the case that good and sufficient reason exists for the way things are done. But it is also often the case that companies and the public are inconvenienced, or worse, by decisions the computer people make and then hide with their claim of technical necessity. ☞

They have really stupid switches now on computers that look Scientific. Zero means Off, see, because that's no current, and 1 means On, because it's, uh, a __number__, right?

Actually, this was just a compromise so they wouldn't have to print switch-plates in different languages. But it sure is stupid. Zero could also mean On. These codes are __arbitrary__.

"COMPUTERS AND THEIR PRIESTS"

"First get it through your head that computers are big, expensive, fast, dumb adding-machine-typewriters. Then realize that most of the computer technicians that you're likely to meet or hire are complicators, not simplifiers. They're trying to make it look tough. Not easy. They're building a mystique, a priesthood, their own mumbo-jumbo ritual to keep you from knowing what they— and you—are doing."

—Robert Townsend,
Up The Organization (Knopf), p. 36.

In the movie "Fail-Safe," they showed you lots of fake tape drives with the reels constantly turning in one direction. This they called a "computer." Calling any sinister box "a computer" is a widespread trick. Gives people the willies. Keeps 'em in line.

"If it can't be done in COBOL, I just tell people it can't be done by computer. It saves a lot of trouble."

Attributed to somebody in Rochester. (See "COBOL," p. 61)

A BASIC REJOINDER

we should all practice and have ready at the tip of our tongues: WHY THE HELL NOT? *YOU'RE* THE ONES WITH THE COMPUTERS, NOT ME!

Let's froth up a little citizen indignation here.

Except maybe now that we __do__ have computers, we can find an even better way (and fair⌐ᴉy) to get back at inconsiderate companies.

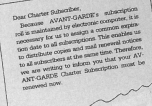
REASONS FOR CYBERCRUD (ALL BAD)

1) to manipulate situations.

2) to control others.

3) to fool.

4) to look like hot stuff.

5) to keep outsiders from seeing through something.

6) to sell something.

7) to put someone down.

8) to conceal.

9) general secretiveness.

10) low expectation of others' mentality.

11) seeking to be the broker and middleman for all relations with the computer.

12) vagueness sounds profound.

13) you don't have to show what you're not sure of.

14) your public image is monolithic.

15) you really don't know.

Fig. 2. Ted Nelson, *Computer Lib/Dream Machines*.

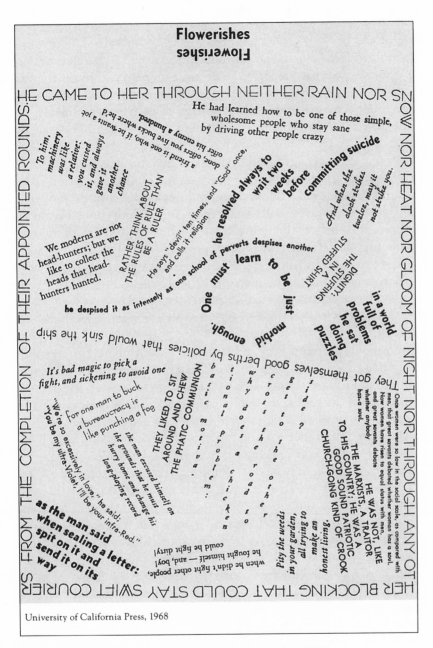

Fig. 3. Kenneth Burke, *Collected Poems, 1915–1967*.

aware of the book as a physical presence in our hands. The printed surface is rendered opaque rather than transparent by changes in type face, font size, and sequencing. Text must be read top to bottom as well as left to right, back to front, in a circle, every which way. Type design thus becomes an aspect of meaning. Does "a grandfather clock, run by gravity," mean something different because it is presented in Gothic type? Typography becomes allegorical, a writer-controlled expressive parameter, just as it does on an electronic screen.

The most revered and central function of the literary canon is to transmit the *canonical* wisdom found quintessentially in the proverb. Here Burke deliberately calls that tradition into question, breaking the "literacy compact" that Havelock so brilliantly isolated for us, and introducing visual patterns and typographical allegories to suggest that proverbial wisdom never really comes into the world purely transparent and disembodied, totally serious, unconditioned by game and play, by the gross physicality of its display. There is no formal cause without a material one. Again, the electronic parallels are manifest.

The struggle between icon and alphabet is nothing new, to be sure, as illuminated manuscripts so often illustrate. Almost any anthology of illuminated manuscripts will provide illustrations of the iconic impulse trying to gobble up alphabetic space like a hungry cookie monster. The same wind that carried away the authoritative text has also ventilated the canonical solemnity with which we viewed it. The *canonical* image of this *anticanonicity* that is usually cited is Marcel Duchamp's urinal, but my favorite emblem of compromised canonicity is John Baldessari's 1967 painting, *Quality Material*. Baldessari, by a radical reversal of alphabetic and iconic information, denies an absolute beauty or fitness of things independent of humankind that it is our business first to discover and then breathlessly to adore. The painting suggests that such fitness is neither out there in "reality" nor in sacred texts—the timeless, unchangeable, self-explanatory, and canonical, excerpts of which will impart the healing touch of sacred relics. Instead of a divine icon, we have a human text that substitutes interpretation for the thing interpreted.

Doesn't electronic text often practice a similar comic reversal? The fundamental motivational structure of electronic text is as comic as print is serious. We can illustrate this reversed polarity of seriousness

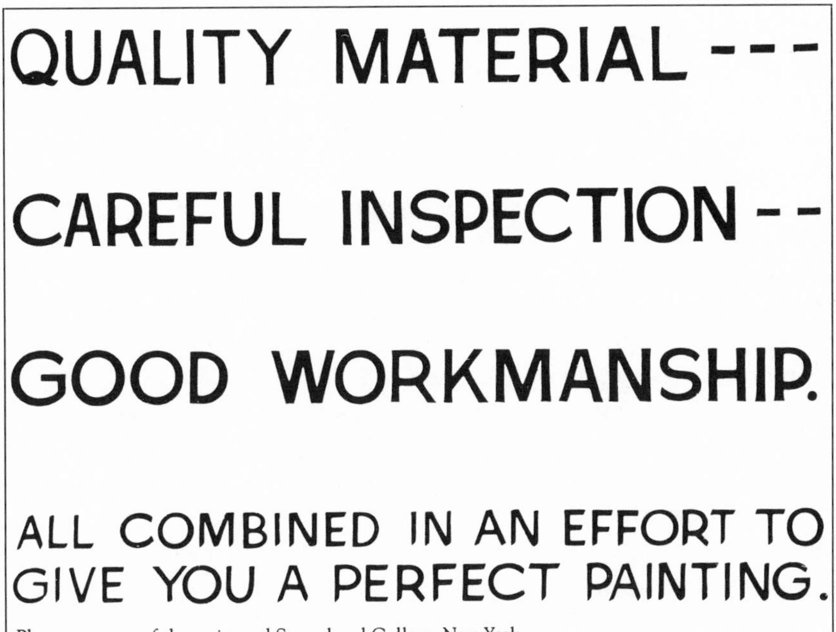

QUALITY MATERIAL - - -

CAREFUL INSPECTION - -

GOOD WORKMANSHIP.

ALL COMBINED IN AN EFFORT TO GIVE YOU A PERFECT PAINTING.

Photo courtesy of the artist and Sonnabend Gallery, New York

Fig. 4. John Baldessari, *Quality Material*, 1967.

with another familiar pre-electronic icon, Duchamp's most famous "Readymade," the mustachioed Mona Lisa. The title of this work, the letters *L.H.O.O.Q.*, if pronounced phonetically in French yield— learned commentators tell us—the words "Elle a chaud au cul" or, in fractured French, "This chick has hot pants." What, in the process, has happened to "Mona Baby"? First of all, she seems to have undergone a devastatingly effective and economical sex-change oper- ation. By thus desecrating Perfection, Duchamp has elicited a sexual ambiguity in the picture we had not seen before and could come to see in no other way. Outrageous Art is Didactic Criticism once again. Second, Duchamp calls our attention to a powerful canonical con- straint. The timeless perfection which Mona Baby represents con- demns us to passivity. No interaction allowed. Canonical vision moves in only one direction, does justice to an external reality that exists independent of us, but never recreates that reality in the act of perceiving it. The traditional idea of an artistic canon brings with it, by the very immortality it strives for, both a passive beholder and a passive reality—waiting to be perceived, the best that has been thought, said, or painted, perhaps, but unchangeable in its perfection, a goddess we can adore but never ask out to play. And so Duchamp asks her out to play. Criticism again. And, again, not so much an attack on the artistic canon as a meditation on the psychology of perception that canon implies. One perceptive critic has called this Readymade full of "quiet savagery." Not at all; playful didacticism rather. Interactivity *compromises* solemnity—just as it does electronic text. If we need a tutelary goddess for digital writing and reading, Mona Mustache is just the girl for the job.

We can see the interactive comic drive replacing Arnoldian solemnity in the work of the Swiss sculptor Jean Tinguely. In Tinguely's exhibitions of junk contraptions that crash, bang, thump, and even ask for a small coin donation, the people in attendance often figure prominently. I saw this myself when I went to the Tate exhibit. In place of a reverential art-gallery hush, the place was a symphony of sounds, not only the whangs, bangs, and whistles of the sculptures but the exclamations of the participants—for that is what we were—and the wonderful outcries of children. Most of them had speedily found the great *Rotozaza*, a sculpture that takes balls and, after moving them through a series of Rube Goldberg maneuvers, flings them out into the crowd. Kids of all ages then retrieve them and feed them back into the machine.

Part of the show was the part of the Tate that was not officially part of the show, the galleries that still preserved the reverential quiet of a conventional exhibition. But now you heard this silence as one of Cage's "silences," something you consciously attended to, that you began to "hear." Don't these conventional galleries allegorize the printed text, as read in a digital age? They are still the same, and yet we listen to them in a different way and hear silences we have not heard before.

With this kind of junk sculpture comes, needless to say, a flood of Marxist moralizing. Here is the detritus of modern capitalism, the sordid remnants of a junk culture, and so on. The machines themselves, though, when they are working in their native environment—moving, clanking, and whistling, the spectators busy catching balls, pushing buttons, commissioning abstract drawings for a sixpence—don't work this way at all. The machines exude high spirits and good humor. They do not damn a machine culture; they redeem it by returning it to play.

Let me report my own embodiment of this process when standing before *Autoportrait Conjugal,* a machine from 1960. Two objects depend from the bottom of the machine, a weight and a stuffed bird. When the machine goes into action, the ladder in the middle moves from side to side, and the weight acts as a pendulum, imparting to the stuffed bird a pendulous twitch. I went to the exhibit with an old friend, a tolerant and sophisticated woman with a wonderful sense of humor who is also a keen bird-watcher. She had, in fact, just arrived in London from a strenuous birding trip to the Pribilof Islands. She immediately noticed the dead bird and, after identifying it, began to excoriate Tinguely. She knows me well, and when she saw me trying to flail my face into something resembling moral outrage she remarked, "I'll bet you find this funny, don't you?"—meaning, by "this," the stuffed bird swinging back and forth at the bottom of a bungee cord, her outrage at it (which I expected), along with my efforts to prevent her from seeing that I did indeed think the dangling bird was, for reasons I could not explain, extremely funny. Finally I burst into laughter. And so did she. Tinguely had written a comedy, and both of us had played our parts. I think we have all come to see, through essays like those collected in this volume, how often electronic text contrives interactive events of just this sort, leavens with comedy the serious if not solemn business of clear, brief, and sincere human communication, just as classical rhetoric had for 2,000 years recommended.

Perhaps the most widely debated, though far from the most important, issue involving electronic text has been whether writing on a computer creates verbal flatulence. Certainly it reinstates the centrality of a fundamental aspect of classical rhetoric: the use of *topics,* of preformed arguments, phrases, whole chunks of verbal boilerplate, which can be electronically cut, pasted, and repeated at will. Classical rhetoric argued that repetition, without intrinsically changing the object repeated, changes it *absolutely.* Modern philosophers like Andy Warhol have dwelt upon this theme repeatedly. In *Thirty Are Better Than One* (1963), Mona's priceless canonical rarity vanishes even as we bring it to self-consciousness, simply by being repeated thirty times. The same aesthetic operates at the center of electronic text, though we seldom notice it for what it is—an aesthetic of collage. This

Photo courtesy of Oeffentliche Kunstsammlung Basel, Kunstmuseum

Fig. 5. Jean Tinguely, *Autoportrait conjugal*, 1960.

is now a commonplace narrative technique, as well as a technique in
the visual arts (for example, in David Hockney's recent work with

photo collage and color Xeroxes). My favorite example remains a golden oldie from the 1950s, Richard Hamilton's *Just What Is It That Makes Today's Homes So Different, So Appealing?* Hamilton's exercise in ironic juxtaposition may tell us something about Today's Desktops as well, collaged up with clip art as they are, often with something of the effect here. Perhaps this fundamental technique of the topos ought not surprise us; the iconographic desktop, after all, was modeled after

©Richard Hamilton/VAGA, New York 1991. Photo courtesy of Kunsthalle Tübingen

Fig. 6. Richard Hamilton, *Just What Is It That Makes Today's Homes So Different, So Appealing?*, 1956.

the memory system in classical Greek rhetoric—or so, at least, says Nicholas Negroponte (Brand 138).

To replicate and juxtapose at will, as collage does, is to alter scale, and scaling change is—as we have discussed—one of the truly enzymatic powers of electronic text. When you click in the Zoom Box, you make a big decision; you are deciding on the central decorum of a human event, on the boundary-conditions within which that event is to be staged, and hence on the nature of the event itself. To change scale is, as with repetition, to transform reality utterly without changing it at all. To make art of scaling changes means finally to make us self-conscious about perceptual distance and the conventions, neural and social, that cluster around it. That distance itself can so change an object—give it, to use Duchamp's phrase, a "new idea"—locks us into a conception of art as fundamentally interactive, the very opposite of canonical passivity.

To render a baseball bat epic in scale, as Claes Oldenburg did in his famous 100-foot *Batcolumn*, erected in Chicago's Loop in 1977, perpetrates one of those play/purpose reversals so common in pop art and beyond. Is this not the same kind of reversal we create when we zoom in on a letter until we dissolve its meaning into the abstract formal pleasure of the pixel patterns themselves (Havelock's decorative letters on Greek vases again)? Oldenburg's bat ceases to be an instrument to hit a ball with and becomes an object to be contemplated, to crane your neck up at, a skyscraper of a baseball bat. Yet the eye, less adaptive than the mind, still wants it to be a bat of normal size and, so, yearns to make everything else increase in scale to fit it, conjures up an enormous ball diamond with gigantic players scaled to fit the bat. If the skyscrapers surrounding it dwarf us, then the *Batcolumn* expands us again, restores a more equal relationship with our environment, a playful epic scale. The *Batcolumn* is a thing of beauty, a new shape, but it is also, and more importantly, one of Duchamp's "new ideas," the idea of scale. Twentieth-century art has often aimed at re-creating epic scale in a new form; here by scaling up an everyday object. Epic scale, then, but radically democratized. We do the same thing when we zoom on the screen—we draw far closer to the text than ever we could with the naked eye, and in the magic world we thus enter the text becomes gigantic, enormously weighty, a physical space, a writing sheet large enough to wrap around the world.

Language does indeed become a field of meaning, over which we wander. A zooming session leaves the student of rhetoric with a renewed and expanded sense of how much basic decisions about reading, writing, and speaking have to do with scaling arguments, fitting them to time and place. Enlarging and diminishing them is the basic figure/ground decision that empowers human vision. Thus the scaling powers of electronic text create an extraordinary *allegory*, almost a continual visual punning, of the fundamental stage sets implied by written discourse. The future of rhetorical figuration, which McLuhan in an inspired phrase in *The Gutenberg Galaxy* called "the postures of the mind," looks, after a long hiatus, once again promising.

Perhaps the most epic engagement with scale-change in our time has been Roy Lichtenstein's comic-book paintings, where a form of commercial art usually presented in a format a couple of inches square suddenly finds a meticulous rendering almost six-by-eight feet. Again, an artifact of daily life is wrenched, through huge scale-change, into the domain of art. But here another profound reversal operates. As these images appear in the funny papers, they function purely transparently and provide immediate access to the narrative they depict. They are the graphic equivalent of Havelock's "literate compact"; they trigger no self-consciousness and provide a pictographic "pure story"—Romance at its most mythically simplified, most unselfconscious. Lichtenstein reverses this convention. The surface is rendered maximally self-conscious. We look at the surface pattern, *at* the design, rather than *through* it.

Lichtenstein points this out in a small sixteen-by-sixteen-inch black-and-white from 1963 called *Magnifying Glass*. Here the microdot pattern (which, in this printing technique, constitutes the main transparent means for creating the narrative image) is deliberately framed, made into a self-conscious and opaque design motif, something we look at and not through. So too with the characters in the narrative. "I use them for purely *formal* reasons," Lichtenstein has said, "and that's not what those heroes were invented for."

This kind of at/through reversal, a favorite Lichtenstein motif, seems to me the most powerful attribute of the electronic textual aesthetic. Print wants the gaze to remain *through* and unselfconscious all the time. Lichtenstein's *Magnifying Glass*, like the electronic screen, insists on the continual oscillation between unselfconscious expression and self-conscious design, which provided the center of classical rhetoric's art and pedagogy. *Magnifying Glass* is a painting about a different kind of seriousness, a different kind of perception, one that forgets intermittently—but must never forget forever—the means of perception, the carefully tuned illusions from which Western social reality has always been constructed. It is a painting, too, about what happens to text when it is painted onto an electronic screen, when we can change fonts, zoom in on the pixels until their meaning metamorphoses into purely formal pleasure. This oscillation

Collection Pier Luigi Pero. © Roy Lichtenstein/VAGA, New York 1991. Photo: Rudy Burckhardt

Fig. 7. Roy Lichtenstein, *Magnifying Glass*, 1963.

happens continually in electronic text without our recognizing it for what it is or seeing how deeply runs its fundamental allegory.

We can see an architectural version of the same oscillation in one of the most controversial attempts at postmodern monumentality, the Centre Pompidou in Paris, the "Beaubourg" as it is called, designed by Richard Rodgers and Renzo Piano. This now-famous facade restates a dominant motif in contemporary architecture, the reversal of use and ornament. The architects here have turned the building inside out and put its plumbing on the outside instead of hiding it in utility shafts. They have made decoration out of ducts, play out of purpose, much as Duchamp did with the *Fountain*. The building thus becomes not only a museum but an allegory of motive, a visual representation of the play/purpose reversal at the heart of postmodern architecture.

One can see this fundamental oscillation between use and orna-ment, between purpose and play, everywhere one looks in the history of computers, and especially of private desktop ones which—Ted Nelson notwithstanding—I think work differently from big ones. Play continually animates the operant purpose, indeed often becomes it. The play impulse, as so often in the academic world, has come to symbolize purity of motive in the computer world, and its loss has seemed the loss of innocence itself. I would urge the opposite case— play is as native to electronic text as it is to rhetoric itself.

Classical rhetoric was built on a single dominant exercise—model-ing. The central form was the oration, and this was rehearsed in every possible form and context, just as we today model pretty nearly all of human effort in digital simulations. Declamation (as it came to be called) stood at the center of Western educational technique, just as computer modeling is coming to do today. Again, we need not look far in contemporary art for an embodiment of this kind of rehearsal-reality and everything it implies. It has formed the basis for a series of gigantic works by the environmental artist Christo Javacheff. I want to consider in some detail his epic *declamatio* of the modern integrated visual arts, a didactic rehearsal-reality event of the greatest scale, grandeur, beauty, and meaning, his famous *Running Fence, Sonoma and Marin Counties, California, 1972–76.*

In October 1972 Christo made the first drawings of a gigantic fence projected to run through farmland and end in the sea. He began to look for a site in northern California or Oregon. The fence was to run for twenty-four-and-a-half miles and was to be built in segments eighteen feet high and from sixty to eighty feet wide. By July of the following summer he had settled on an area around Petaluma, California, formed the Running Fence Corporation, and placed an order for 165,000 yards of woven nylon fabric. The period from July 1973 to April 1976 was taken up by eighteen public hearings to get the permits to build the fence, by several court sessions, a huge Environmental Impact Statement, and applications to fifteen government agencies, these activities all made possible through the kind offices of nine lawyers. Finally, after a tense final hearing, the project was free to proceed. Cables were laid on the ground and holes were dug. Poles were erected, wires strung, the fabric was bent to the poles and threaded to the cables. On 7 September 1976, the part-time army of fabric installation workers, 360 strong, deployed the fence.

The wind took the fabric, and the project set sail for temporary immortality. It took three days to erect the full twenty-four-and-a-half miles. *Running Fence* turned out to be more beautiful even than Christo had imagined, sailing through the early morning fog, celebrating cows in their fields and the rolling hills in their glory, sailing like a silver ribbon toward the sea, punctuating the day from the dusk, scaling, scaling, forever scaling the landscape with its band of silver white, making from the air a ribbon of light across the earth, until at dusk it plunged into the sea.

Running Fence sounded all the notes in our current aesthetic chord. It was calculated to be of an age and not for all time, mortal rather than immortal, to represent what man cannot do forever and should not do for long to the land, to allegorize not his vainglory but his solemn sense of his own limitations. It was completed at noon on 10 September and stood for fourteen days. Then the dismantling began and by 23 October, eight days ahead of schedule, the whole fence had been removed and the pole anchors each driven three feet into the ground. The power of this allegory was not lost on the beholders. As one businessman wrote in the local paper:

> the Running Fence will depict the evolution of man from the sea, his enormous efforts to survive and build on the land, and the ultimate destruction of that for which he has strived with such intensity for so very long. It is, indeed, a true artist and

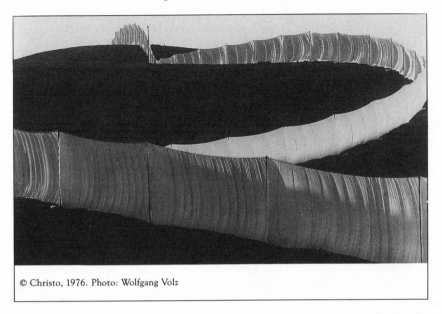

© Christo, 1976. Photo: Wolfgang Volz

Fig. 8. Christo, *Running Fence, Sonoma and Marin Counties, California, 1972–76.*

businessman that can conceive and execute so huge a philosophical symbol of the determination of man and the futile and transitory nature of his efforts. . . . In all this I know whereof I speak. I am retired after forty years as an industrialist and rancher and all the businesses and enterprises that I developed are now gone. Little remains to show they were ever here. I have no regrets, it was great fun, but that is the way it is. (*The Running Fence Project: Christo*)

Christo earned praise as a businessman for financing this project, as he has done all his gargantuan projects, entirely himself. *Running Fence* cost three million dollars; this sum was raised by selling sketches, a film, small sections of cable, nylon and other souvenir remnants, and by making a huge book about the creation of the fence. Christo signed three thousand copies of the book, which includes, besides a full history of *Running Fence* and hundreds of gorgeous photographs, copies of the relevant government documents, film stills, and also a relic of the project, a small square of its nylon cloth. I own copy number 133, and what a book it is. For it is no more a normal codex book than the fence is a normal fence. Like the square of cloth it contains, it is not a book about a work of art, a work past or present that stands detached from it. The book is part of the work of art and formed part of its essence and design from the beginning. Christo has reached out in time as well as space, included in his work of art not only the object itself but all the processes from the beginning that brought it into, and out of, being. And this insistence on art as process rather than product, interactive temporal event rather than untouchable timeless masterpiece, I take to stand at the center of contemporary thinking about art, and about more than art.

I would also take the *Running Fence* book as a model of how codex books will work in an electronic world. We will see them not as absolute entities but as part of an expressive process both alphabetic and iconic, an entity whose physicality is manifest, whose rhetoric is perfectly self-conscious—that is to say whose place in a complex matrix of behavior forms a native part of its expression. Obviously enough, books will not vanish. However, they will, like *Running Fence* the book, send out nerve tendrils to the complex expressive world surrounding them.

I would also take *Running Fence* itself as a model for how the digital computer might function in the everyday world of work. Christo testified before the Sonoma county board of supervisors that "the work is not only the physical object of the fence. The work of art is really right now, and here [that hearing itself]. Everybody is part of the art, that is through the project of the *Running Fence*, and it is a most exciting thing, and there is not one single element in this project that is make-believe" (Christo). Christo has chosen to work, that is, not only in canvas and light but in behavior, in human motive; he has chosen to make art out of economic cooperation, out of the processes of collective work. In America nowadays, these are all bureaucratic processes, and it is just these processes that Christo has transformed into self-conscious art. By subtracting the practical purpose, the enduring object (fence, pipeline, or building), from the process, he has allowed everyone involved (and that includes all of us) to focus on and become self-conscious of the process involved, the process of human cooperation. To look at it rather than through it. I think we can use electronic text in the same way and for the same purpose. The self-consciousness of the device, at least, beckons us along this path far more cordially than ever print did.

I suggest, then, that we can use the digital computer, and more explicitly electronic text, as a work of art very like Christo's *Running Fence*. Electronic text invites us to play with ordinary experience rather than exploit it, to tickle a text or image a little while using it, to defamiliarize it into art. As with scaling change, as with both the actors and the objects in *Running Fence*—the hearing, the plan, the rendering, the Environmental Impact Statement, the construction worker, the councilman, the artist—human purpose will be both the same and utterly transformed. Is this radical democratization of art, this interweaving of play and purpose, so different from the range of hopes that computers inspired in the first generation of hackers who developed them?

I have been using some examples from the visual arts to sketch out what is often called the postmodern critique, an argument whose elements we have now before us: art defined as attention, beholder as well as object; thus an art that includes its beholder, and the beholder's beholder, an outward frame expanding, an infinite progress rather than regress; interactive text, that is, art and criticism mixed together, and so art and life as well; a continually shifting series of scale-changes, of contextualisms (as literary criticism calls them); a resolute use of self-consciousness to turn transparent attention to opaque contemplation (especially in regard to the typographical conventions of fully literate reading); above all, a pervasive reversal of use and ornament, a turning of purpose to play and game, a continual effort not, as with the Arnoldian canon, to purify our motives, but to keep them in a continual, roiling, rich mixture of play, game, and purpose. All this yields a body of work that is active not passive, a canon not frozen in perfection but volatile with contending human motives.

Is this not the aesthetic of the personal computer? And is this aesthetic not part of a worldview that is larger still—as I have tried to suggest by choosing my illustrative images from the pre-electronic world? This larger worldview occurs not only in the visual arts from which I have taken my examples, but in perception psychology from transactional analysis onward (the work upon which the pop artists drew so heavily); in American role theory from George Herbert Mead to Erving Goffman; in evolutionary biology from the New Darwinian Synthesis onward; in Havelock and Ong's formulation of the literate/oral polarity in Western discourse from classical Greece to the present day; in the East/West polarity that, using Balinese culture as Ur-type, first Margaret Mead and Gregory Bateson and then Clifford Geertz have established; and in literary theory, which encapsulates much of this thinking (without footnoting it). In fact, it occurs practically everywhere we care to look in the contemporary intellectual landscape.

This larger worldview presents itself with special insistence in a field that literary scholars do not usually consider—copyright law. We have dwelt so long under the successful umbrella of intellectual accomplishment as defensible property that we have forgotten how fragile that umbrella really is. It stands like literate Homo sapiens on two legs, Romantic Originality and the Fixed Printed Text. The computer aesthetic we have seen emerging in the visual arts and across the whole intellectual landscape threatens both central conceptions. Suppose you digitally sample a song, convert the sample into a drawing, practice a Fourier transform on the drawing, then convert it back to sound, edit that, and play it all on a synthesizer? Who owns what finally comes out of the synth?

Law is rhetoric's ultimate home, the arena from which it originally came. We shall find, I think, that the fundamental alteration in our conceptual and aesthetic universe brought about by digital information will find its first real resolution in the copyright courts. It is litigation that we should all be watching. Theory and Practice will come to focus in the debate about Property. Judge and jury cannot engage in what Gerald Graff has recently called the Deconstructive Two-Step. They must decide. In no field will the radical democratization of art and information offered to us by the computer be more rigorously opposed by the concepts of fixed property created by print. In no field will the debate be more illuminating. My own guess is that democratization will win, and not only because technology leads us that way.

For, I have been arguing, technology really isn't *leading* us that way. The arts and the theoretical debate that tags along after them have done the leading, and digitization has emerged as their condign embodiment. I would argue, then, that we don't have to worry about digital determinism. The central issue to be explained is the extraordinary convergence of twentieth-century thinking over its whole intellectual spectrum with the digital means that now give it expression. It is the *computer as fulfillment of social thought* that needs explication.

What frame is wide enough to provide such explication? To explain reading and writing on computers, I would assert (I haven't space to develop the case here), we need to go back to original Western thinking about reading and writing — the rhetorical paideia that provided the backbone of Western education for 2,000 years. The means of digital expression prove to be a fulfillment, not only of the postmodern aesthetic but also of a larger phenomenon that comprehends and explains that aesthetic — the return of the basic traditional pattern of Western education and Western thinking about words and how they are used. We are still bemused by the 300 years of the Great Newtonian Simplification, a way of thinking that made *Rhetoric* a dirty word; but we are beginning to outgrow this simplified way of thinking. The final Promise of Online Literacy is not, then, a revolutionary but a conservative one, an attempt to reclaim and rethink basic Western wisdom about words. I think the Perils of Online Literacy will prove to be the familiar perils that have always lurked in the divided, unstable, protean Western self.

I have not discussed here what is perhaps the central issue in digitization — the question of ethics. But let me close by observing what I have all along been implying. To debate the ethics of digital text is to debate the ethics of the whole post-Newtonian, post-Darwinian, post-print conception of human life that we have seen emerging in our own time. The computer with its digital display is no technological *vis a tergo* but the condign medium for expressing how we nowadays think of ourselves and our world. I suspect that few of us find this way of thinking altogether comfortable, but we must not blame the computer for that. Do not blame the medium for the message.

How We Knew, How We Know, How We Will Know

Pamela McCorduck

Everyone knows the old rule of thumb all teachers use to test whether a student knows something: can that student rephrase the knowledge in his or her own words? It's a good rule of thumb, for we know from experience that representation—*re-presentation*—is a splendid way of demonstrating that one knows something.

My high-school English teacher—and for all I know, everyone's high-school English teacher—used to insist that if we couldn't put it into writing, then we couldn't claim to know it. Miss Fletcher herself didn't know, but she was taking part in what Sir Herbert Read would call the Hegelian heresy, the identification of human intelligence with discursive reasoning, "as though one could say that Plato was 'more intelligent' than Praxiteles; or that Freud was 'more intelligent' than Cezanne" (Read).

I was on my way to becoming a professional writer, so it never occurred to me then that Miss Fletcher might be taking a rather narrow-minded view of what it means to know. I have spent the rest of my life putting it into writing. I mean that in the most literal sense: like E. M. Forster's old lady, I don't know what I mean until I say it, and being a relatively silent person to say it for me means to write it down. To write it down is to know it.

However, I'd like to suggest that knowledge can be embodied in different kinds of representations and some kinds of knowledge lend themselves better to certain representations than to others; and that the privileged position text has occupied in our schools, indeed in our intellectual lives, is coming to an end.

The equivalence between text and knowledge is one of the great unacknowledged assumptions of education in the past few centuries:

of the three Rs, only 'rithmetic isn't text, although Alfred North Whitehead argued that mathematics is certainly a language. This is the unspoken assumption that makes my own students hesitant to use diagrams or charts when they write essays for my science-writing class. "Is it all right?" they ask nervously. That tells me Miss Fletcher is alive and well in our schools today, insisting on text and excluding other forms of representation, as if text were the most suitable, most useful, and fullest representation for every kind of knowledge, in pursuit of all kinds of purposes.

This is nonsense. Our classrooms are saturated with text because text was the first cheap, mass-produced form of knowledge representation we had: it is called printing, and it made a revolution. I do not want to denigrate the advantages of text—as a professional writer I spend my life manipulating text. Moreover, Walter Ong (among others) tells us that literacy in its most literal meaning, the ability to read and write, confers all sorts of unexpected cognitive benefits. For example, literate people can grasp abstractions better than nonliterate people can—an illiterate might know the difference between *hot* and *cold* but would not grasp what the metaphorical *hot stuff* is. Nonliterates also have greater difficulty verbalizing connections between cause and effect, or the differences between past, present, and future. They tend to move less easily from the personal to the impersonal and to experience greater difficulty grasping a multiplicity of points of view. The ability to generalize seems to be one of the exemplary benefits of knowing one's way around text (Coughlin).

How did we *know* before text? How did we represent what we knew before we could put it in writing? No surprise: we drew pictures. Visual images as the representation of knowledge occur in many places and persist in our own Western tradition of art.

A writer will be forgiven for pointing out that the equivalence between seeing and knowing is embedded in the Indo-European languages. The Indo-European root *ueid* means "to look at" and hence "to know." Thus there is the Sanskrit *veda*, which is "sacred knowledge," and thus the Greek words deriving from *eidos*, "form": for example, *idea*, "a form in the mind"; not to mention *histor*, "having known," hence "history," shortened sometimes to "story." Latin offers *videre*, "to know." The Celts took the root *ueid* and formed from it "white" or "easily seen"; hence "winter," the white season, and *Druid* (*dru-vid*), "oak-knowing." In the Germanic languages, early Anglo-Saxon offers *wit*, which first meant "the faculty of understanding"; *witness*, *wisdom*, and *wizard*. The suffix *-wise* means "in the shape of" or "resembling": *likewise* (Shipley).

I shall argue that the visual representation of knowledge begins with Paleolithic art; it appears in different ways in European art of the sixteenth, seventeenth, and eighteenth centuries; and it emerges, most surprisingly, in late twentieth-century art, with an artist who has made a unique and unexpected marriage between art and artificial intelligence, Harold Cohen. This leads me to speculations about *how we will know* in the future. You'll see as we go along that not only what we know changes over time, but how we know it changes too.

Take, for example, the first art we have records of, European art of the Upper Paleolithic. Art historians have called these artifacts handsome and accomplished, and so they are, while anthropologists speculated they probably had to do with ritual, in some cases the hunt, in other cases (particularly with the statuettes of stylized females) fertility.

Recently anthropologists have asked why there was a sudden explosion of art in the late Pleistocene. The cave paintings of southern France and northern Spain are the most famous but by no means the only examples of Upper Paleolithic art. To say these marvelous artifacts are connected with ritual only begs the question.

We know this much: our earlier hominid forebears went through tens of thousands of generations using technological traditions of, to us, unthinkable monotony. During the Upper Paleolithic, all this began to change. Change was slow at first, then accelerated; at a point about 20,000 years ago, it's fair to say the first information explosion took place.

The cause (and carrier) of all this change was the appearance of the Cro-Magnons, *Homo sapiens sapiens*. Not as strong and rugged as their Neanderthal cousins, the Cro-Magnons had to substitute brain for brawn in unforgiving times—the nearly eternal winter of successive glaciations and the inevitable famines that then prevailed over the European landscape.

Luckily, brains they had. And what brains. They were smaller by measure than those of the Neanderthals but had one outstanding characteristic that was to lead to everything else: the neocortex.

It came upon us all of a sudden, it seems; a swelling of the brainstem that would come to contain two-thirds of our brain's neuronal mass, and three-quarters of all its synapses. The neocortex is the structure that most distinctively sets us apart from other species, and it is intimately involved in those complex higher cognitive functions such as language, facial recognition, and spatial orientation that are intimately involved in all symbolic processing.

Cro-Magnons and their neocortexes are responsible for the famous cave paintings, sculptures, and carvings. The caves themselves are organized in elaborate patterns, and the paintings and other artifacts are now thought to be part of larger organized expressions, all connected with ritual. The question is, What kind of ritual? What ceremonies would have been considered so essential that they drew initiators and initiates alike into the exacting, time-consuming activities of art making, and away from the sheer effort of survival in that arduous climate? The only answer that makes sense, as John Pfeiffer suggests, is that the caves with their paintings and sculptures — and, it's reasonable to speculate, the body painting, the clothing decoration and other adornments, the dancing and singing and music making and storytelling and drama — were as essential to survival as protein.

And so, along with anthropologists, we ask a simple and profound question, What is art for?

Here is a human activity as universal as eating, sleeping, language, and sexual reproduction. What has been its adaptive utility, its survival value, for the human species? We know why sex and eating and language have survival value, and thus are pleasurable, but why art? What's in it for us as a biological species?

Art functions in many ways for us: it echoes and reflects the natural world; it adds significance and delight; it exercises and trains our perceptions, preparing us for the unfamiliar and making us see the familiar afresh; it permits direct sense experience, perhaps in danger of atrophy in a culture as cut off from such experience as ours is getting to be.

Yet valid as each of these functions is, none alone answers the question of why art-making behavior arose in humans in the first place.

Art making shares many characteristics both with play and with ritual. Each seeks to evoke or represent an alternative reality, a world that exists outside the everyday, the ordinary. Making art particularly aspires toward the extraordinary, and its results, the artifacts themselves, speak more or less eloquently for that process, depending on our inclinations and situation (consider the famous snowshovel, before and after Duchamp.)

But receiving art—permitting its evocations—also demands a heightened attention, a special concentration, an engagement, on the beholder's part.

Given the universality among humans of art-making behavior, an ethologist would have to conclude that there's an evolutionary reason for its persistence. (Some brain scientists, such as William Calvin, don't buy that at all. They speculate that art and language are possibly evolutionary side steps, accidental and unexpected dividends of the sequencing neurons we developed to throw and hammer. But this doesn't alter my main point.)

One ethologist who has looked hardest at this subject, Ellen Dissanayake, has written a rich and persuasive book called *What Is Art For?* I'm going to summarize—even caricature—her argument this way: Art-making behavior (what Dissanayake calls "making special") was selected during the biological evolution of human beings because it facilitated or sugarcoated socially important behavior, especially ceremonies, where group values and knowledge, often of a sacred or spiritual nature, were encoded, expressed, and transmitted (Dissanayake).

Let me put it another way. The common explanation for cave paintings is that they were connected with the ritual of the hunt. This may be so; but as I have said, that explanation begs the question. The Neanderthals also, after all, depended on the hunt for survival, but there is no evidence they painted on cave walls or used animal images in any kind of ceremony. No, the record suggests that after hundreds of thousands of years of monotonously repetitive behavior, a sharp increase in ritual and ceremony takes place beginning about 30,000 years ago, with art the lasting memento. Why?

Cro-Magnon appeared, and with it we brought our modern and magnificent neocortex. This is what changed tool technology from the traditions followed monotonously for thousands of years, first slowly, and then more and more quickly. The human neocortex entered into a fast feedback loop with the environment, which included other humans, and the process began to change tools and techniques, began the organization of information networks, established more permanent dwellings, and left the first signs of social hierarchy. That fast feedback loop, as Pfeiffer suggests, was nothing less than a swiftly evolving cultural change that demanded a response to new ways of looking at life, new social complexities, and (most important to my point here) new ways of storing and disseminating information.

In the new world of Homo sapiens, survival demanded new ways of transmitting, from generation to generation and before writing was invented, the contents of an expanding tribal encyclopedia, a body of new rules and old traditions about how to do things and how to relate to others. Viewed in this context, ceremony is a form of communication. The mystery and the illusions and all the planning that went into selection of the caves, the locations wherein images were placed, served to imprint vital knowledge about how things must be done. It surely also served to manage conflict, to reinforce group cohesion, and transfer knowledge quickly, fully, and effectively.

Cast against the other events of the Upper Paleolithic—the emergence of Homo sapiens and our powerful neocortex; the population explosion that also took place; the difficulties of mere survival in the glacial periods—it seems not only plausible but probable that the arts were employed socially, to organize knowledge for effective, long-term retention and retrieval, the visual arts taking advantage of the neocortex's singular capacity for image processing: perceiving images, storing, and recalling them in a code of such breathtaking economy that we still don't fully understand the process.

A contemporary example of art put to such uses (and then some) is Australian aboriginal art, the oldest continuous human art form in the world, known as Dreamings. Dreamings are founding or creation stories, when all the elements of the known world were created. But the Dreaming is also the inner, the spiritual dimension of the present. Thus we find encoded upon a piece of painted bark from, say, North Arnhemland in northern Australia, an entire cosmogony that reminds initiates not only where they came from, but how they must behave. The images are sacred texts, where each element stands for knowledge that will be passed from one generation to the next in a particular kinship group.

Let me make it clear: these images of the Dreamings—and we now believe it to be the case with Paleolithic art—are not mere illustrations. Rather, they contain encoded knowledge that can be imparted to and later evoked in the human brain by attending to the significance of their visual symbols.

What have we here, then, but the first art as a representation of knowledge?

Well. This is strange indeed for those of us raised in the modernist tradition of art, where the artist's task has been to invent a personal reality within and then represent it in a public formalization. It's stranger still to those of us raised in the tradition of texts as the best and perhaps the only legitimate source of knowledge.

Then we're reminded by art historian E. H. Grombrich that for hundreds of years, even Western painting was considered to be the premiere cumulative discipline. The painter's task was to represent knowledge about the world faithfully, whether human or spiritual, whether visual or textual—to attain, in short, true knowledge.

For the reciprocal exchanges between art and knowledge do not end with the Upper Paleolithic. Everybody is familiar with the ultimate renaissance man, Leonardo, who did not believe he knew something until he could realize it in a drawing or a painting, until he could make a visual representation of his knowledge. In his notebooks he wrote: "If poetry deals with moral philosophy, painting deals with natural philosophy. Poetry describes the action of the mind, painting considers what the mind may effect by the motions of the body." He knew a great deal—he was simultaneously a theoretician, an experimentalist, a speculator, an idiosyncratic tease.

Moving beyond Leonardo, art historian Svetlana Alpers makes a persuasive case that northern art of the seventeenth century, particularly Dutch painting, is part of a larger cultural fascination and delight in the observation of things seen and set forth in words and pictures as the basis for new knowledge. The seventeenth-century Dutch believed that knowledge is visible and possible. Thus all those still lifes, landscapes, and elaborate maps are the embodiments—not the symbols or the signs, but the very embodiments—of knowledge. The Dutch tradition is concerned not with the similarities between things, but the individual identity of each thing and each person in the world: such particularity was the era's notion of truth. The seventeenth-century Dutch trusted their eyes, and trusted them augmented by lenses—the microscope, telescope, or ordinary eye-glasses—and held that visual representations offered new and concrete knowledge of the real world. (This was the first time, by the way, that images appeared in textbooks, thanks largely to the ideas of Johann Comenius, who proposed a shift from instruction in words to instruction in the things to which the words referred—visual representations of those things, images of them, systematically arranged. He argued that seeing a dissection was more instructive than reading about one, and it was at his urging that children's books were illustrated, to aid the acquisition of knowledge.)

Dutch art is the representation of knowledge: it is art where the world and the human crafting of it meet, art that gives us the capacity to comprehend—to know—ourselves.

For example, in *Cows and Herdsmen by a River* by Albert Cuyp, now in the Frick Collection, we have an embodiment of distinct knowledge: knowledge of a real, not idealized, human being; real, not idealized cows, birds, clouds—the real thing, so carefully observed that at last it is known. However, such particularity offended practitioners in other traditions. Consider what Sir Joshua Reynolds said about this painting nearly a hundred years later: "Cattle and a shepherd by Albert Cuyp, the best I ever saw of him; the figure is likewise better than usual: but the employment which he has given the shepherd in his solitude is not very poetical; it must, however, be allowed to be truth and nature; he is catching fleas or something worse" (Alpers).

Poor Sir Joshua. He wrote those words lamenting the distance between truth and poetry in 1781. In 1816, not half a century later, another British painter, John Constable, would say this: "Painting is a science and should be pursued as an inquiry into the laws of nature. Why, then, may not landscape painting be considered as a branch of natural philosophy, or which pictures are but the experiments?" (Gombrich).

He meant this literally. Painting was a means of doing physics. And what you could know about the physical world must then be represented—not transcribed, but re-presented—in a medium called painting. We take Constable's illusionism very much for granted these days, but he wasn't making copies of landscapes, he was making *reminders* (as he put it), a *model* we would now say, of the true nature of clouds and sky, trees and thatched roofs and a horse on a barge. Constable was trying to produce what he called "the evanescent effects of nature's chiaroscuro" on a canvas using a medium (oil paints) that did not permit perfect matching between the thing to be represented and the medium. Gombrich puts it:

> What a painter inquires into is not the nature of the physical world but the nature of our reactions to it. He is not concerned with causes but with the mechanisms of certain effects. His is a psychological problem — that of conjuring up a convincing image despite the fact that not one individual shade corresponds to what we call "reality." In order to understand this puzzle — as far as we can claim to understand it as yet — science has had to explore the capacity of our minds to register relationships rather than individual elements.

The knowledge embodied in a Constable painting is the knowledge of how the mind processes retinal images. Yes, we say, that certainly is a country scene; that certainly is Salisbury Cathedral. But it isn't. It's John Constable's knowledge of how the retina processes, embodied in paint on canvas. The Impressionists couldn't be far behind, and they weren't.

It all makes great sense once we stop to remember how much of our brain is taken up by the visual cortex. We catch on fast when somebody draws us a picture. Only primates have the visual subsystem that permits sustained and detailed scrutiny of shape, color, and surface properties of objects, thus giving us the ability to assign multiple visual attributes to an object and correlate its parts; in fact to perceive objects just as the early twentieth-century Gestalt psychologists were sure (but could not prove) humans perceived visually. At present scientists speculate that this ability is tied to the temporal lobes, part of the fabulous neocortex we've already met as engine for the Paleolithic information explosion (Livingstone and Hubel).

If the current view of paleo-anthropologists is tenable, that Paleolithic art was a tribal memory, intended to preserve and disseminate tribal wisdom; and if Svetlana Alpers's claim for Dutch art as the embodiment of knowledge is a plausible one; we must nevertheless take care not to fall into the simplistic assumption that images are mere containers, amphoras from which we pour information or knowledge as needed. The matter is much more subtle. *How* we represent knowledge visually—which visual mode, which scopic regime we choose—makes a profound difference. And this is true of other representations as well, including language, text, music, and mathematics.

In the early 1950s, Herbert Read was already addressing this question. Art has been and still is the essential instrument in the development of human consciousness, Read declared, adding what he called an "immensely presumptuous claim": art is the activity that permits symbolic discourse, and religion, philosophy, and science follow as consequent modes of thought. Art is—and guides—the expansion of human consciousness. The history of the human intellect is the history of artistic development, and not vice versa. As Read writes, "It is only in so far as the artist establishes symbols for the representation of reality that mind, as a structure of thought, can take shape. The artist establishes these symbols by becoming conscious of new aspects of reality, and by representing his consciousness of these new aspects of reality in plastic or poetic images." I hesitate to go quite so far, though Read has not a little historical evidence on his side. But will it be so in the future?

Surely much of the world has proved to be invisible to our eyes. (Since visible matter accounts for perhaps only 2 or 3 percent of the universe, astrophysicists like to joke that, chances are, everything we see is only a statistical error on a cosmic scale.) The topics of deepest interest to know about now—the fundamental nature of matter; the behavior of various natural systems, human and otherwise; the behavior of artificial systems created by humans—are invisible in another way. These topics can only be described in terms of schemata: their very complexity hides their order, though order we believe it to be. All this confounds our European-derived faith that seeing appearances is knowing reality.

So this is how we have known; this is how we know, how we demonstrate that we know: by means of images, by means of the text . . . although, as can be seen throughout this volume, this is in fact changing before our eyes.

We are accustomed to going to *texts* for knowledge. Despite the slightly pejorative air of "book learning," scholars, at least, still think of texts as the ultimate representation. If we go to images for knowledge, they're usually documentaries on public television, *Nova, Nature,* and the like. Entertaining as these films are, their technology, a determinate process, does not give us the participatory or experiential knowledge we get other ways, by being there on the African savanna, or even by absorbing knowledge with the participation required of us by texts (or for that matter by art, which is not the same thing as visual images, but that's a different story).

I am speculating here that text encodes knowledge with great economy and abstraction, and imparts new knowledge about the world, but just as important, imparts new ways of knowing. I am also speculating that another reason for the prevalence of text, along with its technological advantages of cheap mass production, is the level of attentiveness it demands from us to get anything at all out of it. We can scan visual images more casually, with less effort and focus, but we get less out of them in that state of mind too. There is no text equivalent to background music.

How *will* we know? The answer: We will know many different ways. The primacy of text is over, though text is hardly dead.

Roland Barthes famously declared the death of the author twenty years ago, innocent of the fact that three years earlier, Ted Nelson had already summoned the execution squad in the form of hypertext. The lone author dons the silk blindfold and stands against the wall, but text is here to stay. It will be joined by other epistemologies or ways of knowing, and high among them will be a return to visual knowledge. But, I suspect, for that way of knowing to be as effective as text, knowledge must be encoded in a way that will demand the same level of attentiveness that text now does.

And here, I hope, we will be very careful, very self-conscious of how we do this, thinking more rigorously about the many choices we can make in visual representations and about which is best for each purpose. This might seem a capitulation to trends in our culture that make even ordinary levels of literacy difficult, but I think not; I believe it's a separate problem that must be addressed in its own right.

Computers couldn't always exhibit images, just as they couldn't always exhibit text: their first output was numbers. When the first computer-generated images began to appear in the mid-1960s, one enthusiastic fellow said: "Wonderful! Nature provided us with vocal cords and language to express ideas as fast as we think, but didn't give us the capacity to make pictures as fast as we can visualize images; now the computer is going to make up for nature's neglect." You don't need to have read Michel Foucault to detect a certain degree of naivete here.

The ability to make images as fast as we imagine them hasn't quite happened yet, and an artist whose work I have recently studied and written about, Harold Cohen, would argue vehemently that most computer imaging has nothing at all to do with the way we make images in our heads. For one thing, most computer imaging is a straight adaptation of photographic representation—the *appearance* of things, the way things appear to our retinas—whereas other visual modes of representation, and possibly the ones we use in our heads, aren't photographic at all but deal with the *structure* of things—they deal, in other words, with what we know, not just the light and shadow and shapes that fire cones on the retina. The act of seeing, he'd say, includes what happens behind the retina too. For a creature with human intelligence, seeing mainly takes place behind the retina. To put it another way, what we see is shaped by what we know.

Harold Cohen first began constructing his computer program called Aaron nearly twenty years ago to explore certain hypotheses he entertained about human art-making behavior. This autonomous program has evolved over the years, and the drawings it makes have changed accordingly: what accounts for the change in the drawings is the program's acquisition of new knowledge (supplied, I should say, by Harold Cohen, since Aaron has no way of acquiring knowledge on its own: its autonomy lies in its ability to make drawings without human intervention once knowledge is acquired).

At its earliest point, the program had very little knowledge, and the shapes, as charming as they are, are simple and straightforward. In its intermediate stages, the artist began supplying the program with some knowledge of occlusion, of space, of composition on the picture plane. Finally, as the program went figurative, a great deal of knowledge had to be given it—knowledge not only about how to draw, how to represent, but also knowledge about the real world.

For example, objects called humans consist of a trunk, a head, two arms, and two legs, and they hold themselves a certain way and can only move in certain ways; such things as rocks and plants also exist in the world, and they have certain special properties. The different degree of sophistication the images exhibit rests solely on the different amounts of knowledge embedded, first, in the program's representational structures and second, following from the first, in the drawing's representations.

Cohen's singular achievement has been to represent knowledge about the process of art making, as opposed to merely presenting its product, although that knowledge resides in a dynamic computer program. But even the images the program produces are unique among computer graphical representations. Most computer graphics, as I argue in *Aaron's Code*, have until recently relied on a kind of photographic realism, representing the appearance, as opposed to the structure, of things in the world.

However, now comes a modern parallel to the seventeenth-century Dutch and their intention to capture knowledge by images: the newly celebrated power of "visualizing" supercomputer output. When scientists realized they could not make anything out of the billions of closely spaced numbers that blast out of a high-speed computation, firehose style, they turned to visual representations of those patterns. Such representations, such visualizations — of the dynamics of storms, of cellular behavior, of colliding galaxies, of orthopedic prostheses, of virtually anything scientists know how to describe formally — employ color, shading, two and three dimensions, and above all movement over time. They too serve the purposes most seventeenth-century Dutch art served: to exhibit careful observations, permit corrections; to inspire scientists to understand further, and therefore to elucidate the world. The supercomputer visualizations represent what is known and, more important, suggest what might further be known.

So we're in a transitional stage, and I must predict gingerly about how we will, in the future, know.

I have mentioned two ways of knowing, textual and visual, without saying how either way of knowing expands knowledge or enlarges our grasp of the world. Herbert Read, you remember, asserted that art did this: art, he claimed, is the essential instrument in the development of human consciousness. He meant the visual arts, though like every good equal-opportunity employer, he mentions poetics too. I think one thing he was driving at was the variety of visual representations art permits: each mode, each scopic regime, whether Cartesian perspective or Baroque painterliness, "photographic realism" or abstract and stylized carving, is superb for some purposes and impossible for others.

I certainly concur with Read that human consciousness develops by being able to envisage alternative realities. Consciousness, what was once called the faculty of contemplation, is, according to Susan Sontag, "wider and more varied than action"; we can think about things without necessarily acting them out. That faculty is nourished by art and speculative thought. Read, I think, means the same thing when he claims art is a representation of new aspects of reality that reshape the structure of thought, keeping the sensations vivid, the power of reasoning keen. This all puts me in mind of virtual realities.

Virtual realities are computer simulations that permit the sensation of participating in a reality that doesn't really exist: it is virtual, not actual. Virtual realities don't have to look like cinematographic depictions of life as we know it. They can be like dreams (indeed, dreams are precomputational virtual realities). And like dreams, virtual realities sometimes offer the opportunity for experiential knowledge, as opposed to book learning.

Though the idea seems science fiction, its nonfictional development is under way by hardheaded types who can see many applications: as a powerful information and entertainment medium, as a means of training, as a means of long-range planning. Business executives also suspect that productivity in an information-based society might rest as much with consumers of information as with information producers, and what better way to increase their productivity than to open new realities to them? Again, the dream is a good analogy: we can simultaneously participate in the action of a dream and be a spectator; logic in dreams is idiosyncratic; and the symbolic content of dreams is fascinating, no matter which school of psychological interpretation you subscribe to.

I came across some of these ideas in a discussion carried on electronically within a group of executives and futurists. But there was an important dissent. It came from Rusty Schweickart, who first reminded everyone that he wasn't antisimulation, since as an astronaut he had entrusted his life to what he'd learned from simulations.

But he wondered whether these virtual realities under discussion would simply be somebody else's idea of the future, or would they—more usefully—provoke the viewer to imagine his or her own future?

A pertinent question. A correct answer to that question means choosing the best representation, whether visual, textual, or for all I know audial, tactile, olfactory, or a clever combination of several modes, for the purpose at hand, depending on what knowledge is to be represented, and for which purposes. It means recognizing that within each of those major modes of representation there are many possibilities, and being aware of what might be the best for the particular purpose at hand.

Our culture has much knowledge to pass on to its young, to outsiders, to its forgetful elders, and, contrary to Allan Bloom and the die-hard Western cultural supremacists, there is essential knowledge from other cultures that merits being learned. Finally, there is what we would *like* to know; what could possibly be valuable to know in the future.

In sum, knowledge of different kinds is best represented in all its complexity for different purposes by different kinds of knowledge representations. Choosing *la representation juste* (words, images, or anything else) is not at all an obvious thing: in fact, it's magnificently delicate. But we have not had much choice until now because text, whether the best representation for certain purposes or not, has dominated our intellectual lives until now. The computer is changing this.

In this world we are each, as the initiates once were in the European caves, a little anxious, a little puzzled, led forward into the unknown by guides and mentors, humbled before the responsibility of learning the tribal wisdom, secretly harboring a hope that someday we might add to it ourselves. In the computer, we have fashioned for ourselves a means of taking advantage of all our biological capacities to learn and to know, and to seek and find new knowledge; and this is—someday—how we *will* know.

Discussion

TUMAN.   I wonder if you fear that over time, as more and more "reading" (information processing?) takes place at a computer terminal, text and graphics may follow Gresham's law, with the more popular currency of graphics inevitably driving out the less popular text. While there does seem to be something of a balance between the two — in, for example, print advertising (admittedly, hardly a reassuring thought to some) — text seems to have only a marginal role in a medium like television or film where there are moving pictures accompanied by sound.

LANHAM.   Your phrasing doesn't quite conceal how the question prejudices the answer. Greshman's law shows how "bad money" drives out "good money." To compare the icon/alphabet ratio to Gresham's law is to imply that visual information is "bad" information as against the "good" information of alphabetical text. This is certainly how the text-based academic world is going to see the matter, but we ought to formulate the question in a more neutral way.

Is it not the case that information which is more easily and effectively communicated graphically rather than alphabetically will increasingly be communicated in the easier and more effective way? Clearly, the answer is Yes, and a good thing too. We will find, I would guess, that all kinds of information will lend itself to graphic presentation, and often in unexpected ways. The current explosion in scientific visualization is providing a case in point.

Perhaps too we can begin to model conceptual thinking in three-dimensional graphic ways. I have been playing around, for example, with how we might model rhetorical figuration — model how it works, what lines of force it exerts — using three-dimensional animation. Perhaps all prose style, and not only prose style, can be modeled in this way.

Computer animation has been hailed by several commentators as the final emancipation of the visual thinker, of the right-brainer, of the *bricoleur* as against the theoretician. We all know people who can watch something being done and then replicate it but have a hard time learning the same process from books. Computer graphics just re-moves the alphabetic roadblock.

I also think that computer graphics offer great opportunities for instructional programs for "remedial" learning of all sorts. Much of the "backwardness" thus addressed may be just that some people learn better by sight and sound than by alphabetic language. Why not use this ability, not to bypass the world of alphabetic reading, but to introduce these different kinds of learners to it?

TUMAN. Doesn't the promise of true multimedia computer plat-forms over the next decade spell the end, not the mere modification, of print literacy as we have known it?

LANHAM. No, I don't for a moment think so. We will certainly learn, in ways not known before, what print is really good for and what graphics can do better. We will certainly see new mixtures of sight, sound, and alphabet; and we may, *horresco referens*, see the multi-media presentation of the sacred alphabetic texts of the political and literary canons. All these developments seem to me to promise an expansion of human learning and expression. Print literacy may not be dominant, as it has been in the past, but so what? It will be complemented and enhanced, not weakened. In fact, my bet would be that its powers emerge enhanced, when the revolution has taken a full turn or two. Certainly things will be different. And certainly this difference will be revolutionary for the diploma elite, in and out of the university—and they hardly seemed to be prepared!

TUMAN. While IBM, Apple, and Radio Shack continue strug-gling to convince us we all need personal computers in our homes, in part to help prepare our children for the new technological age, we are only slowly realizing that our children are already spending countless hours with computers, albeit in the form of ever more sophisticated video games attached to our television sets. Your essay suggests that our children are undoubtedly learning something about the world through these games, but most of us haven't a clue as to what that might be.

MCCORDUCK. I'm not sure I have a clue as to what kids are learning in front of their screens. I've asked. Most of them are too young to articulate it, and anyway, how do you describe the air you breathe? I suspect—I think I detect—a whole different way of looking at the world, an ease with virtual reality, cyberspace, that people who haven't grown up with computing simply can't have. We still talk about, believe in, uppercase Reality in a way they don't—or perhaps our reality is subsumed as no more than a special case of their reality.

And that sounds to me like they're not learning much about the world, at least our world, in front of those screens, so much as they're constructing a new reality, a new world. This has happened several times in human history, and it's a nice debate to try and decide whether technology precipitates such changes or whether technology comes along in time to enable a change that was taking place any way.

So: they're the ones who are going to have to reinterpret the First, Fourth, and Fifth Amendments to make sure that the electronic frontier is as wonderful as it can be. They're going to make our philosophizing about it look as dopey as current biology makes natural philosophy look. The best our generation can do is keep things technologically and legally fluid until the new generation is old enough to have some wisdom about these matters.

PROVENZO.   As I discuss in *Video Kids*, video games, television, and motion pictures are increasingly linked with one another. Four of the ten most popular television programs listed by children in grades one through six at a local elementary school were based on video games. These included *Teenage Mutant Ninja Turtles*, *Chip and Dale Rescue Rangers*, the *Mario Brothers Super Show*, and *Duck Tales*. Although these results are limited to a survey in a single school, it is probably reasonable to assume that these figures are typical for other parts of the country.

The culture of computers in the form of video games is becoming increasingly merged with that of other media such as television. Combined with the advent of hypertext and hypermedia the implications are profound.

Final Thoughts

It would be helpful to close this volume with some practical advice for classroom teachers—answers, drawn from all these speculations about computers and literacy, to the proverbial question, How to prepare for Monday morning? As indicated in the introduction, all teachers and administrators concerned with language education must soon make difficult, concrete decisions regarding computers. It is in the process of contemplating these changes that educators rightly seek out sound advice (until recently, mostly about word processing) at workshops and in print—What impact will it have on my students' writing? Will it really encourage them to revise more? Or (the subject of a current debate) does it matter if they do it on Macintosh or IBM computers?— the very questions that, as a rule, have not been directly addressed here.

The distinction between practical advice and theoretical specula-tion may not be nearly as great as it seems. The IBM-versus-Macintosh debate for example, which we may be tempted to dismiss as a foolish feud between partisans, is in fact deeply enmeshed in the very theoretical speculations that form the center of this volume: Is writing going to continue to be what it largely has been, at least for the last century—the linear arrangement of pure text—or is it going to become something else perhaps, text integrated with graphics, either printed as complex documents (with headlines and other graphical cues serving rhetorical purposes) or displayed as a nonlinear series of artfully designed screens? In other words, are we to consider writing mainly in terms of the internal structure of ideas, and thus choose a character-based (MS-DOS) word processor, one that favors the ma-nipulation of text, or are we to expand our notion of writing to include pictures, page design, and eventually screen presentation, and thus choose a graphics-based (Macintosh, or alternately a new Microsoft Windows) word processor?

Or perhaps the question itself is backward: that it is the personal selection of the word processor (and operating system) that largely determines one's understanding of the future of literacy; that theories about wholesale changes in the nature of literacy (as presented by most of the contributors here), in some key ways, reflect the decision these individual writers have already made in selecting their own word processors. Reduced to a trivial level, one is tempted to say that theories about the death of the linear text and the triumph of hypermedia reflect the fact that these writers themselves are using Macintosh computers. But this point may really be not that trivial; beneath may lie the realization that technology (here the ability to integrate text and graphics and to work with screens in a nonlinear fashion) is finally a driving force in how we communicate and in turn establish, through curriculum and elsewhere, the norms for proper communication—that is, what it means to be *literate*.

To the extent that we are driven by technology, then certain things may not be hard to predict. At least for the foreseeable future, it seems that most of the technological improvements in both hardware and software will be directed at better integrating pictures (and sound) with text; or, stated differently, that the fairly primitive, inexpensive computers and basic software now widely available already provide students with most of the text-editing power they are ever likely to need for producing "better" traditional writing (better organized school essays, with more evidence, better transitions, and so on). Thus, if we want only to continue writing as we have in the past, the computer revolution in some sense may already be over.

No one, however, believes the computer revolution is in fact over, and, while individual teachers and perhaps entire institutions may be able to freeze certain aspects of their curriculum, we also need to recognize that our role as educators is likely to turn out to be far less important than the changes already happening around us—more precisely, above and below us—almost entirely outside our (or any-body's) control. Specifically, from below, children are increasingly exposed to various forms of computer-driven, interactive video technologies. As discussed by McCorduck and Provenzo, Nintendo with its novel, hypertextual means of presenting narrative as a series of choices or challenges is here to stay, as is Prodigy and other electronic information-gathering systems. As Ulmer demonstrates, our students are likely to come to us deeply acculturated in the notion of "reading" as a kind of literal exploration of new territory and "writing" as a kind of pasting together of diverse materials. Meanwhile, from above, that is, from the workplace, more college graduates will earn their living by mastering the ability to move effortlessly through massive information storage and retrieval systems that already provide the basis of much economic and professional activity. Indeed, the most radical changes in freshman composition programs (for better or worse) are already occurring as a result of this downward pressure, in writing programs at those high-tech universities with close ties to successful information-based institutions—corporate and governmental.

Faced with a host of changes we cannot control—and over time may be unable to resist—the single most important question before us may finally have less to do with practice and more with attitude: How we as teachers (or parents, administrators, citizens) should react to the computerization of print. Should we celebrate or despair over the changes that seem imminent? And here there is agreement among many of these contributors that computers offer us real possibility for progress. Some, like George Landow, would have us see new forms of computer-based literacy as strengthening the critical skills that remain widely accepted as the goal of college education: hence the belief that hypermedia makes all students better readers of traditional English literature. Others, like Richard Lanham, would have us see new forms of computer-based literacy as geometrically expanding (through both interactivity and graphics) the range of human experience involved in thinking critically: hence the belief that hypermedia radically alters (for the better) the kinds of things students do when they study English literature.

Yet the "peril" in the title of this volume and in comments scattered throughout its contents suggest a possibility that the very notion of critical thought may be tied to print technology and, thus, that new computer-based forms of literacy may well engender different and not necessarily better (or more "critical") modes of thought. This is an especially difficult matter to address, given that all of us, contributors and readers alike, are masters of the very print discourse that is under possible duress. Hence the question we cannot answer is, What the study of English literature (or, more generally, the literacy of the past) is likely to become—not for today's literate authors and their students turned on to hypermedia after years of successfully working with print, but for future students and teachers, those in the year 2092, who grow up in a world where even the oldest adults have themselves been fully submersed in an electronic culture where text, sound, and pictures (moving as well as still) are all regularly accessed through the same computer monitor. There will obviously still be books, in such a world, and people studying literature—the question is whether such activities will be any more pertinent to the main business of education then, than the study of calligraphy (a remnant of a still earlier literacy technology) is today.

Those of us with miserable handwriting, and little prospect of mastering such a small motor skill, have little to lament about this particular change. One would be hard put to argue that human culture has somehow been impoverished by the loss of handwriting skills brought on by the introduction of typewriters and then word processors. Even if we can agree that the computers will make us less critical, less "literate" in some old sense (something we obviously cannot agree on), we still may not have sufficient reason to decry the future. The reading and writing practices of print technology only became widely incorporated into the curriculum in the last hundred years—and certainly not everyone is convinced that the literacy curriculum during this period has done much to advance our collective well-being. A heavy indoctrination into print culture has not seemed to cure the world of many ills this past century, and some would argue it may have even contributed to them. Surely we cannot dismiss the possibility that an entirely different sort of computer-based literacy may offer us surer grounds for human progress in the next century. The difficulty here is that none of us really knows. "Whither computers and literacy?" I once prompted Pamela McCorduck; "Get set to be surprised," she aptly responded. Those of us who pose as experts are finally not as helpful as we'd like to be. What we see in the future—promise or peril—too often reflects our sense of the past: the Whigs among us (and in this collection they are the majority) see progress; the Tories, doom.

Seeking a more unifying note on which to close, I asked McCorduck another question: What are we most likely to miss if books disappear entirely? After musing about her own children's reading and the fact that authors, unlike most people she meets, are more interesting in print than in person, she concluded with a resonant afterthought: "Perhaps we really are the last generation that cares about such things. After all, the whole thrust of the computer revolution is to transcend the limits of the physical. So coming generations won't miss what they never had."

Here then was a major chord on which to close, the undeniable value of documenting this change in a volume such as this. The attitudes collected here constitute a time-capsule—preserving for future students of literacy a record of what the thinkers, so successfully acculturated into print culture (possibly "the last [such] generation"), had to say about the profound impact, for better or worse, that nearly everyone agrees computers are about to have on our practice of reading and writing.

Works Cited
Notes on Contributors

Works Cited

Aho, Alfred V., and Jeffrey D. Ullman. *Theory of Parsing, Translation, and Compiling.* Vol. 1, *Parsing.* Englewood Hills, N.J.: Prentice Hall, 1973.

Alpers, Svetlana. *The Art of Describing: Dutch Art in the Seventeenth Century.* Chicago: University of Chicago Press, 1983.

Alschuler, Liora. "Hand-Crafted Hypertext—Lessons from the ACM Experiment," in *The Society of Text.* Edited by Edward Barrett. Cambridge, Mass.: MIT Press, 1989.

Ambron, Sueann, and Kristina Hooper, eds. *Interactive Multimedia.* Redmond, Wash.: Microsoft Press, 1988.

Andriole, Stephen J., ed. *Applications in Artificial Intelligence.* Princeton, N.J.: Petrocelli Books, 1985.

Aristotle. "Organon." *The Basic Works of Aristotle.* Edited by Richard McKeon. New York: Random, 1941.

Balestri, Diane Pelkus. "Softcopy and Hard: Wordprocessing and Writing Process." *Academic Computing* (Feb. 1988): 14-17, 41-45.

Barthes, Roland. "From Work to Text." In *Textual Strategies: Perspectives in Post-Structural Criticism,* edited by Josue V. Harari, 73–81. Ithaca, N.Y.: Cornell University Press, 1979.

———. *S/Z.* Translated by Richard Miller. New York: Hill and Wang, 1974.

Bateson, Gregory. *Steps to an Ecology of Mind.* New York: Ballantine, 1972.

Baudry, Jean-Louis. "The Apparatus." In *Apparatus,* edited by Theresa Hak Kyung Cha. New York: Tanam, 1980.

Beeman, William O., Kenneth T. Anderson, Gail Bader, James Larkin, Anne P. McClard, Patrick McQuillan, and Mark Shields. *Intermedia: A Case Study of Innovation in Higher Education.* Providence, R.I.: Office of Program Analysis, Institute for Research in Information and Scholarship, 1988.

Benjamin, Walter. *Reflections: Essays, Aphorisms, Autobiographical Writings.* Translated by Edmund Jephcott. New York: Harcourt Brace Jovanovich, 1978.

———. "The Work of Art in the Age of Mechanical Reproduction." In *Illuminations,* edited by Hannah Arendt. New York: Schocken, 1967.

Bennett, William. *To Reclaim a Legacy: A Report on the Humanities in Higher Education.* Washington, D.C.: National Endowment for the Humanities, 1984.

Bentham, Jeremy. *Panopticon; or the Inspection-House.* Vol. 4 of *The Works of Jeremy Bentham.* New York: Russell & Russell, 1962.

Billington, Ray Allen. "Foreword." In *Trails West.* Washington, D.C.: National Geographic. 1979.

Birnbaum, Lawrence, and Mallory Selfridge. "Conceptual Analysis of Natural Language." In *Inside Computer Understanding,* edited by Roger C. Schank and Christopher Riesbeck, 318–53. Hillsdale, N.J.: Erlbaum, 1981.

Bobrow, Daniel, and Terry Winograd. "An Overview of KRL, a Knowledge Representation Language." *Cognitive Science* 1 (1977): 3–46.

Bolter, Jay David. "Beyond Word Processing: The Computer as a New Writing Space." *Language and Communication* 9 (1989): 129–42.

———. *Turing's Man: Western Culture in the Computer Age.* Chapel Hill: University of North Carolina Press, 1984.

———. *Writing Space: The Computer, Hypertext, and the History of Writing.* Hillsdale, N.J.: Erlbaum, 1991.

Bolter, Jay, Michael Joyce, and John B. Smith. *Storyspace.* Computer software. Apple Macintosh. Eastgate Systems, 1990.

Boughton, John M. "The Surrender of Control: Computer Literacy as Political Socialization of the Child." In *The Computer in Education: A Critical Perspective,* edited by Douglas Sloan. New York: Teachers College Press, 1984.

Bowers, C. A. *The Cultural Dimensions of Educational Computing: Understanding the Non-Neutrality of Technology.* New York: Teachers College Press, 1988.

Brachman, Ronald J. "On the Epistemological Status of Semantic Networks." In *Associative Networks: Representation and Use of Knowledge by Computers,* edited by Nicholas V. Findler, 3–50. New York: Academic Press, 1979.

Brand, Stewart. *The Media Lab: Inventing the Future at M.I.T.* New York: Viking, 1988.

Bridwell, Lillian, Geoffrey Sirc, and Robert Brooke. "Revising and Computing: Case Studies of Student Writers." In *The Acquisition of Written Language: Revision and Response,* edited by Sarah Freedman, 172–94. Norwood, N.J.: Ablex, 1985.

Bridwell-Bowles, Lillian, Parker Johnson, and Steven Brehe. "Composing and Computers: Case Studies of Experienced Writers." In *Writing in Real Time: Modelling Production Processes,* edited by A. Matsuhashi, 81–107. Norwood, N.J.: Ablex, 1987.

Burke, Kenneth. *Collected Poems.* Berkeley: University of California Press, 1968.

Calvin, William H. *The Cerebral Symphony: Seashore Reflections on the Structure of Consciousness.* New York: Bantam, 1990.

———. "Darwinian View of Language: A Well-Formed Sentence as Analogous to Speciation and the Immune Response." *Society of Neuroscience Abstracts* 15 (1989).

Campbell, Jeremy. *The Improbable Machine.* New York: Simon and Schuster, 1989.

Carbonell, Jaime G. "The Role of User Modeling in Natural Language Interface Design." In *Applications in Artificial Intelligence,* edited by Stephen J. Andriole, 213–26. Princeton, N.J.: Petrocelli Books, 1985.

Carroll, Lewis. *The Philosopher's Alice.* Edited by Peter Heat. New York: St. Martin's, 1974.

Case, Donald P. "Processing Professorial Words: Personal Computers and the Writing Habits of University Professors." *College Composition and Communication* 36 (1985): 317-22.

Chapman, Paul H. *The Man Who Led Columbus to America.* Atlanta, Ga.: Judson, 1973.

Chardak, Burt. "Domino's Pizza Plans a 'Big Brother' Act." *Miami Herald,* 10 September 1989: 1f.

Charrow, Veda. *Let the Rewriter Beware.* Washington, D.C.: Document Design Center, American Institutes for Research, 1979.

Christo: Running Fence—Sonoma and Marin Counties, California 1972–76. Photographs by Gianfranco Corgoni. Chronicle by Calvin Tomkins. Narrative by David Bourdon. New York: Harry N. Abrams, 1978.

Collis, Betty. "Manipulating Critical Variables: A Framework for Improving the Impact of Computers in the School Environment." Presentation at EURIT88, Lausanne, July 1988.

Conklin, Jeffrey. "Hypertext: An Introduction and a Survey." *IEEE Computer* 20 (1987): 17–41.

Coughlin, Ellen K. "Literacy: Excitement of New Field Attracts Scholars of Literature." *Chronicle of Higher Education* 9 January 1985: 1, 10.

Crary, Jonathan. "Eclipse of the Spectacle." In Wallis, 183–94.

Crimp, Douglas. "The Museum in Ruins." In *Anti-Aesthetic: Essays on Postmodern Culture,* edited by Hal Foster. Bay City, Wash.: Bay City Press, 1983.

Cullingford, Richard E., and B. A. Onyshkevych. "Lexicon-driven Machine Translation." In *Proceedings of the Conference on Theoretical and Methodological Issues in Machine Translation of Natural Languages,* edited by Sergei Nirenburg, 75–115. Hamilton, N.Y.: Colgate University, August 1985.

da Vinci, Leonardo. *The Notebooks.* Vol. 1. Compiled and edited by Jean Paul Richter. New York: Dover, 1970.

Davis, Mike. *Prisoners of the American Dream: Politics and Economy in the History of the U.S. Working Class.* London: Verso, 1987.

de Certeau, Michael. *The Practice of Everyday Life.* Translated by Steven Rendall. Berkeley: University of California Press, 1984.

De Maria, Luciana, ed. *Martinetti e il futurismo.* Milano: Mondadori, 1973.

Derber, Charles. *Power in the Highest Degree: Professionals and the New Mandarin Order.* New York: Oxford University Press, 1990.

Derrida, Jacques. "Chora." In *Poikilia: Etudes offertes a Jean Pierre Verdant,* 265–96. Paris: HESS, 1987.

Dissanayake, Ellen. *What Is Art For?* Seattle: University of Washington Press, 1988.

Dover, Victor B. "Image Network: Visualizing Future Environments." *Cadence,* February 1987.

Drexler, Eric. *Engines of Creation.* Garden City, N. Y.: Doubleday, 1986.

Dreyfus, Hubert. *What Computers Can't Do: The Limits of Artificial Intelligence.* Revised edition. New York: Harper, 1979.

Dreyfus, Herbert L., and Stuart E. Dreyfus. "Putting Computers in Their Proper Place." In *The Computer in Education: A Critical Perspective,* edited by Douglas Sloan. New York: Teachers College Press, 1984.

Ehrenreich, Barbara. *Fear of Falling: The Inner Life of the Middle Class.* New York: Pantheon, 1989.

Eisenstein, Elizabeth. *The Printing Press as an Agent of Change: Communications and Cultural Transformations in Early-Modern Europe.* 2 vols. Cambridge: Cambridge University Press, 1979.

————. *The Printing Revolution in Early Europe.* Cambridge: Cambridge University Press, 1984.

Ellul, Jacques. *The Technological Society.* New York: Alfred A. Knopf, 1980.

Englebart, Doug, and Kristina Hooper. "The Augmentation System Framework." In *Interactive Multimedia,* edited by Sueann Ambron and Kristina Hooper. Redmond, Wash.: Microsoft Press, 1988

English Coalition. *Conference Report: Democracy through Language.* Ed. Richard Lloyd-Jones and Andrea Lunsford. Urbana, Ill.: NCTE, 1989.

Erdman, Richard C., ed. *Proceedings of the Conference on Applied Military Decision Aids and Support Systems: Technology, Engineering, and Opportunities.* Fort Wayne, Ind.: Magnavox DACE, 1986.

Fass, D. *Collative Semantics: A Description of the Meta5 Program.* Technical Report MCCS-86-23. New Mexico State University, Computer Research Laboratory, 1986.

Fish, Stanley. "Literature in the Reader: Affective Stylistics." In *Reader-Response Criticism: From Formalism to Post-Structuralism,* edited by Jane P. Tompkins, 70–100. Baltimore, Md.: Johns Hopkins University Press, 1980.

Flower, Linda, John R. Hayes, Linda Carey, Karen Schriver, and James Stratman. "Detection, Diagnosis, and the Strategies." *College Composition and Communication* 37 (February 1986): 16–55.

Foucault, Michel. *Discipline and Punish.* Translated by Alan Sheridan. New York: Random House, 1979.

Frank, Joseph. *The Widening Gyre: Crisis and Mastery in Modern Literature.* New Brunswick, N.J.: Rutgers University Press, 1963.

Franklin, Wayne. *Discoverers, Explorers, Settlers: The Diligent Writers of Early America.* Chicago: University of Chicago Press, 1979.

Freire, Paolo. *Pedagogy of the Oppressed.* Translated by Myra Bergman Ramos. New York: Continuum, 1988.

Gazdar, Gerald. "Unbounded Dependencies and Coordinate Structure." *Linguistic Inquiry* 12 (1981): 155–84.

Goffman, Erving. *Frame Analysis: An Essay on the Organization of Human Experience.* New York: Harper and Row, 1974.

Gombrich, E. H. *Art and Illusion: A Study in the Psychology of Pictorial Representation.* Princeton, N.J.: Princeton University Press, 1960.

Gould, Stephen Jay. *The Mismeasure of Man.* New York: Norton, 1981.

Grow, Gerald. "Lessons from the Computer Writing Problems of Professionals." *College Composition and Communication* 39.2 (May 1988): 217-20.

Haas, Christina. "How the Writing Medium Shapes the Writing Process: Effects of Word Processing on Planning." *Research in the Teaching of English* 23.2 (May 1989): 181-207.

Haas, Christina, and John R. Hayes. "'What Did I Just Say?' Reading Problems in Writing with the Machine." *Research in the Teaching of English* 20.1 (1986): 22-35.

Hansen, Wilfred J., and Christina Haas. "Reading and Writing with Computers: A Framework for Explaining Differences in Performance." *Communications of the ACM* 31 (1988): 1080-89.

Hastings, A. Waller. "Where Ideas Come From: The Computer and Collaborative Learning About Literature." Conference on College Composition and Communication, Seattle, March 1989.

Havelock, Eric A. *The Muse Learns to Write.* New Haven, Conn.: Yale University Press, 1986.

Heath, Stephen. "The Cinematic Apparatus: Technology as Historical and Cultural Form." In *The Cinematic Apparatus,* edited by Teresa de Lauretis and Stephen Heath. New York: St. Martin's, 1980.

Heidegger, Martin. *The Question Concerning Technology and Other Essays.* New York: Harper, 1972.

Hinton, Geoffrey E., and James A. Anderson, eds. *Parallel Models of Associative Memory.* Hillsdale, N.J.: Erlbaum. 1981.

Hirsch, E. D. *Cultural Literacy.* Boston: Houghton Mifflin, 1987.

Hirst, Graeme. *Semantic Interpretation Against Ambiguity.* CS-83-25, Brown University, 1983.

————. *Semantic Interpretation and the Resolution of Ambiguity.* ACL Series "Studies in Natural Language Processing." Cambridge: Cambridge University Press, 1987.

Hobbs, Jerry R. "Overview of the Tacitus Project." *Computational Linguistics* 12.3 (1986): 220–22.

Hoffman, Lily M. *The Politics of Knowledge: Activist Movements in Medicine and Planning.* Albany, N. Y.: State University of New York Press, 1990.

Howard, Alan. "Hypermedia and the Future of Ethnography." *Cultural Anthropology* 3 (1988): 304–15.

Iser, Wolfgang. *The Act of Reading.* Baltimore, Md.: Johns Hopkins University Press, 1978.

————. "The Reading Process: A Phenomenological Approach." In *Reader-Response Criticism: From Formalism to Post-Structuralism,* edited by Jane P. Tompkins, 50–69. Baltimore, Md.: Johns Hopkins University Press, 1980.

Joshi, Aravind, L. S. Levy, and M. Takahashi. "Tree Adjoining Grammars." *Journal of Computer Systems and Sciences* (March 1975): 75–84.

Joyce, Michael. "Siren Shapes: Exploratory and Constructive Hypertexts." *Academic Computing* (November 1988): 10–14, 37–42.

Katz, Ephraim. *The Film Encyclopedia.* New York: Perigee, 1979.

Knabb, Ken, ed. *Situationist International Anthology.* Berkeley, Calif.: Bureau of Public Secrets, 1981.

Kochan, Thomas, Harry Katz, and Robert McKersie. *The Transformation of Industrial Relations.* New York: Basic, 1986.

Kozma, Robert. *Learning Tool.* Computer software. Apple Macintosh.

Kuhn, Thomas. *The Structure of Scientific Revolutions.* 2nd. ed. Chicago: University of Chicago Press, 1970.

Landow, George. "Course Assignments Using Hypertext: The Example of Intermedia." *Journal of Research on Computing in Education* 21 (1989): 349–65.

————. "Hypertext and Collaborative Work: The Example of Intermedia." In *Intellectual Teamwork*, edited by Robert Kraut and Jolene Galegher, 407–28. Hillsdale, N.J.: Erlbaum, 1990.

————. "Hypertext in Literary Education, Criticism, and Scholarship." *Computers and the Humanities* 23 (1989): 173–98.

————. "The Rhetoric of Hypermedia: Some Rules for Authors." *Journal of Computing in Higher Education* 1 (1989): 39–64.

Lanham, Richard. "The Electronic Word: Literary Study and the Digital Revolution." *New Literary History* 20 (1989): 265–90.

————. *Literacy and the Survival of Humanism.* New Haven, Conn.: Yale University Press, 1984.

Larson, Magali Sarfatti. *The Rise of Professionalism: A Sociological Analysis.* Berkeley: University of California Press, 1977.

Latour, Bruno. *Science in Action: How to Follow Scientists and Engineers Through Society.* Cambridge, Mass.: Harvard University Press, 1986.

Levy, Richard, and Richard Lewonthin. *The Dialectical Biologist.* Cambridge, Mass.: Harvard University Press, 1986.

Levy, Steven. *The Hackers: Heroes of the Computer Revolution.* Garden City, N.Y.: Doubleday, 1984.

Livingstone, Margaret, and David Hubel. "Segregation of Form, Color, Movement, and Depth: Anatomy, Physiology and Perception." *Science,* 6 May 1988: 740–49.

McClintock, Robert. "Marking the Second Frontier." *Teachers College Record* 89 (1988): 345–51.

McCorduck, Pamela. *Aaron's Code: Meta-Art, Artificial Intelligence, and the Work of Harold Cohen.* New York: W. H. Freeman, 1990.

————. *Machines Who Think: A Personal Inquiry into the History and Prospects of Artificial Intelligence.* San Francisco, Calif.: W. H. Freeman, 1979.

McLuhan, Marshall. *The Gutenberg Galaxy.* Toronto: University of Toronto Press, 1962.

————. *Understanding Media: The Extensions of Man.* New York: McGraw-Hill, 1964.

Madden, Frank. "Desperately Seeking Literary Response." *Computers and Composition* 4.3 (August 1987): 17-34.

————. *Literature Journal.* Computer software. Westchester Community College.

Marcuse, Herbert. *One-Dimensional Man: Studies in the Ideology of Advanced Industrial Society.* Boston: Beacon, 1964.

Mayr, Ernst. *The Growth of Biological Thought: Diversity, Evolution, and Inheritance.* Cambridge, Mass.: Harvard University Press, 1982.

Moi, Toril. *Sexual/Textual Politics: Feminist Literary Theory.* New York: Methuen, 1985.

Moulthrop, Stuart. "Forking Paths." Hypertext application for Storyspace, based on Borges's "The Garden of Forking Paths." Macintosh. Unpublished manuscript.

Mumford, Lewis. *Technics and Civilization.* New York: Harcourt Brace Jovanovich, 1934.

Negri, Antonio. *The Politics of Subversion*. New York: Basil Blackwell, 1987.

Nelson, Ted. *Computer Lib*. Redmond, Wash.: Microsoft Press, 1987.

Nirenburg, Sergei, ed. *Proceedings of the Conference on Theoretical and Methodological Issues in Machine Translation of Natural Languages*. Hamilton, N.Y.: Colgate University, August 1985.

————. *Machine Translation: Theoretical and Methodological Issues*. ACL Series, Studies in Natural Language Processing. Cambridge: Cambridge University Press, 1987.

Nirenburg, Sergei, and Victor Raskin. "A Metric for Computational Analysis of Meaning: Toward an Applied Theory of Linguistic Semantics." In *Proceedings of the XI International Conference on Computational Linguistics, COLING 1986*, 338–40. Bonn, Germany, August 1986.

————. "The Subworld Concept Lexicon and the Lexicon Management System." *Computational Linguistics* 13.3–4 (1987): 276–89.

————. *Computational Linguistic Semantics*. Amsterdam, Holland: Elsevier (1991, in press).

Nyce, James M., and Paul Kahn. "Innovation, Pragmatism, and Technological Continuity: Vannevar Bush's Memex." *Journal of the American Society for Information Science* 40 (1989): 214–20.

Ong, Walter J. *Orality and Literacy: The Technologizing of the Word*. London: Methuen, 1982.

Oring, Elliott. *The Jokes of Sigmund Freud: A Study in Humor and Jewish Identity*. Philadelphia: University of Pennsylvania Press, 1984.

Owens, Craig. "The Allegorical Impulse: Toward a Theory of Postmodernism." In Wallis, 103–35.

Papert, Seymour. *Mindstorms: Children Computers, and Powerful Ideas*. New York: Basic Books, 1980.

Payne, Robert. *The Life and Death of Lenin*. New York: Simon and Schuster, 1964.

Pfeiffer, John E. *The Creative Explosion: An Inquiry into the Origins of Art and Religion*. New York: Harper, 1982.

Poundstone, William. *Labyrinths of Reason: Paradox, Puzzles, and the Frailty of Knowledge*. New York: Doubleday, 1988.

Pressman, Rebecca. *Legislative and Regulatory Progress on the Readability of Insurance Policies*. Washington, D.C.: Document Design Center, American Institute for Research, 1979.

Provenzo, Eugene, Jr. "Bar Access to Computer Data on Individuals." *Miami News*, 22 October 1987: 15a.

————. *Beyond the Gutenberg Galaxy: Microcomputers and the Emergence of Post-Typographic Culture*. New York: Teachers College Press, 1986.

————. *Video Kids: Making Sense of Nintendo*. Cambridge, Mass.: Harvard University Press, 1991.

Radway, Janice. *Reading the Romance: Women, Patriarchy, and Popular Literature*. Chapel Hill: University of North Carolina Press, 1984.

Raskin, Victor. *Semantic Mechanisms of Humor*. Dordrecht, Holland: D. Reidel, 1985.

————. "Script-based Semantics." In *Contemporary Issues in Language and Discourse Processes*, edited by D. G. Ellis and W. A. Donohue, 23–61. Hillsdale, N.J.: Erlbaum, 1986.

————. "Linguistics and Natural Language Processing." In *Machine Translation: Theoretical and Methodological Issues*, edited by Sergei Nirenburg, 42–58. ACL Series, Studies in Natural Language Processing. Cambridge: Cambridge University Press, 1987.

————. "What Is There in Linguistic Semantics for Natural Language Processing?" In *Proceedings of Natural Language Planning Workshop*. Blue Mountain Lake, N. Y.: RADC, Paper 5. 1987.

Read, Herbert. *Icon and Idea: The Function of Art in the Development of Human Consciousness*. London: Faber and Faber, 1955.

Redish, Janice. "The Plain English Movement." In *The English Language Today*, ed. S. Greenbaum, 125–38. Elmsford, N. Y.: Pergamon Press, 1985.

Reibling, Lyle. "The Application of AI to Combat Aircraft Trajectory Control." Paper 17, in *Proceedings of the Conference on Applied Military Decision Aids and Support Systems: Technology, Engineering, and Opportunities*, edited by Richard C. Erdman, 1–19. Fort Wayne, Ind.: Magnavox DACE, 1986.

Rosenblatt, Louise M. *Literature as Exploration*. 3d edition. New York: MLA, 1983.

Ross, Andrew, ed. *Technoculture*. Minneapolis: University of Minneapolis Press, 1991.

Roszak, Theodore. *The Cult of Information: The Folklore of Computers and the True Art of Thinking*. New York: Pantheon, 1986.

The Running Fence Project: Christo. Text by Werner Spies. Photographs by Wolfgang Volz. New York: Harry N. Abrams, 1980.

Schank, Roger C. "Identification of Conceptualizations Underlying Natural Language." In *Computer Models of Thought and Language*, edited by R. C. Schank and K. M. Colby, 187–247. San Francisco, Calif.: Freeman, 1973.

————. *Conceptual Information Processing*. Amsterdam: North Holland, 1975.

————. "Reminding and Memory Organization: An Introduction to MOPs." In *Strategies for Natural Language Processing*, edited by W. Lehnert and M. Ringle, 455–93. Hillsdale, N.J.: Erlbaum, 1982.

Schank, Roger C., and Robert Abelson. *Scripts, Plans, Goals and Understanding*. Hillsdale, N.J.: Erlbaum, 1977.

Schank, Roger C., and S. P. Shwartz. "The Role of Knowledge Engineering in Natural Language Systems." In *Applications in Artificial Intelligence*, edited by Stephen J. Andriole, 193–211. Princeton, N.J.: Petrocelli Books, 1985.

Scholes, Robert. "Aiming a Canon at the Curriculum." *Salmagundi* 72 (1986): 101–17.

Schwartz, Helen J. "SEEN: A Tutorial and User Network for Hypothesis Testing." *Computers in Composition Instruction*, edited by William Wresch. Urbana, Ill.: NCTE, 1984.

————. *SEEN*. Computer software. IBM and Apple II. Iowa City: CONDUIT, 1989.

————. "Teaching Stylistic Simplicity with a Computerized Readability Formula." International Conference of the American Business Communication Association. Washington, D.C. December 1980. ERIC ED 196 014.

_____. "Reading Literature to Write: How Novices and Experts Interpret With and Without CAI," Conference on College Compositional Communication. Seattle, Wash.: March 1989.

_____. "The 21st-Century Scholars Project: Electronic Mail for the Urban Commuter Learner." Conference on College Composition and Communication. Boston, March 1991.

Selfe, Cynthia L. "Redining Literacy: The Multilayered Grammars of Computers." In *Critical Perspectives on Computers and Composition,* edited by Gail E. Hawisher and Cynthia L. Selfe, 3–15. New York: Teachers College Press, 1989.

Seltzer, Jack. "What Constitutes a Readable Technical Style?" In *New Essays in Technical and Scientific Communication,* edited by P. Anderson et al., 71–89. Baywood, N.J.: Baywood Press, 1983.

Shipley, Joseph T. *The Origins of English Words.* Baltimore, Md.: Johns Hopkins Press, 1984.

Simon, Herbert. *Models of Thought.* New Haven, Conn.: Yale University Press, 1979.

Sloan, Douglas, ed. *The Computer in Education: A Critical Perspective.* New York: Teachers College Press, 1984.

Sontag, Susan. "On Style." In *A Susan Sontag Reader.* New York: Vintage, 1983.

Spencer, Sharon. *Space, Time and Structure in the Modern Novel.* New York: New York University Press, 1971.

Sudol, Ronald A. "Applied Word Processing: Notes on Authority, Responsibility and Revision in a Workshop Model." *College Composition and Communication* 36 (1985): 331–39.

Tedlock, Dennis. "Mayan Linguistic Ideology." In *On the Ethnography of Communication: The Legacy of Sapir,* edited by P. V. Kroskrity. Los Angeles: University of California Press, 1988.

Tompkins, Jane P., ed. *Reader-Response Criticism: From Formalism to Post-Structuralism.* Baltimore, Md.: Johns Hopkins University Press, 1980.

Tuman, Myron C. *A Preface to Literacy: An Inquiry into Pedagogy, Practice, and Progress.* Tuscaloosa: University of Alabama Press, 1987.

Ulmer, Greg. *Teletheory.* New York: Routledge, 1989.

Walker, Pat, ed. *Between Labor and Capital.* Boston: South End, 1976.

Wallis, Brian, ed. *Art After Modernism: Rethinking Representation.* New York: New Museum of Contemporary Art, 1984.

Walter, Eugene Victor. *Placeways: A Theory of the Human Environment.* Chapel Hill: University of North Carolina Press, 1988.

Weizenbaum, Joseph. *Computer Power and Human Reason: From Judgment to Calculation.* San Francisco, Calif.: W. H. Freeman, 1976.

Weyer, Stephen A. "As We May Learn." In *Interactive Multimedia,* edited by Sueann Ambron and Kristina Hooper. Redmond, Wash.: Microsoft Press, 1988.

Wilensky, Robert. *Planning and Understanding.* Reading, Mass.: Addison-Wesley, 1983.

Wilks, Yorick A., and D. Fass. "Preference Semantics, Ill-formedness and Metaphor." *American Journal of Computational Linguistics* 9 (1984): 178–87.

Williams, Raymond. *Keywords: A Vocabulary of Culture and Society*. New York: Oxford University Press, 1976.

Winograd, Terry. *Language as a Cognitive Process*. Vol. 1, *Syntax*. Reading, Mass.: Addison-Wesley, 1983.

Winston, Brian. *Misunderstanding Media*. Cambridge, Mass.: Harvard University Press, 1986.

Woods, William A. "Transition Network Grammars for Natural Language Analysis." CACM 13.10 (1970): 591–606.

Writing Is Thinking. Computer software. IBM. Dallas, Tex.: Kapstrom, 1984.

Yankelovich, Nicole, Bernard Haan, Norman K. Meyrowitz, and Stephen Drucker. "Intermedia: The Concept and Construction of a Seamless Information Environment." *IEEE Computer* 21 (1988): 81–96.

Yankelovich, Nicole, Norman K. Meyrowitz, and Andries van Dam. "Reading and Writing the Electronic Book." *IEEE Computer* 18 (1985): 15–30.

Zimmer, Carl. "Floppy Fiction." *Discover* (November 1989): 35–36.

Zuboff, Shoshana. *In the Age of the Smart Machine: The Future of Work and Power*. New York: Basic Books, 188.

Notes on Contributors

STANLEY ARONOWITZ   Sociology Department, Graduate Center of the City University of New York. Co-author, with Henry Giroux, of *Postmodern Education* (1991) and *Education Under Siege* (1985); author of *Politics of Identity* (1991) and numerous other books of political and cultural criticism.

JAY DAVID BOLTER   Professor of Rhetoric, Georgia Institute of Technology. Author of *Turing's Man: Western Culture in the Computer Age* (1984) and *Writing Space: The Computer, Hypertext and the History of Writing* (1990).

GEORGE P. LANDOW   Professor of English and Art, and Faculty Fellow, Institute for Research in Information and Scholarship, Brown University. Author of numerous books on Victorian art and culture, and most recently co-author of *Hypermedia and Literary Studies* (1991), and author of *Hypertext: The Convergence of Contemporary Critical Theory and Technology* (1991).

RICHARD A. LANHAM   Professor of English, University of California at Los Angeles. Author of *Literacy and the Survival of Humanism* (1983), *Analyzing Prose* (1983), *Revising Prose* (1981, 1986); *Style: An Anti-Textbook* (1978), and numerous essays on the future of rhetoric.

PAMELA MCCORDUCK   Author or co-author of five books on computers and technology, including *Machines Who Think: A Personal Inquiry Into the History and Prospects of Artificial Intelligence* (1979), *The Universal Machine: Confessions of a Technological Optimist* (1985), and, most recently, *Aaron's Code: Meta-Art, Artificial Intelligence, and the Work of Harold Cohen* (1990).

THEODOR HOLM NELSON   Computer pioneer and coiner of the term *hypertext* in 1965; author of one of the earliest studies of the computer revolution, *Computer Lib/Dream Machines* (1974, rev. ed. 1987). Creator of the hypermedia project *Xanadu*, presently under development by Autodesk.

EUGENE F. PROVENZO, JR.   Professor of Education, University of Miami. Author of numerous books on American education, including a series of works with special interest in electronic technology: *Beyond the Gutenberg Galaxy: Microcomputers and the Emergence of Post-Typographic Culture* (1986), *Video Kids: Making Sense of Nintendo* (1991), and, with Arlene Brett, *Computers and Adaptive Technology* (1992).

VICTOR RASKIN   Professor of English and Chair of the Interdepartmental Program in Linguistics, Purdue University. Co-author of *Semantics of Lying* as well as numerous books on semantic theory and applications.

HELEN J. SCHWARTZ   Professor of English, Indiana University/Purdue University at Indianapolis. Author of *Interactive Writing: Composing with a Word Processor* (1985) and developer of the composition software programs *Seen* (1988) and *Organize* (1988).

MYRON C. TUMAN   Professor of English, University of Alabama. Author of two critical studies, *A Preface to Literacy: An Inquiry Into Pedagogy, Practice, and Progress* (1987) and *Word Perfect: Literacy in the Computer Age* (1992), as well as the online handbook and a textbook used with *Norton Textra Writer*.

GREGORY L. ULMER   Professor of English, University of Florida. Author of *Applied Grammatology* (1985), *Teletheory: Grammatology in the Age of Video* (1989), and *Euretics* (forthcoming).

Pittsburgh Series in Composition, Literacy, and Culture

David Bartholomae and Jean Ferguson Carr, Editors

Academic Discourse and Critical Consciousness
Patricia Bizzell

Eating on the Street: Teaching Literacy in a Multicultural Society
David Schaafsma

Fragments of Rationality: Postmodernity and the Subject of Composition
Lester Faigley

Literacy Online: The Promise (and Peril) of Reading and Writing with Computers
Myron C. Tuman, Editor

Word Perfect: Literacy in the Computer Age
Myron C. Tuman